James_The_Second – Primary Source Edition

Hilaire belloc

JAMES THE SECOND

JAMES
THE SECOND

By
Hilaire Belloc

'*Preserve the Mastery of the Sea*'

(James's instructions to his heir as King of England)

PHILADELPHIA

J. B. Lippincott Company

1928

DEDICATED TO

R. B. CUNNINGHAME-GRAHAM

PREFACE

THIS essay is not a biography, still less a chronicle. It is an attempt to portray a character of capital interest to English and European History, of which our academic historians give but a caricature. Were it either a biography or a chronicle, a great mass of detail would have been added, with which the book has no concern. Were it a biography, it would have been essential to describe all the main facts of the subject's life; were it a chronicle, it would have had to include a conspectus of the world contemporary with James at home and abroad and to give the sequence of events in a regular and dated order. Neither of these tasks appears in the pages that follow. Thus, James was conspicuous and successful as a British Admiral in two great naval engagements—the most important of those fought by the fleet which he had created, and the chief actions of the century. I have given the story of one only, as typical of his attitude in command. He was attacked and betrayed by a good score of men in the small clique of great fortunes—all allied by marriage—which destroyed the ancient monarchy of the English. I have described but two, as typical of their set, Shaftesbury and his brother-in-law Sunderland. He presided over, and in great part initiated, the making of the British Navy—his chief work. That in itself would be material for a volume. I have given it but a chapter, and in that chapter have emphasized but two main points: his new corps of professional officers; his new idea of a National Fleet independent of pressed merchant auxiliaries. But these are sufficient to show his creative rôle in the setting up of that service. The characters and careers of his numerous mistresses would be essential to a life: I have concerned myself only with the very difficult problem of his own emotions in such amours, for *that* is the point of character.

I have thus deliberately selected, because it is surely by such selection of special points in connexion with his temperament, achievement and failures that he can be best presented: and, I think, in no other way. But that he should be presented truly is of the first value in understanding England during and since his day. The Revolution of 1688 completed the work of the Reformation. From it dates the Modern Aristocratic England which is nearly all the nineteenth century (and our own) can conceive of as English. To know the man whose failure produced that Revolution is a thing the nineteenth century (and our own) has hardly attempted. It is high time the attempt should be made. I trust that in doing so I have exaggerated neither his vice, nor—as is the temptation in face of our academic text-books—his virtues: neither his capacities, which were great and remarkable, nor his deficiencies which were startlingly pronounced and, combined with certain high moral qualities, led to his ruin.

HILAIRE BELLOC

King's Land
Shipley
Horsham

CONTENTS

FRONTISPIECE

PORTRAIT OF JAMES II, AS DUKE OF YORK
Reproduced from the painting by John Greenhill, in the Dulwich College Picture Gallery, by kind permission of the Governors.

JAMES THE SECOND

I

THE CHARACTER

JAMES II of England and Ireland, VII of Scotland, last legitimate king of the three kingdoms and maker of the British Navy, was born on Wednesday, the 12th October, 1633, in St. James's Palace of Westminster. His mother, the Bourbon Princess, daughter of Henry IV of France, when she heard it was a boy, ordered her choir to sing the Magnificat. He died, very finely, an exile in the palace of St. Germans, near Paris, on Friday, the 16th September, 1701.

The interval, a life of sixty-eight years, was filled with the strangest accidents that ever have befallen a man of such standing. His early childhood was coloured by the splendour of a court still apparently powerful and in all externals glorious. Before he was 9 years old he was in the camp of Edge Hill, the first battle of the rebellion which destroyed that external glory and apparent power. At 13 he is a prisoner of the rebels: at 14 an exile, after a flight for life so perilous and moving as to leave upon him a permanent impress of adventure and of the sea. At 15 he hears that his father, for whom he had established a boy's worship increased by absence, has been murdered.

Thenceforward, through all the formative years, he suffered the increasing embarrassment and humiliations of poverty and of those whose cause seems lost: yet it is clear that under such pressure he was annealed. He dignified his entry into young manhood by a vigorous profession of arms: he immediately and justly acquired a name for conspicuous courage, and (what is rarer in a young officer from superiors grown old in war) aptitude in action, quick and sane judgment upon a situation, firmness and judgment in command.

In such a career the time—which was made for soldiers —would have raised him quickly to eminence. He grows mature in the practice of his trade and his career is open. But, suddenly, in his twenty-seventh year the whole scene changes. He finds himself restored, his brother upon the throne, and he, during the active middle of his life, for twenty-five years, the next heir to the crown: the centre of that close grapple between the strongly rising power of the rich and the failing monarchy. His adversaries and the King's have for their chief instrument a widespread hatred of the Catholic Church, especially among the greatest merchants of London and their train. In such a juncture he accepts Catholicism openly, risking all. None the less, after political adventures not less violent than those earlier physical ones of exile and battle, he accedes upon his brother's death. The forces, now nearly triumphant, which are determined upon the destruction of kingship, watch him opposed. A challenger by nature, he accepts the challenge. He rules determinedly and by authority: the King of these three kingdoms, independent, conspicuous in Europe.

But organized wealth and universal cunning are far too strong for him. He is lied to on every side, a man easily deceived; he is deserted in battle by his dependants who owed him most gratitude, by his own children, by all. His energy attempts the hopeless task of recovery. It fails; and he passes a dozen years, the ageing remainder of so tragic a life, in yet another impoverished exile, illuminated by a religious doctrine long established in better days and growing in intensity as he approaches death; and death he meets with a holiness and a renunciation that should exalt his memory.

What kind of man was it that passed through this doubly repeated ordeal of splendour and poverty, of power and dishonour? That had such courage, such energy, such tenacity, such a misapprehension of the forces about him—and of the social scheme? That saw so clearly the true proportion of things, never sacrificing the eternal to the temporal, yet that saw men's baseness so little and could never grasp its effect? That was so amative of women, so excellent a leader in combat, so capable a master of ships and yet raised no devotion in his kind—dying almost alone?

There is the question set to any who would examine that strange life. Its answer is not easy. I will attempt it.

Two qualities are the bases of James's character: strength and limitation. From each proceeds a whole series of attributes which appear in his every action as in his voluminous writing. From his strength—or in association with it—are discovered his prolonged physical vigour, his courage, his sincerity, his tenacity, his industry: from his limitation, his failure to comprehend his fellows, his misjudgment of every situation, and his lack of diversity. He had very little humour, no wit. He imputed to other men his own emotions. This all tend to do; but James imputed them wholly and could conceive of no others. He foresaw no probable consequence of one man's ambitions, fears and appetites: still less the combination of such in many and various men. He never shrank from an encounter, and so long as its elements were plain he grasped them at once. But let them be tortuous or concealed, and he missed them altogether.

On this last account a false judgment has often been passed upon his intelligence. He has even been called dull

—a term quite inapplicable to one who organized closely
and exceptionally well, who followed at once a train of
reasoning, and who worked with rapidity and decision.
He was not dull; but he was cut off. His mind was
isolated, and to a whole group of appreciations impervious.
It was the lively who most condemned him in this, the
experienced in the comedy of this world who were most
impatient with him. What woman in that generation was
most vivacious, keen to feel all and transmit it? Madame
de Sévigné. And what was her conclusion—passed, it is
true, when the worst blows had fallen—upon his faculties? *'Bien du courage, mais un esprit commun.'*

Complexity did not bewilder him, rather he missed it
altogether; slyness he despised as an evil thing, and there
he was right; but he neglected it as an element in public
men, and there he was immensely wrong. He could scheme
with things but not against schemers. He could make a
plan better than most men and would and did pursue it
with more assiduity than any; but to modify it with
occasion, to maintain a general direction through ceaseless
concession and recovery, to reach a goal by steering right
and left alternately, he could not. He did not know
that such an art existed. He thought in straight lines.

The convention of fiction and the stage associates
restriction and isolation in a man with a lack of generosity
and even a lack of valour: certainly with a lack of adventure. Upon this facile association of ideas was drawn the
caricature of James which did duty for his portrait in the
nineteenth century. But the convention is a convention
only. It is suitable for making up the simple puppet of a
play or the Hero or Villain of a novel. It has no relation
to real life. How many have we not known who were
circumscribed in judgment, defective in their handling of
inferiors, insistent out of season, yet at the same time
open-handed and always ready for a risk?

It was so with this man. His generosity played some part in his ruin; it played a constant and conspicuous part in his common action. On the most critical occasion of his reign when he was compelled to break with his brother-in-law he added to the Treasury grants with which he loaded that disappointed politician large monies of his own. He gave the discomfited Hyde an income which directly lessened his own sources of revenue, and he gave it in a moment when every hundred helped to decide the mortal struggle between kingship and plutocracy. He did the same by Clarendon. He did the same by those who had befriended him in the dereliction of his youth.

But the most touching examples of this virtue in a mind so deprived of communion, are to be found in his last exile, when he was harassed with a perpetual poverty and yet took almost daily of his little to support those whose loyalty had followed him.

An accompaniment of this generosity was a personal indifference to money exceptional in any age, in that age unique. If we had no record of James save in his prosperity, this disdain of avarice might only be inferred from all the rest we know of him. As heir to the throne he was amply endowed by the Crown; as a victorious admiral, by Parliament. But both as king, in age, and in youth as the young prince of a lost cause—that is, in the two situations where best his attitude towards money may be tested—we have example after example. When he would serve in the army as a boy he borrows on terms from a chance lender just what is necessary for his equipment and no more—what he can and does easily repay. He will not long remain under obligation to Turenne when that great captain, in his admiration of dash and gallantry in action, put his purse at the lad's disposal. Throughout the period of the Commonwealth the young man was thus hampered for money and in grievous need of it. But this embarrassment was not inevitable; it was largely of his own choice; he refused a rich marriage because he thought it an unworthy one. He refused the second offer of an advance. Such an attitude towards money marks all his unfortunate, harassed, soldierly youth in exile.

When, twenty-five years later, he became king, this fine but perilous detachment reappeared under another form: one which contributed to his fall. Money was now a necessary instrument of reign. Had he overcome his scruples in regard to it he could have strengthened himself continuously. He refused. He claimed his own —as, for instance, in the arrears of his brother's payments from Louis XIV—but of further subsidy for himself he would have none. Yet it might have saved him. It is true that another strong motive here appeared, one which always mastered him: his sense of dignity and honour: yet another motive, his sense of kingship: yet another, his pride in England. But had he put money first (as did all his enemies without exception, as did indeed all the leaders of that generation) he would have accepted his cousin's aid. He refused it.

He might further have sold places, honours, policies. He might have confiscated largely: heaven knows he had excuse enough! He might have coined colonial concessions. He might have raised great commercial loans. He did none of these things, and in disdaining them he was, perhaps, to blame. With a sufficiency of funds he could have bribed most successfully the ardent defenders of freedom and religion. They took whatever they could get from whomever would provide, and what Louis did, James could have done. It might have saved him.

Nor was this attitude towards money the facile carelessness of a spendthrift. His instinct was all for provision at the other end: by saving. He maintained the necessary parade of a great court and was generous to his

wife. But he looked closely into expenditure. It went
with his zeal for work, his constant writing, hour by
hour, his long experience of accounts at the Admiralty:
above all it went with his grasp of detail. Yet saving
was not what his situation needed. He got no credit
for the increased sobriety of the court, the careful conduct
of all public affairs. Why should he? His opponents
were not prepared to give him praise for anything. They
were prepared to destroy him, and especially, first, to
lower him in the public mind. Against that form of attack
display and lavishness would have been a better policy.
Display and lavishness are also a consequence of the contempt for gold—but not of the sort that James felt.
The lack of discipline which makes a squanderer was
odious to him.

I have spoken of his courage. How often he gave
example of it in action is notorious. It was native to him
to do so. What needs more emphasis is his sense of adventure. He had but rare occasions after his youth to indulge
it in arms, but it never left him. He was for ever trying
his chance, in battle, in policy. Risk attracted him and
excited his initiative. We shall see it in his first flight from
England, in his military service with France and Spain, in
the two famous sea battles where he commanded and—
where it is less noticed—in his second exile. Both in his
desperate attempt to recover Ireland against all odds,
and (still more) in the determined effort, against all
advice, to neglect Ireland for England as a road to the
recovery of his throne, he was always for the desperate
throw. There are many examples in history of a young
prince perpetually challenging. These are some few of an
old man preserving this fire into his last years. But rare or
absent are examples of what James did: returning to the
attack again, and yet again, after failure apparently decisive, and in the very last years of life. It may have been

attempting the impossible, and certainly his temperament led him into that through its errors in judgment more than through his valour. Yet valour also was required; and he showed it plentifully; ill-calculated, out of place —as in his mere resistance to forces clearly his superiors; but also well exercised and in its right posture—as in his admirable confrontation of abandonment and death.

One effect of his limitations was of a sort that to-day, all would praise exaggeratedly: of a sort which in his day seemed odd. He was filled with an intense Nationalism.

To a heart of wide and diverse sympathies such patriotism would, among royalties, have been impossible. The Kings and Princes were—by definition we might say— of every blood in Europe. They were all cousins. Their faint lines of demarcation lay along differences of religion; not of race or provincial tradition which they could not feel, nor of language which they used either indifferently or in the common medium of French. The Kings and Princes of the seventeenth century stood for national divisions, were at the head of them, represented them. But they had not, and could not have, the intense and circumscribed feelings of local patroitism which were already growing so strong in the middle classes and were to become, a century later, a religion: the religion for which lately so many millions have died. Nor is this true only of the Royalties. It is true also, in a lesser degree, of the Nobles. The great landed families of Europe were also, in the seventeenth century, largely cosmopolitan, in speech, in culture, in experience: and their example reacted upon the lesser squires below them, though these, in France and England especially, were already (and had been for two generations) more French and English than European.

Yet James in such a world was not like those of the

summits to which he belonged by birth and every experience. He was as national as the smallest gentleman.
His Englishry was intense—in the eyes of contemporaries,
absurd. He made no effort to speak or spell French
correctly as did any of his nobility you might choose.
He was remarked for a strong English accent which he
did nothing to correct or excuse: which, were not the
man so sincere and un-theatrical, one might suspect of
being deliberately exaggerated. His pride lent added substance to this emotion of nationalism. He would be king,
as was his due, but King of England—and, only because
King of England, King also of Scotland which he little
loved, of Ireland—a country which even his religion did
not help him to understand and which he refused, as
long as he had the power, to relieve from the spoliation
of an English conquest. Before he was 20, serving on
the opposing side, he boasted to the foreigners among
whom he found himself of the English soldiers' prowess
on the Great Dune at Dunkirk. They were in the service
of the man who had murdered his dear father: they were
of the army that tyrannized over England and kept the
King, his brother, from his rightful throne. Yet, because
they were Englishmen it stirred his blood to see them
roaring up the steep sand and turning out the Spaniards
headlong. When, on the same occasion, he sees the Spanish
boats easily beaten off, he writes with a schoolboy enthusiasm of his countrymen's courage, though it was directed
against himself. A long lifetime later, when he was already old, near 60, he could not restrain himself from
exultation at the sight of British sailors boarding the
French ships below the Norman cliffs whence he was
watching the fight which condemned himself to final
defeat.

His father's blood was Scotch and Danish, his mother's
of Navarre and Italy, yet so he was: violently English

—and it was the isolation of his mind that helped him so to be. Ideas, especially emotional ideas, took strong gnarled root in him. He could not communicate them to others. The entry to his mind from others was also closed. The more did he cherish what ideas he held within, and, among such ideas, England: not the abstraction but the thing itself: the people, the fleet, the character, the tongue: and when so many turned against him he could find no explanation save that, in some strange way, they had been "poisoned."

James's character stands out the more vividly from its contrast with that of his elder brother. They loved each other, but there was constant friction between them on account of that deep divergence.

Charles had despaired. James was incapable of despair. Charles consoled the bitterness of dependence and of a ruined monarchy with diversion, almost with debauch, in which he could half forget that he was enchained by the great fortunes of his masters. James knew not what consolation meant. He did not need it; he did not seek it; and as for the now final subservience of the Crown to the rich, he misapprehended it altogether. He had no conception of how low the last flicker of royalty had fallen or of how high the wealthy families had risen. He rejected that new and permanent reality in politics as a passing irritant to be soon overcome by active and firm opposition, when he should be king.

Charles was impatient of intellectual concentration. He was so by nature perhaps but also, and more, by habit, because he was persuaded (quite rightly) that no amount of application could win the battle: that the majesty of English monarchy was already long lost: therefore, though an active man, Charles thought it waste of effort to work. James was industrious beyond all common measure. He worked morning, noon and night. He planned, executed, wrote, went hither and thither superintending his subordinates in whatever office he might hold, and himself with his own eyes and hand taking the chief part in its activities.

Charles had a very wide knowledge of men and therefore a complete contempt for them. James had no knowledge of men, thought them all like himself, or else (very rarely) crude villains. Most men—nearly all intriguers —he trusted.

Charles was bored by adventures. James sought them. To Charles hardship in life, cramped quarters aboard ship, the chance lodging, the camp, were mighty disagreeable: matters to undertake when it was necessary, but otherwise to avoid. They suited James. He used them continually. He returned to them with appetite. The end before Charles—which he achieved—was to maintain the name at least and the trappings of a king by dexterity and the sacrifice of kingship. The end of James—in which he failed—was to be king indeed: and he attempted it by assault.

Charles, partly from that despair of his, partly from weakness, most of all from his great object of holding the name of king, let men whom he knew to be innocent go to the scaffold, victims to the rich oligarchy of Russells and Coopers and their hired mob: he signed the warrants for the murder of such men as Stafford and Coleman and even jested on it to save appearances. In James such action is inconceivable.

Charles knew early that the Catholic Church is the sole beacon in this night if beacon there be. But Charles postponed his declaration of loyalty to the Faith till there was nothing left to lose by it; he admitted his Lord and his God not immediately at the touching of the wounds but tardily when he himself had no more wounds to fear. James had disliked the Church, had rejected it, came to it late by a process of close reasoning. Having once discovered that reality, he openly proclaimed his adhesion to it under such conditions of sacrifice and peril as weighed upon no other man of his time.

Charles, despising men, and enslaved to women only by their looks and his weakness, praised or noticed all, was open to all, avoided offence, studied to say things that pleased and was glad to raise an air of ease about him. Therefore when he died the baby face of one mistress, the doll's eyes of another, were confused with tears and his insignificant neglected wife swooned with grief. To James his fellow beings were but a furniture. He knew them externally, not otherwise. He said not a true word to please, let alone a false one. He studied no mind. And therefore all his life he was alone and only at the very end did, perhaps, his last little child watch him with affection, and his wife, when he had gone, grieve. Charles was a man who let loose the stirrup, was spent and at large. James was a man trammelled, walled.

Had he enjoyed the sentiment of love, however briefly, that, and perhaps that alone, would have unbound his soul. His brother had had a touch of it, very early, with the depraved Lucy Walters. He retained for her sake a particular fondness for the wretched Monmouth in whom he may have seen, in fugitive moments, some gesture or glance of hers. But James—we may be certain—had no such good fortune. He had strong passions, a man of vigour who preserved his activity nearly to the end of his life. He gratified them with women of his own kind, contemptuous of prettiness, almost indifferent to feature, moved by power of mind and body in a mate, but quite abnormally deprived of tenderness in that relation. Steeped in the idea of royalty, following the conception of his day that royalty might be free from all restraint in the matter of women, he lived at large—to the hurt of

his own soul and to the huge scandal of 1850. He was
never under a woman's control, yet he paid deference to
particular minds—notably to that of his first wife—for
the strength of their vision and for a certain faculty of
comradeship about them. But love he had not known and
never knew, even in the slight fashion which Charles
could remember, occasionally sought to find again in later
years, and never found. Love is perhaps an experience less
common in life than in print. At any rate, James missed
it: and, in the lack of it, something arid in his soul continued unrelieved to the end.

He felt deeply for his children; especially for Anne,
who betrayed him. In his dying years he would smile his
restrained smile when looking on the last, the little girl
born in the moment of his final defeat, and call her 'The
Solace.'

Other strong affections he had not. But he had most
powerful devotions, the strongest of which was to his
public duty as subaltern, as admiral, as head of a department, as king. That was with him a passion, into which
entered and in which converged all his characteristics:
his pride, his sincerity, his nervousness, his sense of
inevitable loneliness. His duty as king to rule; his duty
to master too powerful nobles whom it was his to govern;
his duty to maintain the integrity and independence of
the England which had been entrusted to him, neither
serving a French nor a Dutch interest and keeping her
crown undiminished; his duty to preserve the laws intact,
never to punish unjustly, never to force a conscience,
never to interfere with the course of justice; his duty
to leave even his most immediate and pressing personal
interests—which might be of life and death—to the common processes of the National Courts and their
machinery: above everything, to break the unconstitu-
tional and unjust denial of it by lawyers and prelates;

his duty to grant toleration to all in the distracted religious chaos of his time—these were his obsessing ideals. All such men have this clutch on their task to be done. The chivalric name for it was 'devoir,' and the modern is 'doing one's job.' The simple violent appetite for it in tenacious men does not change with the word. It produces in all ages and places an inflexible attitude, and thus destroys those devoted to it.

This rigidity in Duty was seen, pushed to a very high degree, in the matter of the Faith. As a young man he had held fast to the Establishment. The father whom he worshipped had died for it. The very fact that his Catholic mother pestered him with her religious demands, enhanced his determination. It was the Duty of an English Prince to hold communion with the English Church. It was a Duty also to the Family in which he had so deep a pride, and thus we shall see that when Henrietta Maria made a similar attempt upon his younger brother, the Duke of Gloucester, he vehemently defended the boy from that attack, and insisted, successfully, upon his resisting it. There was here no calculation, no policy, nor even any discussion of principle. He was filled with a conviction of duty to an Institution—the Church of England—not to a Creed.

He was in the thirties before the conception of Religion as a body of doctrine, a fully revealed truth, occurred to him. It worked within him unaided, apparently, by any external influence save that of one very insufficient book [1] written *against* the conclusion to which he was led.

The thing has happened before. The Catholic Church appeals at once when it is seen, and it may be first discovered in any one of a thousand ways: from a hostile

[1] That of Peter Heylin, a man of his father's generation and promoted in the Church by Charles I. He was sub-dean of Westminster and died in 1662. Of his many books the one in question is that upon the Reformation, written in support of the Church of England.

book as much as from a friendly one. Possibly his first wife, Anne Hyde, whose vigorous intellect had come to the same end, influenced his last determination in the matter; for the example of her decision always affected him. He concluded the Catholic Church to be the sole authoritative voice on earth, and thenceforward his integrity, his immovable resolve, are the most remarkable political features of his age. He passed, before his reconciliation with the Church was completed, through one phase which is very common, and not only excusable but, until a full experience of the religion is obtained, almost inevitable. He asked whether a man might not believe and profess and yet, for good motives of policy, conceal his faith from others and leave it a private and secret affair—acting as we do when we know that what we love must be odious to our companions. He was told the doctrine of the Church in the matter—that the Faith cannot be so treated, but, once accepted, must be proclaimed. He immediately obeyed—and from that moment to his death he kept unswerving to the strict path, during the years when it led him first to peril and conflict, then to disgrace and loss of his dearest occupation, then to the destruction of his inheritance and of his son's, then to exile and a dereliction ending only in death.

Through all these successive trials he not only stood firm against surrender but on no single occasion contemplated the least compromise or by a word would modify the impression made. It is like a rod of steel running through thirty years.

With such unswerving moral strength was allied that abnormal limitation in him of political judgment. The wisdom of Machiavelli, the essential truth that a prince is powerful in proportion to his ability in choosing his servants, was never better shown. James chose them ill. He could not divine their betrayals, he missed their motives, he judged their talents wrongly and still more wrongly their loyalty. He allowed the wretched Sunderland to put Petre into the Privy Council as his buffer. He was duped into that grave blunder not by weakness but by its very opposite, by determination—coupled with an extreme ignorance of men and of their baseness.

He thought that an order was sufficient—that the agent would be but an instrument to obey. He thought so of Churchill, of all who held commissions from him, of his magistrates. He was blind to the plot laid against him in the matter of the Seven Bishops. He believed those Bishops, later, in the very crisis of his fate, when they protested their devotion—three of them in active treason at the time! He even believed Compton of London, the ringleader of the conspiracy. But the chief, the cardinal errors on which all the rest turned were these: first, his conception that the love of Justice was a common appetite upon which a ruler can rely in his subordinates: secondly, his conception that gratitude affects the mass of men, even the rich.

For the rest every betrayal and falsehood bewildered him. Each came with a new shock. He learnt from none. He could not believe that his officers would desert him. He could not believe that his daughters would abandon him, usurp his throne. He actually accepted the solemn word of William of Orange! His enemies—at least, those of posterity—find something ridiculous in such naïveté. He should have known better. The trusting man is a fool. But something deeper appears in all this than matter for scorn. A dupe may be noble.

There you may see the character upon which the tragedy fell and upon which the world surrounding it was to work what it did.

His tall figure, his firm, advancing step, his large

determined features, his quick eye, all proclaimed his energy and will: his sensitive mouth that sad reserve which nature, not its own choice, imposed upon this uncompanioned and uncompanionable soul. A man of this kind would, under most conditions, have carried out his life and its intentions. He would have conducted commerce, led troops or fulfilled high duties in a civil service without sympathy but with success. He would have achieved.

He was condemned (under such drawbacks) to contend as Heir and then as King with Circumstance which necessarily overpowered him: with an inherited opposition of which none could have done more than postpone the effects, but of which he accelerated the victory. He went under at once, where another would also have succumbed at last, under the pressure of that Circumstance, of the world around him as three lifetimes of England had made it.

What was that Circumstance? What was the nature of the opposition which destroyed the kings? I will examine it before turning to the episodes which explain James's life, because it is only after a first grasping of the way in which English kingship had been undermined that we can understand its fall.

II

THE CIRCUMSTANCE

THE character I have described was set a certain task. For twenty-five years as heir apparent and chief figure of Council and Parliament, for four years as king, James had set before him the task of restoring the Royal power and through it imposing toleration upon a realm torn by religious quarrel. The structure of society rendered that task impossible.

The Social System in and with which James was compelled to work from 1660 to 1688, had become, in the course of a couple of lifetimes, finally and permanently governed no longer by the king, but by the rich. It was organized under their control and functioned through their individual power as magistrates, their now confirmed power in the great corporations—the Lawyers, the Church, the Universities, the city of London, the two Houses of Parliament. A Ruling Class had come into being: a product of the Reformation in this land. The Crown had long been ruined. Its lands had been filched from it steadily, since the death of Henry VIII, by the great lords and squires. Its income had disappeared. Its remnant of apparent authority depended upon the wealthy class from whom alone it could look for revenue voted grudgingly in Parliament and who were rapidly subjecting the Populace and destroying the support a Populace can give to its Kings. Yet James's object, on which he pondered as heir, which he would bring into effect when he should reign, was to restore Popular Monarchy, or, as he would have said, to insist on its rights and duties; especially its duty of protecting minorities and enforcing justice. He regarded these ancient rights as still existing in their full vigour, and the corresponding duties therefore capable of being performed.

It was an illusion. Popular Monarchy was fallen long ago and could not be revived. In his attempt to revive it James was dealing with material quite intractable. He wholly failed.

His failure was due to the fact that of Popular Monarchy, the bare ash remained: the thin and crumbling shell. It had begun to fail a century since. It was sunk into its last agony before James was born. Its power was dead while he was yet a child.

In his failure the supplanting power which he encountered was Parliament, the organ of the wealth which now governed.

That newly organized power of the wealthy, already supplanting the Crown, was further able to use against James the now widespread hostility to the Catholic Church, of which he was an unmoved adherent. Toleration to include the various dissenting sects he might have achieved. Toleration for Catholics he could not.

We have, therefore, in judging the Circumstance under which James II acted, already as heir but especially later, as King, to seize these three factors.

(1) The main one: the passing of Popular Monarchy and the causes of its having been thus supplanted by an organized oligarchy of wealthy men.

(2) The nature of the Parliament which was the instrument of these wealthy men in their attack on the Crown.

(3) The position of Catholicism in England between 1660 and 1688.

[1]

Popular Monarchy had been from time immemorial, until the upheaval of the Reformation, the natural government of the English and indeed of most Christian peoples.

From the remote Dark Ages, from the Roman monarchy itself, right down to the Reformation the King stood for all men. He was the natural protector of the weak against the strong, the curber of the rich, and above all the maintainer of *custom*—which was law. It was his to check the encroachment of powerful men upon the *customary* rights which maintained the mass of the people secure. His courts ascertained *custom* by local inquiry, enforced it, and, where it had been violated, restored it. He was the jealous guardian of public property—which, in those times, formed a very large part of the total resources of society. The King had possession (in general, and subject to some local exceptions) of minerals. His was the control of navigable waterways and chief roads, with their tolls. He, personally and directly, governed. He levied war and made peace. He summoned those occasional groups of private ships, for transport or for fighting on the sea, which might be necessary for the island in a foreign war. (No royal navy existed till the last years of the Middle Ages, and even then the proportion of 'King's Ships' was very small. The chief work was done, right up till Charles's establishment of Ship money, by merchant or even large fishing vessels ordered for special temporary service by royal authority.) The King also bestowed all major posts in the State. He had always occasionally consulted the Peers—some fifty laymen and rather more abbots and bishops—and, in the last of the Middle Ages, had dealt frequently with 'Parliaments' —great councils occasionally and fitfully summoned to register important legislation, to support or incorporate a new reign, but especially to provide special and abnormal revenue in some crisis.

More important as a power of government than the

Peers and (of course) indefinitely more powerful than the occasional and formal 'Parliament' was the King's *Council*—a small body assembled round one table. When the King was a minor it at once assumed control. Orders from the King in that private session were of particular force. It had prestige of the highest order, and by its small size and the continual conversation between its members it had, in spite of their rivalries, homogeneity. The essential thing to remember with regard to this *Council*, is that it was essentially the *King's*. It had no existence save by the King's will: the group of relatives whom he naturally communicated with and of some other few whose judgment he trusted or whose affection he relied on. It was *his* council, and the idea that he must call to it men whom he either did not trust or who were personally distasteful to him, or who persisted in opposing his will, would have seemed not only monstrous to the King himself, but quite as monstrous to any of his subjects.

The Judges under the old popular monarchy were no more than the King's agents: appointed by him, and removable (a rare necessity) by him: it was theirs to declare Custom, and particularly to watch and punish sedition, and a judge would, of course, be dismissed who used this power in opposition to the King.

When we add that to the King reverted sequestrated estates and land without heirs; that the King alone could warrant death or reprieve; that all administration and its officers, the local administrators, the coinage, the monopolies of gunpowder, artillery, the Press, were in his hands, and that all normal revenue sufficient for public purposes was drawn from his own lands and dues, you may see what a mighty thing kingship had for so long meant to the English when the Reformation began to destroy it.

This great office of English kingship was hereditary.

33

It belonged of right to the blood royal, to descendants of the King's body; first to males in order of seniority, then to females. A king was king through blood and in no other fashion, and right of blood in kingship meant what it meant in private estates. It was a personal inheritance.

Because the King was the mystical embodiment of the whole community an old sacramental form was kept up of appealing at a coronation for the approval of those present; but of election there was no conception, still less of making a king by power of the rich men in Parliament. It was not a mechanical office 'created.' It was of God. It was in the nature of things.

I have used in connexion with it the words 'mystical' and 'sacramental.' They are vividly accurate. They exactly connote the attitude of the English mind towards the King of England—while kingship yet was. The King was consecrated. His coronation was not a festival, still less a political function, least of all an appointment, or installation. It was an act of communion with that Divine Authority which sustains the world. He was *anointed* King. And on his anointment there passed into him the whole nation with which afterwards he was to be identified. He became one with them: not only their spokesman or head or even father, but their very selves.

This conception of Popular Kingship has disappeared in England. But those who cannot imagine it or, because they have not experienced it, neglect its force in the past, are ignorant of their own blood. Their ancestral past is to them a foreign country.

It may be asked why a description of this sort is needed in connexion with James II and the mid-seventeenth century, when all the force of this ancient idea had disappeared and when realities wholly contradicted it. I have already said that James's effort to restore or (as he regarded it) enforce the rights of a king were at issue with the whole structure of his time, even though that effort was directed to the establishment—or continued support—of something very much less than the old kingship. Why then bring that dead thing before the reader?

Because, though the thing had been stricken since 1540 and was, by 1660, long dead, its form remained. It is nearly always so with institutions at their decline and disappearance. Their form survives and even deceives, like a sort of very active ghost, long after their substance has dissolved into air. So the Senatorial power in Imperial Rome under the real power of the Commander-in-Chief, the Emperor. So our Parliamentarians to-day under the real rule of finance. The old titles are still used, the words and phrases are as vigorous as ever, even the functions are carried on—their mechanism at least—as before. But the motive power has changed and proceeds from a new centre.

So it was with the age-long Popular Monarchy of England. More than a century before the Restoration of Charles II it had itself introduced that by which it sickened. In that century—1560 to 1660—it died. What killed it?

To answer this question we must appreciate the essential point that the Popular Monarchy did not tax.

It was endowed. The King received as of right and custom, as his *own*, a certain (very large) income mainly from land and dues on which he supported all public work as well as his private household.

That was the original, the normal, idea of public revenue under Popular Monarchy. The King had a huge private income and out of that must 'live of his own.' Out of that he must not only clothe and feed his Court and raise and repair the buildings he lived in, but also anything else he chose to erect and endow, an abbey or

35

school, his fortifications, his hired troops, his public services and all that belonged to his office.

But to this system there could not but arise exceptions, and they increased as Society developed. Often in war—always when war was on a large scale—sometimes for other unusual necessities, the King had to get an *extra* amount: something beyond his regular income. He had to be 'helped' as the phrase went, to have an 'aid.'

But these sudden strainings on private men's resources, however infrequent, were tolerable only as *exceptional* demands, in supplement of the regular royal income, which remained the normal support of public expense.

At the Reformation—say from 1540 onwards—two changes appeared which ruined the old system and with it the independence and therefore the power of the King. The first, and least important, was the beginning of a great and continuous fall in the purchasing power of money. The second, and far the greatest—of overwhelming effect in the story of England—was the loot of religious wealth by the gentry: that is, by the well-to-do class which made up Parliament, Lords and Commons. The change in the value of money could have been met by corresponding changes in the rents and dues of the King. The Crown, remaining strong, could have reckoned its rents and profits in terms of the prices, as did foreign monarchs and as every private landlord and merchant did. What prevented the English Crown from doing this was the new power of the gentry: the power of their new wealth based on their sudden acquirement of ecclesiastical property.

The Crown had raised up against itself, by its own act in confiscating Church wealth, a formidable rival—the gentry. The loot of religion began with the seizure of the lesser monasteries, in 1536, by King Henry VIII. Then came *all* the monastic land (1540), its treasures,

36

buildings, stocks, the plate and jewels of the altar and of shrines, chantries, hospitals, schools, guilds, large slices out of episcopal endowments, sees left empty and even the fabric of churches (for instance: the cloisters of St. Paul's seized by Somerset). All this torrent of wealth was deflected from the King's treasury to the pockets of the old landed gentry and of a crowd of new adventurers at the Court. Henry VIII, who let loose the avalanche, profited nothing. Partly from weakness, partly from riotous expenditure, partly from the need of support (every single county member of the Reformation Parliament shared in the spoil), partly because the real revenue sank alarmingly decade by decade and necessitated forced sales, the great mass of the stolen property went to the landlords old and new, and their allies and connexions, the wealthier merchants—especially of London.

The worst of the rush was over in a dozen years; but the process went on in the shape of big bites out of ecclesiastical endowments during all the Tudor time to the end of the sixteenth century.

As a parallel effect the Royal Domain began to disappear. Small landlords and great continually and ceaselessly encroached upon the Forests, turning public into private land for their enrichment.[1] Royal manors were exchanged to disadvantage or bought on scandalous terms of purchase [2] or given away.

Meanwhile, with the new gold pouring in from Spanish America all over Europe the purchasing value of money

[1] It was one main cause of Charles I's fall that he tried desperately to check the abuse. One of the counts against him is that he inquired strictly into the thefts of Forest land and made the culprits pay. Cromwell, for instance—once the King was got rid of—filled his pockets with the "conveyance" of Hyde Park. Luckily for London, Charles II made the beneficiaries disgorge; Lambert, his successor in command, got the royal dower lands.

[2] A common one is 10 (nominal) years' purchase. The market rate was 20.

went down and down. When Henry VIII was seizing Westminster Abbey, Glastonbury and the rest, half an ounce of gold was a year's subsistence for a labourer. When Charles I raised his standard at Nottingham a hundred years later three ounces would hardly purchase the same necessaries. To-day some eighteen ounces would be needed. But while the cost to the King's government of labour, materials, provisions, ships, buildings, was thus being multiplied by six between the Reformation and Charles I, the old revenue was being received in the old fixed customary terms—and at the same time its sources in land were being rapidly filched away by the gentry.

By the time of the Restoration, in 1660, the Crown was utterly ruined. What had once been exceptional irregular doles, agreed to by Parliament to supplement the much larger permanent and fixed annual revenue of the King, had become a regular necessary supply. The 'King's own' could not supply one-fifth at the utmost, soon not one-tenth, even in time of peace, of the expense of public services.

Meanwhile a powerful political effect accompanied this economic one. The new wealth of the gentry had made them overwhelmingly great against the poor shadow of kingship. It had also made them greater than they had been against the mass of Englishmen. There was still a peasantry, but it was a peasantry impoverished and it did not grow. Above it a considerable class of substantial small owners survived—perhaps a fifth of the agricultural population (then the bulk of the people). But the squires quite overshadowed them, and in the gradual ascent to the very large territorial fortunes each superior rank had a disproportionate power over that below it. The King of the seventeenth century could not here in England, as he could elsewhere, appeal to the populace against the rich; for by the rich the populace was already controlled.

Kingship then, in 1660, was no more; its resources had disappeared. Its mechanical functions remained and their exercise might deceive one wearing the crown into believing himself strong. He himself still named all ministers, chose his own councillors, appointed to every executive office, declared policy, commissioned all commanders of all forces, and their offices, chose magistrates and judges, made peace and war. But to work the machine, to provide for its activity, he depended on the subsidies allowed him by the new oligarchy, already soon to become the ruling aristocracy of England and to make an end of all but the simulacrum of Monarchy.

On this account the King of that pitiful 'restoration' was far from what the poorer mass of Englishmen still believed him to be: their monarch and protector, and master of their more immediate masters. The gentry took away his right to collect dues from them, and put in its place a tax levied on the mass of Englishmen during *their* good pleasure. They confiscated to their own advantage further masses of peasant land and the King could not prevent them. He had rather become the dependant in action of a few great men, to whom he had always to give way in main matters of legislation, and complete subservience to whom, even in foreign policy, he only escaped by perpetually manœuvring, by playing one millionaire against another and subtly working on the special baseness of each; one's avarice, another's spite, another's terror of exposure, another's vices. To such ignominy had the last fragment of Kingship fallen. Yet only at such a price could even that fragment be maintained by Charles II—and because Charles's brother James would not pay that price, or knew not how to arrange it, he fell.

Now the overt instrument whereby the dominant

wealthy class controlled the King was Parliament. It be-hoves us next, in discovering what world that was against which James, Duke of York, and later King, struggled in vain, to try and answer the question: What was Parliament in that mid-lifetime of his, 1660-1688—the day of his action, the space between his twenty-seventh and his fifty-fifth year?

[2]

We talk, and talk rightly, throughout the English seventeenth century, of 'A conflict between King and Parliament.' It is a conflict in which Parliament is constantly in the ascendant and the Crown rapidly falling.

The process is continuous. First there is the growing mutter of this thing, 'Parliament,' against the Crown before the end of Elizabeth's reign. The voice becomes much louder under James I. Parliament begins to assume a place at the King's side, and on a capital occasion—the Petition of Right in 1628—it imposes its will upon his son Charles I. It takes the whole stage. The King is already so frightened that he dare not summon it. He attempts for many years to suppress it. When at last he is compelled to let it out of its lair it presses him back, yielding, from one position to another, orders him to put to death Strafford, his most loyal defender against its aggressions, then makes war on himself, captures him, and kills him.

By that time, 1649—twenty-one years after its first open victory in the Petition of Right—Parliament is clearly become the chief instrument in the realm for affirming the power of propertied men over their former master the King, and, after the confusion of eleven years' military government, its power reappears stronger than ever.

Throughout the reigns of the murdered man's two children, Charles and James, it fills the first place in

40

English affairs. Parliament—though still doubtfully leaving the mere machinery of government in the King's hands —is used by the new power of wealth to control that machinery *and* the King. Charles II, for years cannot move without the leave and support of its chief members. He admits their right. He submits. Yet even so they remain ready to strike. For a very few years Charles contrived at the end to act freely without the incubus of Parliament. The system could not have lasted. James for a much briefer period attempted so to act and wholly failed. Parliament was master.

Such had been the growth of Parliament as a lever wherewith to overset the national government common to all, and substitute for it the government of money.

But what was it? Parliament, in terms of flesh and blood, meant (mainly) the great landowners and the wealthy commercial families of the towns with whom they were intermarried, and with whom they formed that plutocratic class which was ousting the Crown; but it meant more than that, otherwise we should not talk of that class as 'using Parliament' for its own ends, or of Parliament's being the 'instrument' of that class. A body of men do not use themselves as an instrument. They use something other. The victory of Parliament over the Crown meant on its largest lines the real victory of a growing plutocracy (soon to be an aristocracy) over that popular monarchy which truly represented the whole people of England: but Parliament was not identical with the plutocracy.

Parliament consisted in two assemblies, one called the House of Lords, the other the House of Commons. (The names and forms survive.)

The House of Lords was a growing body of some 80 to 140 men, nearly all of them immensely wealthy, but also of good lineage. Hardly any but had, by this time, three generations of large landownership behind him; and large ownership of land meant a considerable population of dependants, of tenants, and their labourers, small subservient freeholders, servants and patronized writers, clergymen and managers. The House of Lords was the gentry in the most powerful expression of that class. With these laymen sat the two archbishops and the bishops twenty-six in number.

The House of Lords was the more important by far of the two houses because it was far the wealthier; further, it was of a size permitting corporate action, not unwieldy, there were close connexions by marriage within this corporation, and its members had great power in the countrysides over the market towns and the smaller landowners. From the House of Lords were taken nearly all those who entered the King's Council. The royal princes sat there, legitimate and illegitimate. It was the chamber where the King's throne was (and still is—but empty), where he read his addresses and in which he himself appeared, following debates.

The House of Commons had, however, a power of its own, long claimed by custom, which turned on this: that in it alone could subsidies in aid of the Crown be normally originated and discussed. The Lords could negative such proposals. They could not as a rule mould or decide them.

Solemn laws, to be of permanent effect, had (by this time) to be agreed upon by both houses and the Crown. The proposals for them could originate in either house. A decision for or against such proposals was arrived at in either house by an absolute majority of those present and had so been arrived at for a long time past. Further, the Houses of Parliament had gradually arrogated to themselves the powers of courts of justice, and the Commons had usurped the power to order any Englishman's imprisonment by their sole decision.

But Parliament possessed a more terrifying power than that. It could condemn to death. True, the King's warrant was required before the Englishman so condemned could be killed. But, by this time, that warrant could hardly be refused. The victim was presented by a majority decision of the Commons to be tried by the Peers, who, by a majority decision, condemned him to death or less, or acquitted him. The process was called 'Impeachment.' Further, the House of Lords was the last court of appeal in ordinary cases of law.

It will be seen what a formidable weapon Parliament was, whether, as at first, wielded by the wealthy class as a weapon against the old decaying national monarchy, or as, later, the seat of government.

Had the House of Commons been formed entirely on the model of a lesser House of Lords, had it consisted, by right (as it later did), of no one but rich men, only less rich than the few peers, had it been confined to the lesser landed gentry or the restricted and wealthy merchant bodies of the towns, then Parliament under Charles and James would have been identical with that monied class which was rapidly seizing power and dethroning the King. It would not have been an instrument for them to use against the King, it would have been themselves— as it became after James's defeat and remained far into the nineteenth century—that is, as long as it held real power.

Now the House of Commons prior to 1688 was more or less of that nature in practice, but not wholly so even in practice; and in theory not at all so. It was in this point of theory that its value resided as a tool for fashioning the new aristocratic government of England and for cutting down the old monarchy. For the House of Commons was, in theory, representative of something. It was not representative of the People of England, but it could pretend to be representative of a certain fraction of the People of England; and hence it was always possible for those who used it to speak (with their tongues in their cheeks) of the 'people,' the 'Country,' and for more sincere men to claim, with justice, that its decisions had a considerable and socially important body of opinion behind them.

It was formed of two elements closely fused. (*a*) Gentlemen called 'Knights of the Shire' (they were for much the most part landed men, though sometimes rich lawyers) sent up from the villages and countrysides, two for each county; (*b*) Gentlemen, merchants, occasionally lawyers, called 'Burgesses' and sent up from a great number of towns and villages large and small called 'Boroughs.' These 'Boroughs' were originally an arbitrary list of towns decided by the Crown at its discretion: at first on common-sense lines distinguishing the market town from the village; later, under the Tudors, with a good deal of 'packing' keeping back one small place and putting in another to suit the Government. But the principal towns were always included. By the time of the Stuarts this list had crystallized, and though some places in it were dwindled to hamlets or less they continued to send Burgesses, while villages grown into small towns sent none.

The counties were about 50 in number and sent 80 members. The boroughs averaged 200 in number, sending some 400 members: the average number of members voting in a division varied from 250 to over 300.

'Election' to Parliament, in our modern sense of that word, was rare at the Restoration, but became commoner at its close. But even when there were opposing candidates the number of those who could or would come to the county centre to vote was small. But what did give the gentry who were nominated (or nominated themselves) for the counties some sort of moral support was the theoretical right of any one owing land to the value of £2 a year to vote. Many of those below the gentry were prosperous and felt the effects of taxation.

The number of these yeomen at the beginning of the seventeenth century was large. It is probable that before the Civil War a fourth or more of rural England was in this class, if we count in the poorer owners. Later they were less—being eaten up by the gentry, and probably in James's reign not a seventh. The other three-fourths of rural Englishmen, labourers and those who leased land, did not count.

As to the towns, there was an inextricable confusion, and it is impossible to present any general scheme. The greater number of Boroughs (some of them were now not even hamlets, and a great number were but large villages) returned to Parliament two members chosen by mayor or corporation or by a couple of bailiffs sitting in a pub for that purpose, or (in practice) by the local rich land-owner. There were many and large exceptions. In some towns even men who had no freehold in the place and were only leaseholders could vote (when, at the very end of the seventeenth century, voting became general); but in general the Burgesses, like the county members, were simply important local people. It is not quite true to say that the members of Commons appointed themselves, though many did so; but it is true to say that they were essentially a corporation of rich men, the 'tail' as it were of the Lords, who held the really great fortunes of £5,000, £10,000 . and in one exception case even £20,000 a year.[1]

[1] The purchasing value of money in 1660 was about six times what it is to-day. The real wealth of the country per head was a good deal

The average income of Members of the House of Commons under Charles II was vaguely guessed (by Temple—a man of sound judgment) as being roughly about £300 a year, say £2,000 a year in purchasing value to-day and far more in social value.

Such was Parliament. It was not the 'nation' or 'the people.' It was a group of rich men, led by the very rich but in touch with a much larger number—say one-fifth gradually lessening to one-seventh of the nation, including all property owners: of whom a certain fraction actually voted.[2] It was, of course, no *numerical* reflection of the English people. Only a small minority of these could have anything to do with it, and only a small fraction of that minority did actually have anything to do with it. Four-fifths of its membership sat for boroughs. For Agricultural England—the vast majority of the people— sat less than a fifth of the House of Commons. A parliamentary majority had no connexion with a popular majority.

For a proper appreciation of the time it is essential to remember that the bulk of men were not thinking in terms of abstract political theory, but of concrete realities. They saw on the one side a kingship centuries old, of which the tradition was still lively in their minds; they saw on the other a gathering of squires, lawyers and merchants who had already largely usurped, who were trying wholly to usurp, the place of that kingship. When popular ballads ridiculed the 'Parliament' as 'Five Hundred Kings,' they represented the way in which the average man, count-

---

less than it is now, and the population only just over an eighth of what it is now. So the social value of an income of, say, 10,000 a year was far more than the same to-day multiplied by 6. It was not what £60,000 is to-day in England, it was more like (in social scale), what £150,000 or £200,000 is to-day.

[2] For instance, in 1685 in the large and populous county of Essex some 3,000 odd voted—say a twelfth or fifteenth of the adult men.

ing in all, rich and poor, enthusiast and indifferent, looked at the affair. It was a struggle between the kind of government his fathers had always reverenced as legitimate and a new kind of government with certainly no better right. Only that new upstart kind of government could speak for the religious mood of the majority at a time when the King himself and very many educated men were contemptuous of that mood, at a time when James, Duke of York, the man who was brother and heir to the King, had declared his abandonment of that mood, and his adhesion to its opponent.

Towards the end of the long struggle, those really affected by the successes of the Parliament were much fewer than they had been at the beginning. The victorious rebellion of 1688 was the triumph of a small but very wealthy privileged class which had already begun to destroy the yeomen, and was soon to exclude from government all outside its own body.

That small wealthy class had won the battle against the king because it had been able to use Parliament as its instrument, and because Parliament could pretend to some warped and distorted connexion with the most important minority of the nation—the taxpayers.

But it could not have won by relying on Parliament alone. Parliament was too manifestly a selfish, restricted body to be safe in a frontal attack on the national crown. It won by calling in a widely diffused force, one discovered in all classes of the community, intense in less than a third at most, but present in some degree through at least three-quarters of the nation: dislike and dread of the Catholic Church.

This was the agent which the Supplanters of Monarchy found ready to hand and used for their purpose, and we must see how the Catholic Church stood in that Eng-

land of 1660-88 if we are to understand why the throne
fell as early and as suddenly as it did.

[3]

ENGLISH CATHOLICISM

What was the position of Catholicism in England during the reigns of the last Stuarts—between 1660 and
1688?

That is the fundamental question which must be
accurately answered if we are to understand the fortunes
of James II.

The answer will still appear paradoxical to many, and
to some fantastic. For the old official history is, though
demonstrably false, still strong; it is still compulsorily
imposed in the State schools; it is still taken for granted
in every Public School and University, in the universal
test of examinations, in the Press, in fiction, in everything.

Catholicism in the England of the Restoration and
during all those nearly thirty years between the Restoration and the Revolution, held a position which may be
defined as follows:—

(1) It was numerically strong. Its professed adherents
were perhaps a seventh, certainly an eighth of the nation,
while those who in varying degrees sympathized with
or were at least not hostile to that important minority
cannot have come to less than as much again: perhaps
to more.

I leave to a note at the end of this volume the discussion of this truth. The details would interrupt the
reader if I were to print them here. It is enough to say
that every applicable test leads us to such an estimate.

The proportion of the great families (which means
also the proportion of the little worlds they governed,
and of their class in general); the proportion of Catholic

officers, not a score of years earlier, in Charles's armies; the proportion of Catholics noted in the question to Magistrates (1687); the very large number of Catholics who leave London in 1678 rather than make even a temporary concealment of their religion—all these converging evidences point to the same figure: from an eighth to a seventh of the population.

(2) Catholicism in England between 1660 and 1688 was a force upon the up-grade, though the slope was not a steep one. There was a tendency, especially throughout the governing class, to veer towards the Catholic side of things, and in many individual instances to accept the Faith openly.

(3) When Charles II was 21 and his brother James 18, all old people could remember an England in which a Catholic habit of mind was still the national tradition and mood of the England for which Shakespeare wrote his plays—as essentially Catholic in all their tone—in what they took for granted of man, his nature and his faith—as, say, Tennyson's poems are Protestant.

(4) Catholicism was thought even stronger than it was. The turning-point had been the date of the Gunpowder Plot, 1605. After that the anti-Catholic body in England grew rapidly. But we must remember that men's conceptions of society lie in the past; the middle-aged men of 1660, though Catholicism in England had been weakening very rapidly indeed during the preceding half-century, thought of it as more powerful than it really was in that year.

(5) The anti-Catholic feeling was of many shades. The national tone as a whole had become anti-Catholic long before the Restoration of 1660. It was already clearly anti-Catholic before 1625. But the degree in which such moods affect different layers of a society differ greatly. Save in moments of excitement there is a large

section which is almost indifferent, though potentially material for any sudden enthusiasm in their keener neighbours. There is another section not indifferent, but much more concerned with daily life than any ideal. Only a few will anywhere devote themselves over considerable periods of time to the active defence of what is the general mental tone of a much larger number.

There is a section overlapping this last, and larger than this last, which feels very strongly upon the matter and forms a sort of reserve, as it were, which can be mobilized in the cause before there has been time to recruit the mass of the national material.

So it was with the England of the Restoration in 1680 and even of James II's reign, 1685-8. The nation was anti-Catholic; a very large minority of the nation was pronouncedly anti-Catholic; a large minority, a third according to contemporary evidence, felt strongly enough to resist actively any movement towards Catholicism, and within this minority was to be found a smaller but still very large group which made their antagonism to the Faith the chief business of their lives.

(6) The organized wealth of the country, the corporations of the governing class, at a moment when wealth had become the test of governing power, at a moment when the great landlords were eating up the yeomen, at a moment when the body of gentry was replacing the Crown as the source of government, was definitely, officially, permanently and with extreme tenacity, anti-Catholic.

This last point is really the determining one. The official Church, the Legal Corporations, the Universities, the Town Councils, the Gentry in local government, what was left of the London Guilds, were not only, like the mass of Englishmen, now in the anti-Catholic tradition, but were anti-Catholic in essence. The origins of their new power all lay in the Reformation.

That, stated in general terms, seems to me the position between 1660 and 1688.

But to appreciate the matter rightly we must look at it from many other points of view. Catholicism was stronger than its mere numbers might imply from the fact that England had just been relieved of an exceedingly unpopular Puritan despotism. The hatred of Puritanism which filled most men led many to a lenient judgment of what Puritans chiefly foamed against, though they none the less believed it to be an irrational superstition. Another social force, making in the same direction, was the type of literature, the type of architecture, the type of painting, which informed the time. The spirit of all this proceeded in the main from the Catholic culture of Europe. The effect of such things is both subtle and indirect, but it must be noted, for it is strong.

On the other hand, something much stronger was making against Catholicism, and that was jealousy of the power of France. That growing power struck every eye; while the corresponding decline of Spain was not yet grasped. Not only does the populace everywhere hate the foreigner nearest to hand, nor was there only the contrast between Englishmen and Frenchmen, which had developed rapidly since the Reformation—there was also the spectacle in France of a powerful popular monarchy, the very contradiction of that aristocratic plutocracy which was already the main character of the English State. By every instinct, whether conscious in the form of direct policy or only as a vague political mood, the English gentry dreaded the example of the completed kingship across the Channel. Its triumph in the general civilization of Europe would have been the destruction of their power, their wealth, and, in fairness we must add, of their convictions; for they had by this time (most of them) already persuaded themselves of what their descendants have taken for granted for more than two hundred years, that their rule over the mass of their poorer fellow countrymen is in the nature of things; something the negation of which is unnatural and indecent.

In a very different fashion, of great weight also, was the spectacle of Ireland. Ireland, it must be remembered, was not yet ruined, though the process of ruining it had begun. In population it was nothing like equal to Great Britain, but it was probably at least a third (some said rather over a quarter). Its shipping was still very considerable, as was its commerce; and though the Irish had been dispossessed of their land by a spoliation which has no parallel in history, the Irish people in the mass were Catholics. The falling away of the Irish social leaders from Catholicism, though already considerable, was not so universal as it was to become a lifetime and two lifetimes later.

These forces combined made the opposition to Catholicism a very strong, permanent and almost unchangeable thing. The most that the old religion could have done would have been to keep its position, with perhaps some considerable increase of its numbers especially among the educated, but not to have converted the mass of Englishmen.

Supposing by an impossible hypothesis that the defeat of James II had not taken place (a man fighting organized wealth is always defeated), England would presumably have been down to our own time a nation possessed of a large Catholic minority, as is Holland; that minority entering into the professions, the universities, the army, but never determining the general spirit of the nation. It might have had a considerable effect upon English literature. It would, at any rate, have been a great and permanent feature in the nation.

As it was, the Revolution produced an astonishing change. Immediately after it the considerable Catholic body diminishes with startling rapidity. The children forget their fathers' religion or abandon it. All the doubtful or weak give up the struggle. By the time the generation of 1688 was dead, by the years which opened the second half of the eighteenth century (when the last Stuart effort failed), the numerial position of Catholics in England had sunk to nothingness. They were barely one in a hundred of the population and their weight was far less than even such paltry numbers would suggest. They appeared as rarities and in their social spirit had largely merged into the Protestant world around them.

It was not so in the critical years of the Restoration. To-day the Catholic is, to most Englishmen, something alien and the member of an insignificant body. Then he represented a most powerful national tradition not long overcome, very tenacious in all memories, as is our tradition of the old rural England of the early nineteenth century. Any close acquaintance with the mid-seventeenth century in England convinces the student both of the presence of Catholicism on all sides and of the ease with which men passed from one group to the other. Lord Carlisle, Cromwell's adherent, had been a Catholic. Fauconberg, Cromwell's own son-in-law, had been a Catholic. John Milton's brother was a Catholic all his life. Lord Bristol and a dozen of his sort became Catholic when it was least easy. I shall have occasion later in these pages to show how widely the Catholic Church was working on at least the educated England of this time. I will here conclude with only two examples—but they are typical.

Take the case of Sir John Coventry. It is most illumi-

nating. Here was a man typical of the class which made up
Parliament; a squire by birth, Member for Evesham,
returned (by his family) to the Long Parliament thirty
years before Charles II's return, serving as a Cavalier
(wherefore, after five years of membership, the Long
Parliament expelled him), given honours at Charles's
accession, and yet acting soon after in opposition to the
King. He was fond of the bottle, and had wit. He was
also brave in the field and in private quarrel. He could
not resist the chance of making a very gross and insulting
jest against Charles [1] during the debate upon Playhouses.
Perhaps he was drunk when he made it. At any rate, Monmouth and sundry others of the young bloods waylaid
him and slit his nose for it—but he had it sewn up so
well that it hardly showed. Here is a man representative
of all manner of things in his time and of the class which
supplanted the monarchy: a man loving the rapier-play
and the cavalry swordmanship of the seventeenth century:
a boon companion and a challenger to arms: put into
Parliament as a matter of course by his relations because
they were the important family in his district. Does it
not make you understand the nature of the time to learn
that such a man after such adventures, for and against
the Crown, following such professions of arms and politics, and apparently a fairly typical example of his class
in the nation, left an ardent will recommending his soul
to the prayers of Our Lady; asking to be buried in the
Queen's Catholic Chapel in Somerset House; bequeath-
ing the greater part of his wealth to the Jesuits at St.
Omer? Of course the governing class and their lawyers
would not allow the will to stand. But does not the incident throw light upon what masses of men there were

[1] He accused the King of those unnatural vices to which all Charles's
character was alien, but of which opinion accused the Prince of Orange,
his nephew, and his cousin, the brother of Louis XIV.

at that moment who had, in James's own famous words, 'still their religion to choose'? And does it not show how strong the old religious tradition could still prove itself?

My other example, which is most illuminating, shall be that of the Duchess of York herself, Anne Hyde, James's first wife. The reader will later hear some appreciation of her position and character, the part she played, her representative quality: by which I mean that she was not an eccentric but one typical of her class. She was a woman far better known for her judgment than for her wit. She directed her husband's opinion; she influenced that of others; she was a great person at Court; she was presumably the future Queen; it was not in her to do anything which in the eyes of her surrounders at Court, in general Society, or before the Nation, would have seemed extravagant.

Well, Anne Hyde became Catholic. She did so deliberately, and evidently after long thought. She made no concealment of it; she prepared a document which no one can read without being convinced of its sincerity. Those who might pretend that she was under the influence of her husband, know as little of her husband as they do of herself. He would be moved by her far more than she by him, strong character though he was. His respect for her decisions was profound. He abided by them; what is more, I think it nearly certain that at the moment of her reception James had himself not yet been received.

There is more in her case than this; for it helps one also to understand how a believing, deep and pondering mind then acted while yet within the Anglican communion, and this in its turn helps one to understand what the spirit of the Anglican communion—or much of it— was in that day, and why the general fear of its possible reunion with Rome had some grounds.

This woman communicated; not frequently, but once a month. Before every communion she went to confession, having for Confessor and director, as her rank demanded, a member of the Anglican hierarchy, the Bishop of Worcester. She received what she believed to be Canonical absolution from his lips. Until she had so made Auricular Confession and obtained Sacramental absolution, she would not receive the Eucharist—the Body of the Lord, as she believed it to be. The great movement which has recently taken place in modern England may make a story of this kind acceptable enough, but the point for the reader to grasp is, that in the mid-seventeenth century such an attitude was neither combative nor extreme, nor even, properly speaking, exceptional. It took place within the general machinery of the Church of England, and seemed to those who adopted it, and indeed to those who heard of it, no affectation, still less any innovation.

The whole thing is a sharp example; a revelation to modern eyes of what the time was and why the gulf between the Established Church and the Dissenting bodies was then so deep. By all this I do not mean, of course, that Anne Hyde's practice was an average thing, or one that would be found in most of her rank. But though she was Clarendon's daughter, coming of the general run of well-to-do Anglican squires and lawyers, her manner in religion did not connote any violent contrast with her surroundings.

It was then the strength of Catholicism at that date— a strength to-day almost forgotten in England—a strength moral and numerical—which explains both the sudden outbursts of violence against it and renders comprehensible what otherwise makes wild nonsense: the acute fear of that which our popular historians, reading the present into the past, represent as being, in these days, but an insignificant handful of Englishmen quite different from their kind. On the contrary, the Catholics of England under Charles and James formed a most powerful group, and they still represented, in their compact spiritual stronghold, the most ancient tradition of England: the ancestral religion which had been so slowly and painfully rooted out from the stubborn soil where it was native, and the universal presence of which was as near a memory to the contemporaries of Charles and James as the days of the Regency are to ourselves.

It was this strength of Catholicism in numbers here, in the general European culture of the day abroad, in its manifest attraction for the better educated and governing classes, which aroused against its toleration that public resentment upon which the cynical and godless clique arrayed against the last kings of England played with such fatal success.

III

THE FIRST EXILE

WE CAN judge by his actions, as from his great mass of letters and other writings, what James Stuart was: what manner of man we should have found if we had met and spoken with him. But to discover how he came to be this we must particularly note, as with any other man, the formative years.

There is that internal which directs the form of a man. It escapes us. It is the cause of the individual. But there is also, striking like a die upon material more or less plastic, the powerful external influence of experience during the years of transition: the teens. What inward forces inherited, warped, developed out of sight, produced his excellencies and defects, strength and limitations, we shall never discover; but we can follow a period of tossed and shaken youth not undergone by any other man called in later life not only to govern, but to attempt, as duty commanded him, an impossible task.

Remarking the sincere directness of his intentions, always and everywhere, his firmness and venturesome courage, remarking also that odd insufficiency which cut him off from his fellow men, that lack of sympathy which both led him to misunderstand their plots and to lose their devotion, we perceive the whole to be connected with a set of youthful accidents, so unusual, so rapidly contrasted in episodes of good and evil fortune, while yet his mind and body were growing to maturity, as would, in the case of another man, have made him something romantic in history for ever.

When the great rebellion against his father's hereditary government broke out, he was a child of 9; too young to have any conception of the world. When the dreadful news of his father's murder reached Paris he was advanced in his sixteenth year. All in between, which is for most boys the story of regular lessons, of games, with a routine of discipline—the most fixed and secure part of their lives, at school or at home—was with him an amazing sequence of rumour, battle, defeat, peril of imprisonment and death, escape in disguise, great receptions abroad, exile again, abandonment, sharp poverty. The succeeding years, when he passed from boyhood into manhood, were a perpetual employment in arms and successive vivid experiences of battle where his conspicuous valour was tested and loudly praised. All the while he was an abandoned Prince with a ruined cause and a future like night before him—until suddenly, within a few weeks, all changes and he is the brother and heir of a restored king.

What an education and hardening! He profited by it; but he only half profited by it. It strengthened a character already strong, but it did not develop that character. One may say that such experiences tempered and hardened the outer armour of the man, but by so doing separated him from his fellows even more than his natural temper would have done. Adversity made him more intense within; but all this diversity of experience of good and evil, of travel, of courts and camps, poor lodgings and palaces, taught him nothing of mankind.

The first thing to remark in the man so formed is that intense *nationalism* upon which I have already insisted in my introductory sketch of his character. I there said how strange it was to find this in any royalty, and especially in him, who was the product of a marriage between Scotch-Danish blood and French and Italian.

Like all royalties he met men of every region and rank. He was surrounded in boyhood by every Western language, and (as one might think) by every Western influence. He should have turned out, like all royalties, cosmopolitan. Instead of that he was an intense Englishman. Nationalism was his permanent inspiration.

I mean by this word Nationalism what to-day is sometimes rather wrongly called patriotism: not only devotion to one's own country but an ineradicable contempt for all that is not of one's own country: a referring of everything foreign to one's own national habit. This intense nationalism which clung to him during the whole of his life arose in part, as I have said, and largely, from that note of isolation which was native to the man. His moods turned inwards. But so far as the externals of life affected him during the formative years it was due, I think, very largely to his exile; to his having to meet common Netherlands and Frenchmen and Spaniards not as inferiors but as close companions: as men often playing the superior to him, while he nourished in his own heart memories of a royal childhood in England.

Examples of this distilled Englishry in James II you will find scattered all up and down his life, to the very last moments of it. No ship could be a good ship unless it was an English ship. The English courage in battle is for him a unique thing, necessarily and quite obviously superior to the courage of lesser breeds. It is noteworthy that with a French mother and in the highest cosmopolitan surroundings of a court he—Henry IV's grandson!—disdained what was then universal to his class, whether in Holland, Germany or England: the effort to attain French culture and speech. He boasted, as I have said, an insular accent, and when a certain hesitation in his delivery made him, in the eyes of the Frenchmen, ridiculous, he was quite indifferent. Their amusement seemed to him but the folly of an inferior race.

There is a point in connexion with James's Nationalism which, to many modern readers who only know the man through our official historians will sound novel indeed, but which is very evident on reading his own writings. James's religion was English. It was English in him to be intensely Protestant, and, after his conversion to Catholicism, to be so rigid and absorbed in his new convictions.

Here I am dealing with a thing very difficult to describe in words, just as one cannot describe a colour or the tone of an instrument. But there is something quite unmistakable in the way an Englishman takes his religion, whether that religion be Atheism or Calvinism or anything else. He clings to it and he worries about it. And that 'English way of taking religion' you will find in James most strikingly, just as you will find in him the awkwardness, the self-centred isolation of the soul, the lack of expansiveness, and (to introduce a nobler word) the pride which supports in any English tourist to-day his self-respect, but makes him the butt of more gregarious nations. When Victor Hugo said of England, 'It is an island: and every Englishman is an island,' he spoke with vision. James was an island.

Let me return to another source of that first strong Protestantism of his: the worship of his father's memory. It was laudable; it also contained, of course, a great deal of illusion.

That father, while the boy was still a child, goes off to great wars. He is seen by the growing lad at rare intervals as a military figure at the head of an army. He has come from this siege, from that battle. A close intimacy, which might have bred a special affection, could not have nourished hero-worship; but of such close intimacy James had none. I know of few things more pathetic in history than

the single restrained sentence which he wrote down at the
end of a long life telling how his father, when leaving
Oxford after the ruin of his cause, 'had intended to take
the Duke of York with him, but upon consideration
decided to leave him within the town.' Lord! How that
handsome little fellow of 13 must have wished to ride out
with his father and to have shared Charles's high fortune
to the end!

From the moment of his father's leaving, James goes
through adventures which must be known in some detail
if we are to comprehend the character on which their
memory had so deep an effect.

There is the boy, shut up with the Royalist garrison
in Oxford, until the town surrenders to the Parliamentarians on old midsummer's day 1646. He comes for
the first time into direct contact with the rich men who
had destroyed his father's power. He notes their varied
demeanour. There is an absence, in too many, of due
respect; the Commander-in-Chief, Fairfax, does not kiss
his hand. Then he hears the harsh voice of Cromwell and
sees that large, booted man kneeling before him, kissing
his hand, and paying him an especial deference. For
Cromwell was still intriguing for the support of royalty
against his rivals till the right moment should come to
destroy the king and his family.

Thenceforward the boy is a prisoner. He so remains
for months—a new experience of evil, lasting from his
thirteenth to his fifteenth year. And all that while his
father's image stands bright in his mind.

Now for what did the image stand? Charles's devotion
was to the Church of England. It will be remembered
how he withstood that wife of his for all her unquiet
energy and in spite of his devotion to her, when it came
to the matter of the Catholic faith; how he restricted
her services in that communion; how jealously he watched

to prevent her giving any handle to those who complained that the English Crown was not sufficiently opposed to Rome. Can any one forget how, as he rode north to raise his standard, he caused two priests to be disembowelled (or plain hanged—I forget which) as a sort of confirmation of his resistance to the pretensions of their creed? In the last moments of his life Charles protested (and it was with the utmost sincerity) that he died, not only for the English people—and that also was true—but for the rights of the Church of England. She has recently repaid him by striking his name off her calendar.

There came in to reinforce this Protestantism of the young James his natural reaction against the fussiness of his mother. When Henrietta Maria was working to make Gloucester, his younger brother, a Papist, we have seen how he objected and interfered with all his might. He felt himself a sort of guardian to the boy's national traditions and his mother to be taking advantage of their orphanage. He was successful. The Cadet died young, but soundly saved from Rome. When serving as a soldier abroad James's lack of sympathy with his Catholic fellow officers is apparent enough, especially in the case of the Spaniards. His natural sympathy with the Huguenot French officers is equally apparent.

Once more I must introduce what may seem a fantastic point to the modern reader, but it is a true one. The strong Protestantism of James left some tincture in his mind after he had accepted the Catholic faith; it appeared especially towards the end of his life. Here I must steer carefully lest I give a false impression. He was not Jansenist—and no gentleman of that high sort could ever be Puritan. But there are phrases in his voluminous remarkable notes upon religion which lean towards all that side of things the excess of which is Jansenism among the cultured, and Puritanism among the rest. He has not the gaiety of the Faith: and indeed no gaiety. He had not the tenderness of it. I can recall no devotion of his towards the Mother of God.

Now from this strong Protestantism and strong Englishry of the growing lad under his rapidly changing surroundings, turn to that combative love of adventure which marked his whole life. This also was formed during his early years of exile, of peril, of poverty.

Take first the adventure of his escape.

After Oxford he was still left with Sir George Ratcliffe by the generosity or inertness of Fairfax. He was taken to London—his mother interfering as usual, plying him with dangerous correspondence from abroad. He was lodged in St. James's, and there Lord Northumberland, the Percy, governed him and was his gaoler. In the account he himself has given he testifies to the courtesy and good breeding of the man. Indeed James is always just to opponents and even oppressors. It is one of the things which distinguishes him most clearly from his enemies even in his last disasters. *They* lie and exaggerate impudently wherever he is concerned: but his own words are downright and his pledges kept. He owed this generosity in part to ignorance of knaves. It would seem as though to know too much of men were to know too much of evil.

Though thus a prisoner (and he fell ill of an ague, which we would call influenza, in the late winter of 1646-7) he was allowed to see his father at Henley for a moment, in June of the latter year. He never saw him again.

We must remember that at this moment he was not 14 years old, yet he was already beginning his continual attempts at escape. A letter of his in cypher being intercepted (the Bishop of Salisbury's wife was his confidant in the matter) he was bullied by a committee of parliamentarians. They threatened him with the Tower, and that sooner or later would have meant the loss of his life.

Even under their bullyings he refused to betray those who had helped him. But there is in connexion with these attempts to escape from St. James's Palace one most characteristic incident. He gave a solemn promise to these parliamentarians that he would not communicate with the Queen his mother. Another letter came from her. He refused to receive it. This refusal caused the first of their many quarrels. But he said at the time, and repeated it years later, that his honour forbade his breaking his promise. James always had that fine sense of morals. He knew by a right instinct when it is legitimate to lie, and when it is illegitimate. He would not betray his accomplices; but he would not betray, either, his solemnly pledged word.

We have a contemporary drawing of St. James's Palace, where he was kept confined. The little domestic brick building stands with fields and a park on either side: an oak paling runs up north from it towards Piccadilly Lane. The high roof of the Abbey, the lower one of Westminster Hall, show above the trees half a mile away. There is no house visible between; and stretching from the little palace eastwards towards what is now Trafalgar Square are a couple of gardens with their fruit trees.

The episode of his final evasion merits a detailed account; for among a dozen other characteristics of the already ripening character it exemplifies that careful method, that attention to detail, which (divorced from judgment) became in him, a lifetime later, when he had grown elderly, excessive. He had made his two efforts to get away, and had been discovered in each. Now, however, in the early spring of 1648, his chance was to come. What did he do?

For a fortnight before the date agreed upon he started

games of hide and seek with his little sister and brother. There is a curiously boyish boast, written down years afterwards, in which he tells how cleverly he hid himself so that they would be seeking him half an hour, and how he would give himself up at last because they could never have found him. When the right day came, the 20th April, 1648 (he was then, as I have said, in his fifteenth year), after dusk, at seven o'clock the gardener of the Close (called 'Spring Gardens,' at the very end of the palace walks towards the east, the end which gave upon Charing Cross) was sent for and asked for the keys of the door; he was told that they were needed because the Prince would go hunting the next day at a very early hour. The gardener gave him one of his keys. It is presumable that, like the mass of the common people, all his sympathies were with the Crown, for he must have known that the boy was a prisoner.

James waited until nine o'clock on that dark, moonless night; unlocked the door, somewhere near the place where the lane we still call Spring Garden stands—by the old offices of the London County Council—he found outside Colonel Dampfield, who was awaiting him. This companion put a bandage across his face with a shield over the whole of one eye, and part of the forehead, and nose, as though he had to deal with some one who had suffered an accident. Thus disguised, Dampfield led him to a carriage which a certain Mr. Trip had been ordered to bring up for delivery of the Prince. They went quickly to one of the public stairs upon the river shore hard at hand—perhaps those of Whitehall—and drifted down the half ebb-tide (it would seem till near ten) to a house near London Bridge. There James was dressed in petticoats as a girl, took another boat with Dampfield, and followed the last of the tide on to Greenwich.

This second embarkation was on something with sails,

for we know that on approaching Greenwich the Master refused to go farther, saying that as the wind was rising and blowing up-river, it would be better to anchor than to beat slowly down with the chance of meeting the midnight flood against them before they had made much headway.

But the fugitives could not afford to wait. Their lives were at stake—Dampfield's certainly and at once; ultimately the Duke's. That was why it had behoved those who cared for the lad's life to see that he should escape overseas. The fact that Charles I alone of the Royal Family was later murdered must not blind us to the danger which every male member of that family ran. For we must consider the motive. Charles I was put to death upon the main motive that his survival endangered the heads of the chief rebels—particularly Cromwell's. Now it endangered no less the heads of his male descendants. Of his little daughter one cannot say the same thing; but with the young man the heir, already of age to take the throne, and with James his brother, then within a few years of the same age, it was another matter. Because it did not happen, people now cannot imagine the murder of the sons after that of the father. But the people of the day could imagine it well enough, and they were right. Cromwell saw clearly. He was a 'realist,' as the German phrase goes; and whatever he saw needed to be done to his own advantage, that he did. . . .

The real reason the Master of the barge refused to go farther down the river was that he had watched his passengers and had discovered their secret; he had seen through a crack the young lad take off the Order of the Garter which he wore, perceived the incongruity of the ornament upon a girl, made certain that it was some young man of great importance, and suddenly guessed that no lad of such an age would have the Garter save the Duke of York.

He smiled, therefore, when Dampfield begged him to drop farther down-river, urging the peril to this young lady who had most important business to attend to in Holland. The worthy man could only say that he had never heard of young ladies who were Knights of the Garter. Upon this James, boy as he was, boldly risked the throw. He told that bargee that he was Prince of England, Charles's son. He assured him that if he were succoured he would see that the bargee should later be very well rewarded. But there was no need to bribe. Here again the loyalty of the common people served him. Monarchy, of course, was still taken for granted by all the mass of Englishmen, and by this same Thames bargee amongst the rest.

He got them to Gravesend before meeting the flood, pulled in the sweeps with which apparently they were helping to make against the wind, shortened sail, and shot through the gap in the boom which had been thrown across the river—without being noticed by the watch on shore.

It was the most perilous moment of the flight: but it was passed. James went ashore at Tilbury, found a Dutch vessel of some seventy tons which had been provided for him, and which lay there at anchor, and so went on board.

There were still anxious hours to pass: the next ebb did not run till between six and seven o'clock when it had long been broad daylight. But no one hindered them, and they had the luck of a new wind which blew from the west. By the next dawn they were off Flushing, bumped twice on the bar (running in false alarm from a vessel taken for a Parliament frigate), reached Middleburg and so The Hague—where James was received by his sister the Princess of Orange and was safe.

Such things as these happening to a boy before he is 15 powerfully impress the mind; and much more was to follow. After he had seen his sister the Princess of Orange and his brother Charles, his mother called him into France. On the way he stopped at the Abbey of St. Armande, halted because the civil disturbances in France were not yet settled, and it was while he lay there (from early in January 1649 to the 8th February) that, unknown to him, his father was being done to death in London.

He got to Paris on February the 13th. It was not till the 14th or 15th that he heard of what had happened a fortnight before: that Charles the King had been murdered. It is characteristic of him that in his detailed memories of the time he refuses to describe what passed in his mind.

The formal side of his character becomes apparent immediately, even so early in life. His father, Charles I, had been put to death by the rebels? Well, then, his brother Charles was now Charles the Second, and his king. Therefore when his brother Charles asks him to come back to Brussels in the next year, he obeys as a subject, though his mother the Queen violently protests.

He was in Brussels by the 13th October, 1650. His sister's husband, the Prince of Orange, died not long after his arrival, and three days later, on the 14th November, was born that posthumous child William Henry called in English history William III; the man who later was to be a figurehead for those who betrayed James himself and broke the line of English kings.

His sister would not receive him because of their mother's protests at his departure. Further, he was in great poverty. It was not till January of the next year that she accepted him at her court, at The Hague, and only then because Henrietta Maria relented. His brother the King gives another order—he is to go back to Paris; he does so.

He was now nearly a young man; he was in his eighteenth year. Embarrassed for money, as were his brother
and his mother too (though she was the aunt of the French
King), their position was yet such that some great match
might have been made for him, and there was proposed
one of the greatest of heiresses—from over the left;
but James considered his rank, and the French government, that is, the Cardinal, forbade it. Immediately after
came the crash of the Battle of Worcester, and the royal
cause in England seemed lost for good and all.

James felt his increasing poverty. He felt little else.
Of the rights of his blood he could no more doubt than
he could doubt his own name. I think it true to say that
he did not appreciate what an effect Worcester had upon
the mind of Mazarin and the young French king, his own
cousin. After Worcester every one made up their minds
that the Stuart cause was lost; but James's mind remained
as it did throughout his life, lonely and fixed deep in its
own ideas. His brother was King of England. He was
himself brother and heir presumptive to the Crown of
England. Whether he were poor or rich, whether battles
were lost or won, made no difference. Though still under
19, he desires to play the part of his rank, he insists upon
active service. He will enter the French army. He must
have the least sum necessary for his accoutrement, 300
pistoles. He troubles not his family or any equal. He seeks
the sum in the way of business from a man who makes it
his business to lend. He tells us in a sort of aside that he
borrowed those 300 pistoles 'from a Gascon.' He gives
us the Gascon's name: Gautier.

Thence onwards for six years—the most vivid six years
of a man's life—he loses himself in the profession of
arms. He adored it. He was born for it. When, after the
Restoration, his position and the lack of expeditions or a
sufficient force forbade him a military post, he took the

next best thing he could find and commanded at sea—and there found his chief talent. That accident which warps all human record, a great or simple, has hidden from posterity the trade native to James Stuart. He was made to be a soldier or sailor; a commander in battle. That was what suited him; that was what he understood. He had not the capacities of a general-in-chief. He would not have attained them; but he was born for the service and admirably fitted to command a unit in the field, though hardly an army.

During these six young years of his, from his nineteenth to his twenty-fourth year, when he was riding out day after day at the head of his troop, later of his regiment, he discovers everywhere not only the active mind of a man who is suited to command, but an intellectual interest in the affair of arms which distinguishes a special sort of soldier from his fellows. There in the French service among the officers, and especially the Huguenot officers with whom he consorted and whom he understood, he lived the life which he would have wished to live, I suppose, for ever. And that new experience was yet another force moulding him.

For one thing, it gave him an opportunity for showing his courage, and that courage was conspicuous. Condé said of him later, in his Memoirs of past years, that 'in the matter of courage in a man, he desired to see nothing better than the Duke of York.' The great Turenne, his Huguenot General, praised him not only for that, a minor quality (alas!) in the individual soldier, but also for his 'eye,' his quick knowledge of what to do. And by the way, the great Turenne insisted on lending the embarrassed Stuart, so heavily under the weather, another 300 pistoles, as had the Gascon.

James's fighting spirit appeared in his whole life, from the encounter when he drew his sword as a boy in the

Low Countries upon an envoy of Cromwell's responsible for his father's death, to the moment when, more than forty years later, he mustered the force in Normandy for a last effort at recovering his crown. That spirit had full play during these years of service in the French army at war.

There is a certain quality in courage which leads a man who possesses it to tell the story of action in a direct and true fashion, without reticence, and especially without that damnable apology for talking of himself which marks the vain man. James's descriptions of his service show that quality.

He kept a diary during all this time, so that we have a mass of detail on it, and when he himself did anything remarkable or was in any remarkable situation, he put it down.

For instance, at the siege of Mousson in 1653, when he was just 20, he tells how a shot hit three barrels of gunpowder close by him and his fellow officers (they had gone up to the front trenches) and how those three barrels did not explode; and what would have happened if they had. (One thing that would not have happened was the Revolution.) He tells us casually how a spent bullet hit him on the foot; 'the toe of his boot.' He tells us how (two years later, in the summer of '55) he lived during the siege of St. Ghislain in a little hut within musket-shot of the walls, while his brother officers were far back beyond or at extreme cannon range. This he does not quote as an example of courage, so much as an amusing trick; 'for' says he 'the enemy did not believe the hut to be inhabited; so the Duke saw everything from close at hand.'

There is no doubt that this youthful experience of his in the French army coloured his whole life. He was fond of the officers his colleagues, he took on the impress of what was then and for long after the best of all trades, at that moment in life when men are most permanently influenced. This, I think, accounts for his odd, alien, friendship towards the French, which he kept up all his life. But it never obscured in him that schoolboy certitude in what seemed to him the natural, inevitable, supremacy of British blood.

With the end of 1655 there comes an episode which may justly be quoted as a test of the young man's developing character, and of the way in which it was tending.

He was told that an alliance with Cromwell (his father's murderer) was essential to French policy. Cromwell had what was then the best army in Europe—veteran, well paid, highly disciplined, excellent in every way. He put it up to auction, as it were, between France and Spain. And Mazarin, conducting French affairs, explained to the young man that if the Government of the French King did not capture Cromwell's alliance, it would go to Spain and turn the whole war. James's comment was, 'Mazarin serves his master well'; he, James, had no right to complain.

In the treaty with Cromwell, all that the ephemeral despot of England insisted on was that James, if he must remain in the French service, should not fight in Flanders. His reason was obvious. James in Flanders might have been a rallying point at any moment for English desertion. The average Englishman was for the Crown. The Puritan despotism was increasingly unpopular. Indeed, later on, after the battle in front of Dunkirk, Reynolds, who commanded that very fine body of Cromwellian troops which drove the Spaniards from the Dunes, desired an interview with the Duke of York, and in this interview made it clear that his heart was with the royal cause, as were the hearts of all such Englishmen. Of what profit to them was the Parliamentary set and Cromwell?

James was set aside to work with the French armies in Italy. But his brother, permanently exiled by the new alliance between Cromwell and the French, ordered him to leave the service, and it is characteristic of him that he obeyed.

It was a miserable period, this period of James's young manhood, his twenty-third and twenty-fourth years, just before the Restoration.

He was being badgered to get rid of his friends. The wretched, exiled, out-at-elbows crew which was not a court, split up into factions. The Duke of York was asked to sacrifice those intimate servitors who were most devoted to him; and the trade he followed, the trade of arms, which he had begun to love so well, and to enjoy, and in which he had shown so great intelligence, seemed closed to him.

In 1657 he got leave from his brother, now that he could no longer serve with the French, to serve with the Spaniards. He did so with distinction, and his account of what happened in the Battle of the Dunes in front of Dunkirk is the best we possess. You cannot read the writing of the man without seeing how well he understood field operations. But the Spanish service did not suit him. He complains of its formality, and—in that moment of the great decline in Spain—of its lack of perception in war. It is from him that we have the story of how when he, the young man of 24, saw the opportunity of cutting off a big convoy of the enemy's, he was refused leave because Don Juan, the Commander, had given no orders. When he asked that orders should be sought, he was told that Don Juan could not be disturbed; he was having a siesta under a hedge, during the advance of the army in the summer heat.

There are touches in all that description of the Battle of the Dunes which are delightful. One where he praises the courage of his little brother, the Duke of Gloucester. Another where he tells how he was certain that the Anglo-French army was about to advance (on June the 14th, 1658); that he alone of the officers had gone out to the line of sentries and seen to the preparations. How Don Juan would not believe him. And then (most character-istic) his impetuous comment: 'would the enemy have come out in full battalia, with their guns before their horse, to push in outposts?'

There is also in his account that lapidary phrase of the Condé to young Gloucester, confirming his brother's sound eye and judgment in saying that a general action would ensue. For Condé said to Gloucester, 'Have you ever seen a battle?'

'No,' said the boy.

'Well,' said the other grimly, 'in half an hour you will see one.'

But best of all (to return to the note I have struck so often) is the English heart of James. He finds himself with certain troops, English indeed, but exiled like him-self, pitted against English regiments; they now appeared on those sand-hills so recently in our own time drenched with English blood. The English regiments opposed to him were those coming under the orders of the man who had killed his father. The English ships standing off the shore were cannonading his own forces. Yet in all he writes, his heart is with the other side.

When Cromwell's regiments in their red coats charge the big sand-hill with a roar and turn the Spaniards off it, he writes of them with an enthusiasm that might make you think he was engaged in their own ranks. He himself leads his mounted men against the position and is beaten back. He makes you feel that it was the courage of those English troops which forbade his success. And when he tells the story of the Spanish boats going out to attack the English ships, and turning tail at the first shots, his pride is in England and with the English sailor.

That is how the man was formed: in exile, worried by a fussing mother, reacting against that fuss strongly, so as to detest her religion, proud of his Protestant training, devoted to his Protestant father's memory, passionate for the England from which he had been exiled, unable to think highly of anything not English, but friends with, and keeping as a permanent memory, his French companions in arms: of the Spanish contemptuous.

There comes a last act. Those who understand England know by the late autumn of 1659 that the Restoration is afoot. Foreigners will not believe it. His brother Charles, who was in Spain negotiating, was not even allowed to pass through the French territory on his way back, so little did any one at the French Court believe that what was coming, *was* coming. James in disguise at Boulogne (the last of these innumerable adventures—and how exciting!) only just escaped from capture at the hands of the Governor of the town and his garrison—because they had to prevent anything being done by the English Pretenders, and believed, even at this late hour, that the monarchy in England was ruined for ever.

Yet the Restoration was immediately at hand—and it was at this moment that the young man, as yet tardy in such affairs, was caught by Anne Hyde.

James was 26 years old. He was not easily accessible. In spite of his military reputation he had not had the love of women. Perhaps he had not that of Anne Hyde; but to be approached at all was a novelty and she approached him. She was 22—yet she was older than he, and really knew the world, which, to the end of his life, he did not understand. He was there, lonely, in the half-court of his sister the widowed Princess of Orange with her little sharp-eyed, stunted, wizened boy, his nephew,

William, at her side—a boy then still innocent and even timid, but peevish. Anne made of James her companion —and more. The opportunity was flagrant. She was the Princess's maid of honour: a stuff of which Queens had been made.

She was the daughter of that Edward Hyde whom history knows as Lord Clarendon. A lawyer born of the landed gentry but of no great family, he served Charles I consistently though half-hearted in his cause—feeling, like most of his rank, that the gentry had a right to withstand the Crown. He had been Charles's chief minister and advisor, had accompanied his sons into exile and was sincere in his horror at his master's murder. A podgy, self-satisfied man (it is to his credit that he knew good cooking), he should by rights of his face have been short; he was, against all the rules with such a face, of at least medium stature. He felt himself in a half-paternal relationship to the exiles. He wrote admirably; on which account his famous History of the Great Rebellion has misled posterity not through its numerous errors of fact nor through its military incapacity, but by the fact that his service of the King makes it pass for a fair statement of the legitimate cause—whereas, in truth, his heart perpetually hankered after his kin, the squires and lawyers, the upper-class in revolt and conquering the Crown. He had married the wealthy daughter of the too wealthy Aylesbury, mathematician and master of the Mint. She had borne him, among other children, this daughter Anne in 1637.

Anne Hyde was dark, she was ugly, she was vivacious, she was intelligent. She had will. She had also what is rarer, and not often an accompaniment of these: judgment. Her large mouth uttered sense and her blobby eyes—for they were bulging—looked firmly and strongly at mankind, comprehended it, and conveyed decisions.

In all this she had nothing from her father save some power of planning, but inherited perhaps from her mother, perhaps from an earlier strain. Such was the woman who, in the last days of impoverished exile, cast her net over the young man James.

The moment was well chosen. On the 14th November, 1659, Monk at the head of the great Cromwellian army (Cromwell dead a year and more) was preparing to march. The order had gone out for a Parliament. On the 24th November, the news of Monk's action already received at The Hague, a document was dated and signed. It was a promise of marriage between the Duke of York and Anne Hyde, and it bore the hand of James Stuart.

They were not strangers. She had first seen him nearly four years before when, reaching Paris with the Princess of Orange, very early in 1656, she at 18 had met the lad of 22 for a moment—but his fortunes were still falling. She had seen him again for a moment later in the same year when her Court was visiting the Queen Mother, Henrietta Maria. They met once more, the year after, at Breda. But still the fortunes of the exiles fell and there was nothing doing. *Now*, in her opinion, by November 1659, things had changed. The Court of France did not foresee that imminent Restoration. James did not foresee it. She foresaw it.

It is not to be believed that Clarendon was originally a party to his daughter's move. It is certain that when the thing was public in England (in the summer of 1660 after the return of the royal brothers in May) he filled the air with his loud protestations, shouting shrilly that he had rather see his daughter dead than so disgracing the monarchy. It is equally certain that he perceived what advantage might accrue to himself by this marriage—and also what peril. By that time he knew her condition well enough. She had been with child since February 1660.

The Queen Mother stormed against the marriage with even more than her customary vigour: raged and protested. An heir to England married to a lawyer's daughter! The (possibly) future Queen of England a lawyer's daughter! A lawyer's daughter upon *her* throne!

Mazarin, more astute, calmed her, and himself made no overt move. He did not want James to bear a grudge. Yet it was perhaps he who saw to it that certain young bloods should boast Anne to have been their mistress, and so make her affianced husband hesitate. It was a calumny, but an index of how Anne was regarded. James did not hesitate for long. On the 3rd September, 1660, he married her in the dead of night in her father's house. On the 22nd October their first child was born.

It was a boy, called Duke of Cambridge, destined to die within a year. What if he had lived, or any of his younger brothers? But of eight children of that marriage all died young save two: Mary, born on January the 10th, 1662, Anne on February the 16th, 1664. Both to be Queens of England.

Before Christmas the Duchess was acknowledged. The courtiers came to kiss hands as to royalty. She was accepted and at once she dominated. She filled her position with ease, and all men rallied to the admission of it. She acquired immediately the way of her new rank. She was easily the equal of those born to it; and as the years passed without a child to Charles, as she became more fixedly the wife of the heir apparent, in a sort of minor way she reigned.

Her husband had for her an increasing respect. He followed her decisions; he was even led by them. His infidelities she first condoned, then chafed under. But her power over him never diminished, and she alone could ever exercise such power. Had she lived she might have taught him, as King, how to meet the wiles and hypocrisies of his opponents. But after eleven years of intimacy, ten of wifehood, during which she had balanced and, in effect, enlarged that rigid, sadly separated mind, she died.

IV

ADMIRALTY

HAD James II shirked the burden of the Faith; had he denied or concealed reality when he had discovered it, he would be immensely famous in English history as the creator of the Navy.

There is nothing which Englishmen for over two centuries have more regarded as their peculiar pride and the expression of their country than the Navy. Since the beginning of the great change in wealth and numbers the Navy has been their instrument of power and advance. It has given them the markets of the East and the vast expansion of their race overseas. For more than a century —from 1794 to 1914—it remained supreme, easily procuring a complete immunity from foreign aggression (till such aggression came at last to seem incredible) and freedom for action at will upon foreign nations. Between Waterloo and the Boer War—a very long lifetime of eighty-four years—it secured the preponderance of England in Europe and the world.

For a man to stand at the origins of so mighty a thing would be as permanent a title to fame as could be found for him, nor would fame have been spared James II. From what we know of legends in matters of the sea it would certainly have been exaggerated. And yet it would be difficult to exaggerate the effect of his combined industry in naval affairs and passion for ships. It is from him that dates the transition from an irregular to a regular, from a spasmodic to a permanent Service. The regulations take from him their fixed form; he is at the origin of all the chief traditions of the fleet.

Nor did this creative work of his come any too early. The French and the Dutch services were senior and better organized. They had behind them a greater revenue, and if Parliament had succeeded (as it nearly did) in starving the British Navy to death in its origins, the rivals of England would have gained, in the race for naval supremacy, a start which would never have been recovered. As it was, and thanks to the Duke of York, a regular list of ships, sufficient dockyards, a standing personnel came into being and has since grown uninterruptedly.

If we mean by the British Navy any group of ships under the orders of Government, for no matter how short a period, no matter how summarily gathered, manned and equipped, under no matter what ownership, then its origins may be referred at random to Henry VII, Alfred or Carausius: but if we mean a continuous body with unbroken traditions, regularly manned by disciplined seamen, professional, with a fixed corps of officers and of permanent establishment, then that force dates from, and was created by, the Duke of York, later James II of England and VII of Scotland.

He it is who made that instrument on which the strength of modern England has since reposed.

It was his father who had made the thing possible by first insisting upon the complete central control of the national arms. Charles I had had sharp and humiliating experience early in his reign of what the old hotchpotch fashion of mixing a few 'king's ships' with a number of hired or speculative private craft could produce. He could not, with the Government embarrassed for money, create a fleet wholly in its service. He still had to depend largely on private craft. But he set out to form a nucleus of ships solely designed for fighting and transport, owned and commanded by Government.

It should have been clear to any reasonable and patriotic man that such a force was necessary, faced as England was by the new and far superior maritime organization of France under Richelieu, and with the growing power of Holland. The Modern Fleet, regularly and permanently organized for war, was arising among the rivals of England who held the opposite coasts of the narrow seas. There was an imperative necessity for England under Charles I to meet that foreign effort.

But the rich merchants and squires whose organ of action was the House of Commons, and of whom the Reformation had made such increasingly formidable opponents to the national monarchy, were pressing their novel revolutionary claim to forbid revenue save what they might allow, and on their own terms of power; and this, in practice, had meant that they would pay as little as possible. The revenue of the country, as provided by them, fell shamefully low, and they hampered every effort to increase it, preferring their pockets and ambition to their country. To provide for the defence of England they allowed far less than could be raised by the Dutch: but a fraction of what poured into the treasury of the King of France.

Charles I did his best. By the levy of a special fund under writs of 'Ship money' he did produce a fleet—comparable at least to the foreigner's. He commissioned between forty and fifty ships—five of them first-raters of over a thousand tons—and carrying between them nearly 1,500 guns. But the effect could only be spasmodic. The great demonstration of 1636 which for a moment gave England the mastery of the narrow seas was ephemeral; regular financial supply was lacking; and on the eve of the Civil War, in 1639, England could only look on while the Dutch—with all the political weight of Richelieu's France behind them—destroyed the last Spanish fleet of the North within a few miles of Dover.

Nevertheless it was the vessels and naval stores present through Charles's patriotic policy which, though largely out of use from lack of supply, formed the very instrument of his defeat.

On the outbreak of the Parliamentary Rebellion in 1642 the Two Houses controlled London and nearly all the main seaports. They seized Portsmouth, they kept Hull. Save for a short interval after Prince Regent's capture of Bristol the King was blocked from the sea by the Parliament's capture of his own fleet—of the fleet he had built in spite of Parliament. They rigged, munitioned and commissioned Charles's own ships against the King, paying new and high wages to the seamen now hired to man them. The best national work of the National Monarchy became the very instrument of its defeat. One of the first actions of the Parliamentary commanders was to fire, when the Queen had landed, upon the house from which she barely escaped with her life. It was symbolic of the naval power of the rebellion.

That same wealthy class which had been so reluctant to give of their wealth for the country were now lavish of their own and others to defend their domination. For the better part of twenty years (1642-60)—with one interlude of mutiny—a considerable naval force was kept in being, rapidly acquiring cohesion and a professional spirit. During the latter part of this interval—under the despotism called The Commonwealth—the very large resources in money which an absolute ruler can command by force, and which Cromwell chiefly devoted to his armed supremacy, maintained great strength at sea, and the already long experience of naval warfare was confirmed.

But the British Navy was not yet in being. In the

anarchy after Cromwell's death the ships effected nothing, and not even so many years of war had created a tradition or a continuous force—still less a permanent body of officers and men. The old conception still remained in men's minds that ships were to be used only on occasions of crisis; that the craft directly owned by Government should, in such crises, be mixed with private vessels; that in normal times the hulls should lie idle; that they were to be rigged, munitioned and fitted out, and crews gathered, haphazard and only on the threat of war.

What changed all that and began the new phase in English history—the phase of sea-power—was the taking over of active work at the Admiralty by the Duke of York immediately upon his brother's restoration to the throne.

The Duke of York, who had of right been Lord High Admiral of England since his youth, now at the age of 26 hoisted his flag at Schevenig in active command of a united fleet. It was the 23rd of May, 1660, and from that date begins his great work in the founding of the Navy.

The chief difficulty—lack of money—was (for the moment) not pressing. It was only not pressing by the accident of the occasion. Parliament, normally and persistently opposed to furnishing a sufficient revenue, had for the moment provided one. It did not indeed settle a sufficient permanent revenue for the Government, as it should have done—but it did at least provide a nominal revenue of twelve hundred thousand pounds, which in practice might reach a million or less. The Restoration House of Commons did this—characteristically—at the expense of the mass of Englishmen and to the increase of their own fortunes as great landowners. They abolished the feudal dues of the Crown, they replaced and added to them by an excise on articles of general consumption. At any rate, a large sum was immediately available, and in the true tradition of the Stuart monarchy it was mainly used to restore—or create—a navy. Two-thirds of the whole financial power of the Crown was set aside for the proper provisioning of the fleet and for the restoration of the two great arsenals, that in the Thames and the other at Portsmouth.

James's next step was one of capital importance: the first in the establishment of a true national navy. It was the creation of a *permanent* and *professional* body of naval officers.

When the officers present in the ships at the Restoration had been put through a necessary process of examination and selection—to eliminate the disloyal—a certain proportion of the most competent and trustworthy were given a guarantee of continuous employment whether in peace or war, whether in a ship or on shore, by a system of retaining fees which were, in effect, permanent minimum salaries; these were increased on active service, but were at all times sufficient to maintain their recipients. Thus was originated by the Duke of York that corps of professional sailors whom we now call the officers of the Royal Navy.

To this original act of foundation was soon added another: recruitment. The Duke of York set up the Midshipman: the lad who was to be trained from boyhood to the sea, to grow up in the service and so to provide for the constant maintainance of the corps of naval officers. This second and very important step was taken as early as the 7th of May, 1661, less than a year after the Duke's accession to his direction of the Admiralty.

The original title was not that of 'Midshipman'. This was originally applied to certain petty officers, of which we may remark James's personal (and characteristic) decision, that they could not be married and go permanently ashore until they had completed seven full years of sea-service. The young gentlemen who were now, in

May 1661, given places in each king's ship going out were termed 'Vounteers' and later 'King's Letter Boys'. They had, to begin with, the pay of a Midshipman, and thus the old term 'Midshipman', formerly applied to that non-commissioned rank whereto the lads' commissions were affiliated, was gradually transferred, by custom, to them alone.

The new system was not yet exclusive. A man could get a commission from any origin, especially after sea-service in a lower capacity. Nor had the 'King's Letter Boy' a right to promotion. But he was there in his ship with the special object of studying navigation, of rising to be lieutenant and, in practice, of feeding the new organization with a regular supply of trained command.[1]

At the same time a whole new administrative service was set up by James which is the parent, in unbroken succession, of the vast machine in operation to-day. At the head of the financial side was the Treasurer of the Navy; dependent for supplies, of course, upon the Exchequer, but *responsible* to the Duke himself as Lord High Admiral. Three other great officers, subordinate, were the Comptroller, the Surveyor and the Clerk—or as we should say 'Secretary'—each also directly responsible to the Duke. Similar offices, or their predecessors, had already existed at times in a less defined fashion. But the full new organization with its host of subordinates was the creation of the King's brother upon the Restoration, and they served a force afloat which was greatly increased in numbers, tonnage and efficiency from anything that had been known before.

To all this was added (in this same first year of James's active founding of a permanent fleet) the 'Orders' and 'General Instructions' which are the parents of the

---

[1] The first so to be received was young Mr. Thomas Darcy. He is the Adam of Midshipmen.

'King's Regulations and Admiralty Instructions.' Here again there had been previous rough models under the Commonwealth, and some of James's orders copy these; but his work as a whole is new. After its issue (in 44 articles of 'Instructions' and 10 'Orders') the old chaos of separate rules and disciplinary regulations at the caprice of transient fleet commanders in war, was finally displaced by an official, united and national system.

That all this was done in so short a time was due to that characteristic in James which all have noted, some very foolishly ridiculed: his immense industry. He worked, and he made others work; and that in a day when work was not the fashion. For whole hours together the pen was never out of his hand, and in the intervals he was visiting the ships and docks, examining details, suggesting reforms, calling for accounts, checking figures of material.

In so brief an appreciation, let one example serve. It will appeal, I think, to all men interested to-day in the Service, for it is of permanent interest. The industry of the Duke of York and his active application to everything regarding his charge of the sea was particularly effective in his memorandum on the size of Units.

It is a very old quarrel, of which our newspapers and debates were full half a lifetime ago (I know not how the matter stands now), whether at sea one should lean to a majority in the number of gun platforms, that is ships, or to a superiority of power in the individual ship. It is clear one cannot have both. With a certain sum to expend you may build fifty craft each of such and such gun power, and so be able to act dispersed, or twenty-five of double (in practice more than double) the gun power in each, and so dominate the enemy when concentrated. I have no competence in the matter. It is to be presumed, I suppose, that the problem varies with changes in armament, in methods of propulsion, and the rest. But at any rate there can be no doubt that the Duke of York thought clearly at a time when his contemporaries were thinking in a more muddle-headed fashion or (most of them) not thinking at all. He was for the large unit, or at any rate for the unit equal in gun power to the unit of his rivals, the French and Dutch.

Consider the conditions. The French fleet, largely the creation of Richelieu, had been met and countered by Charles I's policy of ship money. But the financial difficulty was always present. Even those thirty years earlier Charles I could only raise the money necessary for the navy by an exceptional and perilous effort; so powerful had the propertied classes already become. Since then those classes had won a great war against the Crown and put the King to death. During the whole of that generation they continued to grow more and more powerful. Their power depended on controlling and therefore hampering government expenditure—and as such expenditure involved taxes on themselves, they were reluctant to allow it. But reluctance in expenditure from any cause tends to produce the small unit in a navy rather than the large one. A given amount of money spent on five large ships will provide more power at sea than the same amount of money spent on eight smaller ones. But the person who is gradually doling out the money by bits is prompted to say, 'Surely now you have enough! What? You need another ship? Well, let it be a small one! What? You need yet another? Well, let it be a small one again!' Parsimony always has these effects of interfering with the quality and size of the individual unit. The result of this reluctance in the propertied class to pay taxes, coupled with its acquiring the control of tax levying, was that, throughout the seventeenth century, and even well on into the eighteenth, the English ship of 100 guns hardly counted as equal to the French ship of 80. The unit was inferior. James insisted upon the righting of this—but he was overruled. Over and over again you thus find his conclusions upon matters of the sea justified by posterity.

It would be of the highest interest to possess and analyse James's own judgment on the behaviour of the craft which he commanded. He was obviously by nature a man that should have followed the sea. He caught the tradition of the great English sailors, and he loved their element. He made himself expert in the matter of design; knew a ship's behaviour, whether she was slow in stays, sluggish or crank; followed changes advised in gear and rigging; saw the advantage and disadvantage of that enormous freeboard (necessary, it was thought, for the high-firing guns of his day) of the great beetling poop of those times; of the too bluff bows: he knew which craft sailed closest to the wind: he had his conclusions upon the advantages and disadvantages of heavy draught; his appreciation of how this or that build behaved in a seaway—and all the rest of it.

In his close concern for design in ship-building he had the useful support of his brother. Charles II was strongly interested in the art of naval design, and, for an amateur, not unskilled in it. He and James were perhaps the two men in the kingdom who most appreciated what a strong navy meant to England and how necessary it was to furnish one: not only by sufficient expenditure to secure quantity, but by attention and intelligent application to secure quality. Certainly there was no sign of any such feeling among the great landlords who spent their lives in hampering the Stuart government. Their descendants, when they had succeeded in ruining the Crown and in making England an Aristocracy, were more awake to the value of sea power than any government in Europe. The grandsons of the Territorials who cast down the last of the English Monarchy were the statesmen who presided over, and often who commanded, those fleets of the eighteenth century which gave England the control of the seas. But in the seventeenth century it was not so. In the seventeenth century it was the failing Crown (or the despotism of Cromwell) which provided ships, crews and guns. The organized wealth of England was for starving the service to save its pockets, and on one famous occasion their refusal of financial support allowed an enemy to enter the Thames.

Among the effects of this perpetual struggle for pence, of which the Government might not enforce payment and which the chief taxpayers refused to provide, was a grave hindrance to manning the fleet for war.

The main difficulty in getting crews together was the pay. It was low; it was not handed over till the end of the year; and it was precarious. It is interesting to note that a common seaman working on the decks of a ship bringing coal to London from the north was paid at the end of his voyage at the rate of £2 a week, which is at least £10 in our money. In those days seafaring was not a trade. It is ridiculous to note that a man in the Royal Navy got only one-sixth of this sum. Moreover, in your average merchant ship the men had beer; on the King's ships they were not denied it, but they were stinted of it. It is true that the collier wages were exceptional, were for short journeys, including frequent risk from war, were hampered by a restricted labour market and yet financed by a wealthy and high demand for their cargoes at the port of delivery, the Capital. It is true, also, that their very high wages included the man's provision during the short time he was at sea, while the man in a king's ship was fed. It is also true that the pay at the *rate* of £2 a week was often or usually for less than a month; the passage was a short one, and employment therefore intermittent. Still, when all allowances are made, the contrast is too great.

James could do nothing to better the pay. Funds were lacking. He had therefore to contend with desertion and even with the danger of delay in setting out a fleet, yet so much labour in every other direction produced, within five years of the Restoration, by far the best fleet England had ever boasted, and it was the creation of one man's tenacity, industry, intelligence and devotion to his department.

With that fleet, in personal command as High Admiral, James gained for England the greatest naval victory she had known within living memory, and, indeed, since the Middle Ages. He was to fight at the head of an English fleet once more; but it was at the end of his command, when his enemies were already closing round him. In that second battle also, against odds and with an incompetent ally, he fought very well and had one ship dismasted before he transferred his flag, another sunk. But in this book, which is not a biography, still less a chronicle, but an appreciation, it is sufficient to take the example of 1665. It shows that James was in command. It shows how easily and deservedly he gained his popularity. It shows by contrast how the one fact of his Conversion to Catholicism changed all.

It was on Friday, June the 1st, 1665, that James stood out from his anchorage off Lowestoft, with eighty-eight sail of the line and four fire-ships all told. The 1st of June is a day propitious to the British fleet. His wife, who had been in his flagship (the *Royal Charles*) with her maids, had landed. The Plague had already appeared in London.

On that same day he pressed into the fleet the crews of

many of the coaling vessels coming down from the north towards the Thames. On that same day, Friday, the 1st of June, while the fleet still lay at anchor, James had had information that the Dutch with 113 sail had been sighted to the SSE. The wind was easterly and light. He beat up against it, and came to anchor at the fall of darkness in that shallow sea.

Here the reader should note something which was so obvious to our immediate ancestry that it hardly needed telling, but which in this day of machinery is getting more and more forgotten: the advantage of the weather-gage.

A man-of-war—and this is particularly true of the heavier and deciding units—could not sail close to the wind. With the wind blowing at right angles to her course she could sail finely: with the wind 2 points—22½ degrees—farther forward (or a trifle more, say 25 degrees of a circle) she could sail, but, closer, she had difficulty in carrying on. A full-rigged craft of the day, such as, for instance, James's own flagship, the *Royal Charles*, might carry on with the wind coming from less than a third of the way from the beam to dead ahead; but it only sailed easily with the wind about a quarter of that distance: or, to put it in the terms of the trade, your first-class man-of-war could sail within six points of the wind but hardly five. For instance, supposing the wind was blowing from the south; your man-of-war in those days could sail east or west with speed; she could also sail a little to the south of east or west, say rather less than a third of the quarter-circle between east and south or between west and south; but if you brought her closer to the wind than that, you could do nothing with her; and if you tried to force her to go closer, you were likely to get into great difficulties—hung up, losing way, and not the master of your movements until you let her go off and your sails filled again—during which interval you were at the mercy of any neighbouring opponent.

Under such conditions to have the wind abaft your beam when you were facing an enemy was a first-rate advantage; and that was called "having the weather-gage."

Thus, suppose two lines of ships stretched out from north to south, and facing each other, the one looking westwards, the other looking eastwards, and suppose the wind to be from the east; then the line which faced westward had the wind behind it, that is, it had the weather-gage, and its ships could manœuvre at will. They could bear down on their enemy or slant off to the right or to the left with freedom. But their opponents could not work at all until they had their bows pointing nearly north or nearly south. They were hampered in the action of their craft. They could not attack directly. They were, as contrasted with their enemies, like a man who can only fight to the right or to the left of his body, while his opponent can fight to the right, to the left, and also in front of him. Over and above this the weather-gage gave its possessor the use of fire ships to drift down on the enemy and set his ships alight.

Now the Dutch on this occasion had the weather-gage, for they lay to the east facing westwards, while the English lay to the west facing eastwards; and the slight wind was, as I have said, easterly.

During the next day—Saturday, the 2nd of June—the Duke of York was painfully working his ships eastward against the wind to approach the Dutch. But he could not force the enemy to action because though the wind began drawing towards the south (and therewith freshened somewhat) it was still easterly and the Dutch still had the weather-gage. So by nightfall of this Saturday, the 2nd of June, the English fleet came to anchor again in that shallow sea.

But during the night England had a stroke of luck. The wind got west of south, and gave her ships the weather-gage.

Hitherto the Dutch had declined action because Opdam, who commanded them, though superior in numbers, doubted the issue. But now, with the wind gone round behind the English, he could not decline again save, indeed, by putting on all sail and breaking away. The politicians who were with him, and were his superiors, compelled him to accept battle. De Witt especially insisted, and he was probably right: the domestic situation in Holland was such that even a lost battle hard fought might be better than a retirement. Moreover, it is not certain that the Dutch fleet could have escaped, for perhaps (we are not certain of this) the average rate of sailing on the English side, even before they had hammered their enemy, was superior.

At any rate, the Dutch line accepted battle, and the gunners opened just in the grey of the dawn, at half-past three in the morning, on Sunday, the 3rd of June, 1665.

The two lines faced each other some thirty-five miles south-south-east from Lowestoft in twenty fathom of water.[1]

The English line, lying roughly from north to south, but a little west of north, headed northward; the Dutch, also lying roughly from north to south but a little east of south, headed southwards; the English ships having the south-westerly wind on the port quarter, the Dutch keeping as close as they could to the wind on the star-

---

[1] It is curious that with such detailed accounts as we have of this action it seems impossible to be certain, within many miles, of where it was engaged. There is a version which places it much nearer the English coast and more to the north. I have taken what seems to me the most probable on the evidence of the number of hours sailed.

board tack, that is, with the south-westerly wind coming somewhat forward of the beam, but not so much as to check their sailing. The three divisions of the British lines were commanded, as to the leading one, or northernmost, by Prince Rupert; the hinder was the Blue Squadron, commanded by Sandwich; while in the centre was the Duke, commanding the whole, and in particular this middle or Red Squadron.

We must envisage the big battle as a thing covering about ten miles of sea, the English fleet thus sailing north at the rate of, say 3½ knots an hour (at the most), and the Dutch passing it exchanged broadsides as they sailed: and this first "round" covered something like one and a half hours of time, or nearly two. The superiority of the English fire had already begun to tell.[1]

It was the object of the Dutch when the manœuvre was over to try and recover the weather-gage by passing behind the English and getting to the west of them. But they failed to do so: and within half an hour, it being about six o'clock, the passage was "charged" as contemporaries put it, having taken well over one and a half hours, from just before four o'clock to later than 5.30. Both lines then went about, the English now sailing southerly and the Dutch northerly, so that each presented to its opponent the guns and sides which in the last passage had been untouched by fire.

So they sailed, each past the other, cannonading at short range; Sandwich of course now leading and Rupert at the tail. A third of these manœuvres followed,

---

[1] It is curious to note that most historians of the battle, allowing a rate of sailing of some 3½ knots and the length of the line to be between 9 and 10 miles, think that the Dutch and English fleets took some three hours to pass each other. They forget that, with the fleets sailing in opposite directions, the time should be halved. The relative speed of passing was not 3½ knots but 7. There is here no necessity to read Einstein.

the English sailing north, the Dutch south again, as at
the beginning, hours before.

It is clear that by this time the Dutch must have been
very heavily damaged, for their leading ships could not
come properly up to the wind, and began to fall away
to leeward. James with immediate decision ordered the
whole fleet to go about, that is, to turn south again and
run parallel with the Dutch, so that they could hammer
the enemy indefinitely, not in passing them, but continuously and at close quarters. He put into the action
something of his own fighting spirit, going close in and
delivering his flagship's whole weight of fire. The cannonade was so well maintained that the Dutch could no
longer properly handle their ships and all their attempts
to go about failed.

The action had already been very costly to the English
side in its leading men: and there was one moment when
James, who had been under heavy fire all day long, was
in special peril. It was just after the order to go about
and run southerly parallel with the Dutch, each ship en-
gaging its opposite number. It so happened that of his
squadron, the Red, all save two had dropped out to refit.
There was for the moment a heavily superior fire concentrated upon his flagship, the *Royal Charles*.

It was in this situation that a chain shot killed at one
blow Lord Falmouth, Lord Muskerry and the son of
Lord Burlington, who were standing close to the Duke.
Their blood covered and soaked the clothes of the Admiral
and a fragment of his friend's skull wounded him in
the hand.

The ships that had dropped out to refit recovered their
places, and it was somewhat later that James effected his
decisive blow. The *Eendracht* was opposite to him, and
there was apparent some confusion upon her decks, which
the intensity of the English fire had caused. He took

97

advantage of it. He ordered fire no longer by broadsides but gun by gun so that it was continuous.[1] The first and second tiers had thus rolled out their thunder; fire had begun from the third, next to the water. The first of its two guns had been successively discharged; the third made, perhaps, a lucky shot into the magazine. At any rate, coincident with its discharge, the *Eendracht* blew up, with all her crew of 500—and Opdam himself amongst them. This of course took place in the centre of the action. The Dutch line was already disorganized. The fighting was resolving itself into detached groups when, upon the disaster to their admiral, the rest of the middle ships of the Dutch line broke away and ran for it before the wind. A big gap was thus made in their line. James took immediate advantage of it and cut right through with the south-west wind behind him. The manœuvre had some distant resemblance to what happened at Trafalgar.

With the enemy formation thus broken the English took on ship for ship, rounding upon their enemies to left and to right; and those enemies fought their way out as best they could, running for the Dutch coast. The son of the great van Tromp fought an admirable rearguard action (as it would be called on land) to protect the retirement of his colleagues.

The long June day ended in that light wind with harbours not yet made, with the English fleet in pursuit, the Dutch flying before them, and in that chase through the night it is possible that the enemy might have been destroyed. But there followed a strange incident.

The leading vessel of the chase on the British side

[1] It took some three minutes to run in the piece, swab, reload, run out again and fire: with this interval between the shots of each gun a full broadside meant a corresponding delay before the next could be delivered, whereas a rolling fire of individual guns one after another had upon a shaken enemy quite a different effect. It could break his nerve.

was of course the flagship, the *Royal Charles*, with James on board.[1] The rest of the fleet was to follow the light upon this vessel. The Master was one John Harman, and he was on the quarter-deck when night fell. James had been in the thick of the action all day long, exposing himself with splendid courage, and, as we have seen, with friends killed at his side. He went below after at least eighteen hours of active, highly concentrated and successful command, and of ceaseless cannonade.

There came up from below one of his gentlemen, called Brouncker or Bronkhard, with orders to John Harman that he should shorten sail, that is, lower topsails and give up the chase. The weather required no such precaution. Harman was astonished and asked for confirmation of the order. Brouncker went away for a short space, returned and said he had orders again confirmed by the Duke himself. Harman after some delay reluctantly obeyed those orders. No vessel in the fleet might pass the light of the leading flagship; all three squadrons dropped a knot or two an hour; the Dutch made away in the night and took refuge in the Texel.

There have been endless discussions upon this order to shorten sail, most of them provoked by the hatred of James on account of his later change in religion.

Common sense is enough to show that there was no sort of reason why James should have given the order. It would have been all to his advantage to have followed up the victory and achieved a decision. On the other hand, Brouncker or Bronkhard had a very good reason for not carrying on, which was, that he was frightened. He had shown terror during the action, and had no appetite for more trouble in the night. We also know that he had approached the Master, Harman, with suggestions for the shortening of sail before saying that he had any

[1] She was of 80 guns.

orders from James, and that only after this did he assert that he had James's positive orders.

Now we have in these affairs to go by our knowledge of how men are made. If there was one character in James which went with his obstinacy, it was his straight-forwardness. And when we couple that with the fact that he had no motive for not following up, but every motive for being still in touch with the enemy at daylight, we may make fairly certain, I think, that the order did not proceed from him; and he himself denies it.

The only apparent difficulty in the affair is why Brouncker or Bronkhard was not punished. But that becomes explicable enough when we read the full narrative.

Brouncker or Bronkhard was a man with a good deal of underhand influence. He was a gentleman by birth. He was a member of that powerful rich clique called the House of Commons. He was a coward, and he had been through a most grueling day under conditions where he could not run away without jumping overboard and drowning. The short June night had fallen. The whole day he had been suffering under a furious cannonade. He had no particular desire that the experience should be prolonged and that action should be renewed by the active pursuit of a defeated enemy.

He was James's Gentleman of the Bedchamber. He had seen his master down for that brief moment of rest. Then came his opportunity.

He came up on deck again, with a pretended order from the Duke that the Master of the Flagship should shorten sail. This man, Harman, was naturally astonished at such an order, and said it must be confirmed before he would obey it. Brouncker then disappeared again as though to return to James's cabin, to which, be it remembered, he was the only man who had the right to approach. But he did not go into the Admiral's cabin. He only went below to deceive those on deck into the belief that he had seen his master. He came up again with pretended renewed orders, and Harman reluctantly shortened sail.

Now before James had concluded that very brief and necessary repose of his, that is, just before dawn of that June morning (Monday, the 4th), whether because the wind had died down or from whatever other reason, the topsails were set up again; and when the Duke came up on deck there was no shortening of sail apparent compared with the time when he went away. He saw the Dutch coast at hand—they were now but a very few miles off those low sands—and the enemy had escaped. But James had no idea that sail had been shortened in the night. He thought the enemy had made good their escape during the darkness.

Much later, when he came to know what had happened, he moved at once for a court martial on Brouncker. But —and here is the rub!—Brouncker formed part of that powerful oligarchy the House of Commons, already the master of the Crown. The Members of the House of Commons took up, as they always do, the case of a corrupt colleague and put up every delay against his examination and punishment. First the dreadful business of the Plague, then the Fire, intervened. While these delays were protracting, he was advised to go and hide himself in France, which he did. Things dragged on. James's narrative concludes by saying that after so many (and such!) months, after all this water had passed under the bridge, it would have been morally impossible to revive a lengthy and belated prosecution—and he was undoubtedly right.

There is no one with a knowledge of Parliaments who will not agree. The House of Commons had got its man off. That same body which was responsible for the shame of the Dutch in the Medway was responsible for the immunity of the fellow who had saved the Dutch fleet from destruction two years before.

Such was the great naval battle of 1665, the victory under James's command. It was never equalled in that generation, nor approached, as proof of English dominion single-handed at sea, till long after the youngest of those who had fought in it was dead. When James was, immediately after, ordered by his brother to give up active service, the fleet was taken over by others. They fought well but with no such effect.

It is essential to remember that this battle was not only a greater success than that generation was to see again, but also, as I have said, by far the greatest naval victory ever yet won by an English fleet, unless we are to call the gatherings of the Middle Ages national fleets (for if we count thus, the Sluys was both much more decisive and on a larger scale). It impressed the national mind strongly. On this account it was of the highest advantage to James himself. It was he who had made this navy what it was; and here, now, in the first years of its new character it had triumphed. For though the victory missed being a decision (and we all know from the last war how little the public understands the difference between a decisive battle and a victory), yet the Dutchman, the national enemy of the day, had been very heavily hit. He had lost 4 admirals, 7,000 killed, maimed or prisoners, and 18 of his sail either captured or burnt.

The English losses had been insignificant in comparison. One ship of 50 guns had been captured early in the affair, but all the killed and wounded only amounted to some 600. The losses in the leaders, however, was heavy. I have already give those of Lord Falmouth, Lord Muskerry, and Boyle (Lord Burlington's son). There also fell two of James's naval commanders trained to the sea, Lawson and Sampson, and Lord Portland and Lord Marlborough.

It was part of James's bad luck that this great success, which had made him for the moment the darling of the nation, and would have kept him permanently popular, fell at a moment when London at least (which was the director of England) was too disturbed to feel its full effects. Already before James had sailed to victory the Plague, starting in St. Giles's Parish in the last days of May, had begun to do its work. When the Admiral and his officers returned to land, the panic was beginning, and some three weeks after the great battle in the North Sea all who could afford it, or nearly all, were fleeing from London. Monk was an honourable exception. He remained at his post.

And here comes a passage which we—who review it so long after—perceive to be most unfortunate for England: though it must be admitted in favour of the men of the time that there were strong reasons for their action. The Duke of York, fresh from victory, with so high and so deserved a reputation for courage and (what was more important) of exceptional talent in marine warfare, was withdrawn by superior authority from actual command at sea.

It seems probable or certain that the King's order to this effect was individual. If the suggestion had come from James's enemies he would have told us, but in his own account the decision is laid down wholly to his brother. Charles feared further risk to the life of his heir.

We should remember how strongly the King must have felt in such a matter at that particular moment. He was by this time doubtful of any issue from his wife. If James were killed there would come next in succession a baby barely three years old and a girl at that. He knew on what a precarious tenure he (and his) alone could hold the throne. He knew how much more powerful than the King the wealthy class had become and how easily a minority might destroy what little initiative the nominal head of the country still possessed. He ardently desired the recovery of some part at least of what had been torn away from the English Crown—and for such a recovery a man was needed. He knew that in James he had a man who delighted in personal risk and who fought with gusto—a 'thruster' as the young men of the Great War called such a comrade. From a fresh action the news might come that his brother had fallen. Further, James's popularity seemed now assured, and it was an important asset. Later, when he had become Catholic and had so given his powerful enemies their advantage, it was as essential to attempt a renewal of that popular support. Therefore— in 1672—he was again allowed to command. Again he showed the highest courage and the strongest determination. But it was too late.

Nevertheless, the recall was a disaster, immediate and also at long range. Had James proceeded to further fighting before the eyes of the country he might have become its permanent idol. His conspicuous valour shone where Englishmen have always most admired it, on the quarter-deck. He had already become a hero in their eyes, this young man in the strength of his thirty-second year. Further renown would have set him on a public pedestal from which he could not have been deposed. The common folk, though inflammable on religion, had no part in the political spite and rancour of their betters, the parliamentary gentry, nor any direct burden of taxation to pay for the fleet. They did not appreciate how far the fall of kingship had gone, and against James as the hero of the nation the intriguers at Westminster might have failed even after his change of religion.

For immediate consequence there was the possibility of crippling once and for all the Dutch power at sea. The Duke of York had defeated it and could defeat it again. He earnestly craved the opportunity of inflicting the final blow. It was denied him: Sandwich was put in command, and all James could obtain was the melancholy privilege of seeing the fleet off on its cruise from the Nore, and the pursuance on land of his duties as Lord High Admiral, overlooking and energizing that Naval Administration which was the great occupation of his life.

His popularity was already such that even the Parliament, when it met at Oxford during that plague year of 1665, had to vote him a hundred and twenty thousand pounds and to connect the endowment openly with his gallantry at sea; while the tradition of his success further compelled them to provide over a million and a quarter for the war.

As we shall see, such unusual generosity on the part of these large taxpayers was of short life. For it was but the next year that their lack of patriotism so crippled the forces of the Nation and the Crown that all the main ships had to be laid up, and that England suffered the disgrace of the Dutch in the Medway, burning and carrying off her great men-of-war and threatening London itself.

The full story is a significant one for any man who prefers history to official legend. The starving of the revenue by Parliament with its double motive of avarice and pretension to rule was a fixed political feature of the whole seventeenth century in this country with which I have dealt in its own place. But the examples of 1665 and 1667 are particularly flagrant and must be emphasized and put in the clearest light if we are to understand the shame of the time, and the indifference of the conspirators to the honour of their country in their hunger to master their king.

There is one last note to be added to this story of the great naval victory of '65. We know with what horror the official historians of the nineteenth century talked of a king's power to suspend laws. But when it comes to suspension in causes which their readers would approve, those historians slur over the facts.

Now one of the most important examples of the suspensory power we have in the whole Stuart period, and of its value, is the action of Charles II in preparing for the Dutch war. The parliamentary organization of the wealthy classes happened to be at the moment enthusiastic for the war and even—what was a rare thing with them—ready to vote money for it. But there was no provision of men. The faulty pay was bad enough, as we have seen. Apart from that, mere numbers were lacking. Handling sailing craft is an expert business. You could not in those days pick up any one at random, as we can now, to shovel coal, pull a lever, or handle things on iron deck. And the number of men trained to the sea, a small proportion of the population, was absorbed by the merchant service. When a fleet had to be got ready for war, men had to be kidnapped, that is, taken by force and put aboard. It was a practice which had grown immensely under the Puritan regime, with its contempt for the poor, and had thus become established. How, when they got aboard, they were trained, one wonders!

Now, the necessity for trained seamen was so great that Charles for the purposes of the war suspended the Navigation Acts which forbade the employment of foreigners in English boats; and helped in this way to secure a sufficiency of English seamen for his crews. It has never occurred to the solemn denunciators of the royal power to attack this salutary action. They reserve their criticism for the use of the same royal faculties in the relief of the oppressed.

It should be remarked in this connexion that the Scotch, who still were a separate nation and of whom most still thought themselves a hostile nation, would have nothing to do with the necessities of England. They denied the right of the English Navy to press men in Scotland (they were obviously justified in this), and indeed many of them served on enemy vessels. The Scotch seaman when he was needy seems to have preferred the Dutch service, because there at least he was regularly paid. There was no king in Holland, and the rich men who governed that country, after the model which was beginning to be imposed on England and later triumphed, saw to their public revenue and expenditure accurately, as, to do them justice, the wealthier classes in England also did when they had thoroughly destroyed the power of the Crown. For though in strong resistance to the popular monarchy they had been grudging of contributions, yet when they were well in the saddle they furnished fleets and armies lavishly enough.

V

THE CONVERSION

THE space of time between the accession of Charles II and his death is twenty-five years (May 1660-February 1685). In General History it is the Period of Louis XIV, of French culture and even of French arms: the rapid decline of Spain: the exhaustion of the Germans from the Thirty Years' War of the preceding generation. In the history of England it is the skilful, vigilant and untiring effort of the King to maintain the last ruins of the Monarchy. But in our understanding of his brother these twenty-five years are of another order. They are the period of his conversion to Catholicism and of the consequent opportunity afforded to the enemies of the Monarchy. James's acceptation of the Faith after eleven years of power made possible that fierce attack upon him, led by the great landed fortunes, aided (in part) by an organized London mob at their disposal and mustered by men in their pay; aided in a much less degree by some minority of the nation at large. That attack just—but only just—failed of its main object, which was to prevent James, whose strong character threatened their supremacy, from becoming King. James acceded in due course to the throne. Once crowned, the full ordeal fell upon him, and, then he failed in his turn through mishandling his problem.

All turns, then, on his conversion. This religious and intellectual change in the character of one man, the manner in which he met the furious assault which he knew he would have to face and which he resisted without yielding a step for a dozen years, until he had triumphed over it, are the history of the time.

The period is entered by James as a young man of 26. He leaves it, a man of 51, advanced in middle age. It covers the most active period of his life, and we note that it is in the full manhood of the earlier part that he discovers and at last accepts the Faith: his subsequent challenge and defence are the business of a mind grown unchangeable and finally determined, the mind of later years.

The two portions are nearly equally divided by the approach of a date critical in most lives: the age of forty. He is near forty when his conversion is generally known in 1672, and the main struggle begins. The boundary between the two is the imposition of the Test Act by the great landlords as a blow against the Crown in early 1673. The Test Act was aimed at excluding Catholics in general (not Nonconformists) from doing any public work as officers or ministers or in any other capacity under the Crown. But its main object was the exclusion of the Duke of York from the Council and the Admiralty. There were plenty of Catholics in such places during the ten years following the Restoration. They occasioned no such action. But the moment James himself was known to be Catholic, action was taken.

Until that date, 1673, James's chief public activity remained at the Admiralty to which he was so devoted and to the fleet which, in spite of the universal and deliberate starving of it by the wealthy intriguers against the throne, he maintained through situations almost desperate, and could still present, after a dozen years of such shameful neglect by Parliament, a predominant instrument of war. In the year *before* the Test Act the fleet is maintaining with renewed vigour the power of England by sea. James himself is again commanding in its flagship. He fights a last action in which, despite the incapacity of an inferior French contingent, he stands up successfully to the superior armament of Holland in the fiercest naval battle of that generation.

The Test Act, coming immediately after, compelled him to be silent on religion or to resign. Undoubtedly the King his brother accepted the Act under the impression that James would give up the public profession of Catholicism and keep his place. He did what perhaps no other man of his station in Europe would have done: he preferred Truth to power and he resigned: and from that day the recurrent supremacy of England in the Narrow Seas is ended for a generation.

The next twelve years present for his great energies few public occasions. He is no longer at the head of the department most vital to England. He can no longer see to it that, subject to continual strains from lack of supply, the fleet shall be supported. He has to stand by and observe its decline. He is not even regularly present, of right, at his brother's side in the Council as heir apparent. He has, once and again, for long months to absent himself from England lest his presence should hamper Charles in the perilous duel between the throne and its more powerful subjects. It is proposed to exile him for ever, to exclude him from the succession, to prefer to him his own daughter, her alien husband or a bastard nephew; and all because he is unflinching not only in his private conviction on the only things that count—any one may be that—but in his publication of them and open, challenging adherence. His steadfast attitude, his brother's tardy and compromising but at last sufficient support exhaust the enemy—for a time—and during the last three years of the reign the heir is at peace.

The background to all this personal story of the man is his brother's struggle to maintain the Crown—or what was left of it. That struggle fills the national history of the time, and though we are not principally concerned with it here, we must understand it if we are also to understand the Duke of York during these years; for when his brother had married Catherine of Braganza, the Princess of Portugal, soon after his restoration, it became more and more doubtful, as the years proceeded, that she would bear him an heir. The Duke of York therefore remained the presumptive heir. Had he been mediocre or even pliant, still more had he been as skilful in political intrigue as he was intelligent and determined, he would have been accepted as the chief man in the kingdom. But he was otherwise. He was ill-suited to such a part. His intelligence, which was strong, his energy and capacity for work, which was exceptional, he could not direct either towards finesse or towards appreciating the motives of others. He did not even watch his opponents. He hardly distinguished their characters, he overestimated their morals, he heavily underestimated their power; and (worst and most dangerous trait of all) he was unable to make friends.

Not so Charles. Charles II carried on for these twenty-five years, from his younger manhood to the approach of age and death, as skilful a contest as we can watch in history. He looked into men's hearts—an unpleasing spectacle; he understood them; he could evolve strong personal attachment in the most worthy.

Charles had to play upon a board of eight chequers, as it were, divided into two sets of four, and to consider the perpetual combinations and recombinations of their innumerable interactions.

To change the metaphor, he had to deal with two groups of four forces, each of the eight changing perpetually within, each having varied relations with the other seven, and all concerned, now as enemies, now as supporters, with his own power.

These eight factors were: *First*, the foreign group: (*a*) Holland, (*b*) France, (*c*) The beginnings of colonial expansion, (*d*) The general European situation—on the whole a situation gradually weakening France as the twenty-five years drew to their close; *Second*, the domestic group: (*a*) The Gentry (and their Parliament), especially the score of very rich men who conducted all; (*b*) London—that is, the great merchants, their dependent population and trade (which was expanding rapidly), the residence of Court, Government and Opposition. London was also of exaggerated effect through the concentration there in one place of immense numbers, a fifteenth of all England; (*c*) The People, for whom his Royal Ancestry had stood, for whom his father had died, who were without organ of expression, but who were there, underneath it all, and still had some latent force in them (they supported him in his years of rule without a parliament); (*d*) The two bodies of dissent, Calvinist [1] and Catholic. The former, the Nonconformist, was of the greater size and, beneath the surface, of one culture with the main body, at least, of the Established Church. The other, the Catholic was considerable in actual numbers; as we have seen, from one-seventh to one-eighth of the people. It was also supported by the broad belt of those who, though not risking a public profession, sympathized with Catholicism, and a much broader belt which tolerated it. On the other hand, these numerous Catholics surviving were already half cowed by generations of fierce persecution and ruin. Government had acted with intensity for a hundred years to extirpate the traditional religion. Only the hardest core

[1] The word is appropriate to British Nonconformity, though but one of its numerous sects accepts the full Calvinist discipline. The spirit of the whole is that proceeding from Geneva in the sixteenth century.

had survived, to represent among Englishmen that which had built up their country through a thousand years..

Through this maze of conflicting and shifting forces Charles manœuvred with the ability of a master. Both brothers were active in thought as in frame, but James was incapable of complexity: Charles comprehended and delighted in it. James had one main object, personal and ideal. Charles also had but one, only it was practical and very terrestrial, to maintain for English kingship what little was left of its power: even (if that were possible—and in some measure he succeeded) to increase that power somewhat: to defend its boundaries by some degree of expansion.

See with what art he works the intricate scheme! The rich men, using Parliament as their instrument, hold him apparently at their mercy. The income of the King was gone. He could employ no men, build neither ship nor barrack, buy neither stores nor guns, save by leave of the merchants and squires. At his restoration they destroy such permanent revenue as remained to the Crown and replace it by a *life* revenue only, based upon taxes of which they relieve their own landed class to levy them upon the mass of the people. They are very careful to see that this revenue shall be insufficient. Even its nominal sum would not maintain the rapidly developing state, and that nominal sum is never nearly reached in practice. The yield of the taxes granted by Parliament is known to be quite insufficient for the purposes of government.

Therefore the King will be bound to come to them again and again for money, and they will only provide it on terms of reducing step by step the small relic of his authority.

But Charles has three cards to play against these rich men opposed to him: Their fears; The Customs Revenue; Subsidy from an ally.

The landed class do not want invasion; they fear the unpopularity of defeat in war. Charles can therefore occasionally—not often, but occasionally—frighten them into providing *temporarily* for the armed forces; and on such votes he can carry on for a while. That is what he did early in the affair, to provide for the first Dutch war in 1664: he did it again with consummate ability, quite outflanking the intriguers, when he made them vote the regiments and the crews of 1671.

With what difficulty this card could be played we know from the disaster of 1667. The masters of Parliament had thought to hold the King when, in the midst of the Plague and the Great Fire, they withheld supply for the fleet. Charles could find no substitute money in time, and as a result the first-raters are laid up, the crews disbanded. As an immediate second result the Dutch are masters of the North Sea, enter the Thames and the Medway, destroy the King's ships, sail to Gravesend and menace London.

The expansion of the Customs the opponents of the Crown had not foreseen. The grant for life to the King was not intended to emancipate him but to provide him with an insufficient dole. Without giving them a handle to attack, without changing rates, Charles watched with a smile the rapidly expanding trade and its fruits in revenue. Before the end of his life it had floated him.

Subsidy from an ally was a more delicate matter, but the King's political genius was never more conspicuous than in his treatment of that resource—and it saved the throne in three moments of great peril.

Of the two main groups into which Europe was divided —France and her lesser supporters, on the one hand: Spain, Holland, the House of Austria, on the other (in perpetual changes this was the main division of the time) —one could pay a price: France. The other could not.

There was money to be had by supporting the one policy only, that of Louis; as later Austria had the money of Pitt to attack Napoleon, as earlier Gustavus Adolphus the money of Richelieu to attack the Empire.

But simply to side with the Bourbons in the European field would be to weaken the English monarchy in two ways: loss of power to turn the tide of European war, and loss of a complete international independence.

It would destroy England's chief international asset, which was that of acting, small as were her numbers, as a balance and makeweight, capable of reinforcing either side at will. England had not (thanks to Parliament) even the revenue of Holland; she had hardly a third—perhaps not much more than a quarter—the population of France, or a third of Spain's. But she had aptitude for the sea, and, in spite of lack of public funds and therefore of bad irregular pay, an unequalled generation of sailors. She had, thanks to the Duke of York, and in spite of Parliament, a fleet which, when spasmodically provided with funds, could defeat an opponent. Her support to the one group or the other was of a value greater than her grudged revenue or population accounted for. This freedom to act at will must be present, or the British Crown would lose its chief instrument of action among its rivals of Spain, France and the powerful wealthy, maritime Dutch Republic—the bank of Europe.

Again, mere permanent alliance with his cousin the King of France would have meant for Charles, in the long run, dependence. If Louis, with his vastly superior revenue, should come to think that the English Crown, lacking his aid, would be delivered into the hands of its opponents, he could exact from the Crown what terms he pleased and make it subservient to his own ends. It was essential to prevent this, and it was prevented by Charles's perpetually retaining *and exercising* the power to take up a contrary policy: the policy of opposing France at will.

When Louis was allied with the Dutch for his effort against Spain in Flanders during 1665, Charles took the other side, and sent out his brother James to fight and defeat them by sea. When he signed peace with the Dutch it was the peace of Breda in '67 which was in effect a challenge to Louis, just when Louis was beginning to change his attitude and to abandon the Dutch. The triple alliance of England, Holland and Sweden in 1678 was a flat defiance of Louis. Charles thus made his support of France a thing anxiously desired and revocable, and when he came to that secret arrangement with Louis called the Treaty of Dover, it was with a temporary French ally far more anxious to pay for his help than the King of England was anxious to receive.

The same decisive play appears in 1677. The great end of Louis at that moment was to prevent a Union between the houses of Stuart and Orange. He was wise. He foresaw the ultimate result. Charles therefore (unfortunately for his country in the long run, but acting intelligently for his diplomatic needs of the moment) insisted precisely upon that marriage, and gave his niece Mary, a Protestant, and not yet 16, to that deplorable husband William in his twenty-seventh year. For the King had already insisted on her being confirmed in the Established Church, and, in spite of her mother's memory and her father's violent protest, brought her up a Protestant.

Watch carefully the succession of advances towards, and withdrawals from, the support of Bourbon power between 1660 and 1685 and you will perceive throughout one brain consistently at work; not the tortuous personal intrigues of the Temples and Halifaxes and Sunderlands, not the doubtful double-faced services of a Digby, not the

more loyal ones of a Clifford, but one mind behind it all
—and that mind is the mind of Charles II. All is calculated to obtain just so much as will save the Crown
from being eaten up by its domestic enemies while at once
making its alliance well worth purchasing; keeping open,
and using continually, the door to reversal of policy.
Throughout the independence of the English Monarchy
was secured from those who could threaten it from within
or from without. What is even more remarkable, secrecy
was preserved.

The crude statement 'Money has come from France'
would have been fatal in its effect on uninstructed opinion
in 1671 as would the statement 'The money comes from
Holland' have been fatal to William's invasion with a
foreign army subsidized by Holland seventeen years later.
In the one case as in the other secrecy was necessary and
was kept. But there was this difference. That the French
money of 1671 was mainly spent on a very necessary
National Navy which otherwise would have rotted, the
Dutch money of 1688 on the upkeep of alien troops supporting a usurper who neither did nor desired to do anything for the strengthening of England amongst the
nations. The French money of 1671 was acquired permanently for English use; the Dutch money of 1688 had to
be repaid by the duped taxpayer of England who had the
additional pleasure of finding the very high interest with
which, all unknown to himself, he was charged. (It fell
in part on his tobacco.)

There is the same patient and successful handling of
the Corporation of London. A mob was managed in
the interest of those who would destroy the monarchy.
Shaftesbury was in touch with it always, and the organized wealth of the great merchants was also *upon the
whole* opposed to Charles, both because the limitation
of taxes was a strong motive with them and because the

Corporation enjoyed great power. It was a factor of high importance because the Franchise was wide—there were some 50,000 of the livery—and because those who worked the election could, as is the cant of mechanical representation, pretend to speak for the whole. And this great body of London, Westminster, and their extensions, was a concentrated mass of population wherein were caught the palace, and the organs of government: a mass perhaps at the end of Charles's reign a twelfth of all England, by 1700 a tenth.

Charles yields sufficiently to those rich men who control London, plays upon its jealousy of Dutch trade, allows it to work its frenzy out in the moments of popular madness nourished by Shaftesbury and his crew—and then, as the fish weakens, he begins to reel in. He knows that the essential point of the opposition is not the mass of liverymen (who were equally divided in party, and, for the vast majority, apathetic), but the organized clique of the Corporation. He uses a half-loyal mayor. He sees to it that a poll is contested. He wins. And when the Charter upon which the old oligarchy of wealth depended is withdrawn, there is no popular weight behind the demand for its renewal.

He, with more difficulty, kept alive the idea of religious toleration: a policy solemnly promised before his restoration, continually thwarted by the Parliament and yet never allowed to disappear. He always gave way on it and always kept it in reserve; so that by the end of his reign it was still lively and familiar.

He saw to the colonial effort of England, then just developing; he acquired the Dutch 'corridor' of the Hudson Valley between New England and Maryland (New York preserves his brother's name). It was not his fault that the French alliance did not procure for the English Crown more American territory at the expense of Spain

—for he had stipulated it should; but the French Crown, considering rather its own opportunities in the new world, did not keep its word.

Charles won his battle and died in the enjoyment of that precarious victory. But he did not win the campaign. He had been compelled to use as his ministers the class which was, of its nature, the enemy of Monarchy, the great landed proprietors. They were a close body, whose relationship is a study. Shaftesbury is Sunderland's brother-in-law. Henry Sydney is Sunderland's uncle (and the lover of Sunderland's wife). Halifax is Sunderland's first cousin—and so on through a score of names. Charles had no advantage over that set but to shuffle them in turn as a man may shuffle the shares of connected companies on a falling market: knowing that in the long run he is bound to lose.

The Duke of York in the first dozen years, while he was still an active power and before the declaration of his conversion had driven him away, supported his brother; but supported him awkwardly. Nevertheless, in the major things he was permanently right and his brother Charles wrong. For Charles had in view an ephemeral thing, and even so struggled to preserve for a brief while what was already doomed, but James had in view clear principles and struggled for political ideas which are not doomed when their expression is defeated. Monarchy did not disappear for ever.

Before examining the Duke of York's action between 1660 and 1673, we must consider the religious revolution in him, on which all turned.

It is strange that we do not know the date upon which he was received into the Church. He kept the point secret; and it is an instance of his rigidity and self-control that after these two and a half centuries, secret it remains. Did we know it, the task of appreciating his actions and their motives between the Restoration and the Test Act—1660 to 1673—would be greatly eased. He had excellent reason for such discretion. It would have damaged the dynasty to let the thing come with a shock. Not that the later excitements raised in London and fomented by the opponents of the Crown should be confused with the spirit of the nation, but that the great majority of the nation was Protestant, and had so been increasingly for half a century, and (what was more important) that the *framework* of the nation, the corporate institutions round and upon which it gathered, were exclusively Protestant. A Catholic heir was at the best an anomaly, at the worst an offence: at the very worst he might even prove (as Charles instinctively felt) a peril to the throne. It was just and politic, therefore, that the news of James's conversion should be delayed and broken, not rushed.

But there is another thing to remember. Reconciliation with the Catholic Church was not, in the England of that day, the complete transition which it is now. There had been no breach of continuity. The Catholic body in the England of the Restoration was as close a part, historically, of the English past as the French royalists are to-day a part of the French past, or the Southerners in the United States of the American. A Catholic in the England of 1660-70 was but one who had preserved what others had not so lately lost or abandoned. He was the son of a man who had formed, in 1600-50, part of a very large still resisting minority, the grandson of one who had formed, in 1560-1600, part of a large majority—though dwindling at the end to but half the nation. The London of the Restoration was full of men, themselves elderly, who had heard from their fathers personal memories of an England evenly divided on religion, as we have heard from our elders personal memories of an England divided, in the American War of Secession between Northern and Southern sympathies. The most rabid Puritan, if he were past middle age, would in most cases have had to admit that his grandfather was a Catholic, or, in rare cases, might prove with pride that the worthy man had stood fast among the little flock persecuted by Mary Tudor.

Moreover, Catholicism was familiar as an international tone in that Europe which was not divided, as ours has come to be, into quite estranged nationalities. And this was especially true of the very large and lively world of the Court, where, since forty or fifty years, the Queen of England had her Mass and its attendants, and where foreign nobility and Irish perpetually came and went, and where the literature, drama and manners of Catholic culture were a general experience.

For one that took the strong step of accepting the Faith, there were a number in that world who had at one time or another considered it, or at the least wondered. For each that accepted the heavy burden, there was one at least who came to the very verge of acceptance and turned back.

Nevertheless, a definite act was required at conversion. The man or woman not born in the Church must, on a determined occasion, accept its authority and communicate with it if they were to call themselves of the Faith. When that definite date fell for James Stuart we do not know: perhaps later research or accident will discover it; but, provisionally, I should put it not earlier than 1671, and certainly not later than the end of 1672, that is, in his thirty-eighth or thirty-ninth year.

Later than the end of 1672 it could not have been. The Test Act was law on March the 29th, 1673, and James, under its provisions, declared himself and gave up, with a heavy heart, the chief occupation of his life: the ships. But though James's reception into the Church cannot be later than 1672, the reader may be surprised to read it just so late as 1671. I repeat, it is only a surmise, but I will give my reasons for it.

James's first wife, Anne Hyde, had a strong influence over him. She was perhaps the only human being who ever impressed the hard material of his mind. Hers was the initiative in that combination, and by her he would largely be guided, not in a conviction but in judgment of what was politic. Now the Duchess was received, as we know, late in 1670. She dispassionately and soberly wrote out her reasons for the step, and they remain to us. They are individual and full of personal decision. They are essential, because she was the mother at the time, of a male heir to the throne. The boy was to die soon after her, but that she could not know. That she and her husband had long discussed the matter of religion there can be no doubt. That his earlier intention moved her to inquiry is probable. That he had taken the momentous step before her is not so.

Then there are the children. Any that survived were, in their order, heirs to England. Many had been born —seven indeed—and at the moment of their mother's reception Mary and Anne, the later sovereigns, were respectively over 8 and 6 years old. Yet they were baptized and brought up as members of the Church of England. It is true that this fitted in with the King's wishes, but we hear of no protest, whereas, when in 1676, after the critical date, Mary was to be confirmed in the Establishment, it could only be done against her father's resistance and at her royal uncle's express desire—or rather order.[1]

Lastly we know that he can hardly have been received before he ceased to communicate in the Royal chapel. For he specially asked—as many another has—whether

[1] It was—as one might expect—*Compton*, Lord Northampton's brother, who urged it most strongly; the leader of the plot against James in the affair of the seven bishops. True, he was Bishop of London, but his urgency was political.

such formal acts were permitted by the discipline of the Faith and had been told that they were not.

The contrary evidence is weak. Our official historians call James—and for that matter Charles himself—'secretly a Catholic,' long before. The use of the phrase shows their ignorance of their subject. Charles and James were both of high European culture and both knew what the traditional religion of that culture was. Charles, probably earlier than James, felt due sympathy with this religion. James at some comparatively early period in his life—perhaps while still at Brussels before the Restoration—had been both impressed and repelled by it far more than his brother. In that sense the phrase 'secretly a Catholic' could be and was used by contemporaries. But that had nothing to do in either case with the man's being or not being a Catholic. One might as well call a man 'secretly a Member of Parliament' before he is duly elected. Charles and James after him could be 'secretly Catholics' with all the vigour in the world and in no way jeopardize the succession. We have all known people (and they are numerous) who are attracted by the Catholic Church and who often or even regularly follow her services, and yet shirk the last and decisive act which may alienate affection or lose income. No, Charles was not a Catholic—however much he may have admitted his duty to his own conscience, till the 5th February, 1685—a few hours before he died. And James was not a Catholic until that same act had been performed by him. When? Presumably it is but a presumption—as late as 1671, at least, and after March of that year: certainly before March, 1673.[1]

On the process of his conversion we have more knowl-

[1] He had so far advanced as to cease to take the Sacrament of the Church of England in 1670, the year of his wife's conversion. But I believe that to have been a preliminary approach, not an effect of the thing done.

edge. It came to that curiously isolated mind finally—
after earlier experiences and impressions—by reading the
book I have mentioned: Heylin's book opposing Catholic
claims. This same book he later introduced to his wife.
It was a process intellectual, not emotional. He was convinced, not filled. His brother the King approached from
a very different and more sympathetic direction: from
scepticism—an excellent entry. But James had been very
definitely Protestant and the curious will remark in his
noble writing upon religion a strong tinge of his earlier
position. His faith, at the end, though sound, was still
of the colour which, earlier in the century, had so powerfully (and gloomily) affected the noblest minds: and
Pascal's.

Though he still avoided (apparently) formal reconciliation with the Church, his sympathies were known;
presumptions therefore arose that he would be received,
and these sufficed to put a strong weapon in the hands
of those who watched with more or less conscious enmity
the dynasty, and a political necessity of whose rank it was
—even in those who believed themselves most loyal—
to undo the monarchy.

The fall and exile of James's father-in-law Clarendon,
in 1667, was due to many other and stronger causes—
the failure of the Navy (for which he had no sort of
responsibility, it was all Parliament's), his too great
wealth, his extravagant Palace,[1] his contempt for others,
his best piece of foreign policy—the sale of Dunkirk—
above all his resistance to the revolutionary encroachments
of the House of Commons. But *among* the causes was the
fact that he was father-in-law to the Duke of York.
He was known to approve of the Declaration of Indul-

---

[1] It stood in the field on the top of St. James's Hill, along Piccadilly
Lane, where Albemarle Street (so called because the Duke of Albemarle
bought the house after Clarendon's fall) is now.

gence for the relief of Dissenters and Catholics—but it
was not his, it was the King's; and it was part of a strong
and constant policy of toleration to which the last Stuarts
consistently kept in spite of numerous set-backs from the
Established Church and from those who used the Parliament. The Kings believed it would give the country
unity.

For the rest James's personal feelings towards Catholicism before his public profession of it little affected
his public action, though it gave opportunity to his
opponents.

His advice on *things* was commonly wise; his advice
on men and ideas otherwise. Thus when in the refusal
of Parliament to vote ·supplies, the Navy was crippled,
he wisely insisted on the advisability of keeping the fleet
in being at any cost (Debt? Sale of lands? A moratorium?
—He mentioned none of these: but where was money to
come from? There was as yet no fleet-money from
France). But he could not tell the Council where to find
the funds. He said (it was his special care) that if you
laid up the First-rates—the Capital Ships—and trusted
to smaller craft as mere protectors of commerce you would
find yourself in an equal expense at last for protecting the
coast.

On the *thing* he was right. We all know what happened.
The Parliament having failed to provide money, the
Dutch men-of-war entered the Thames at will. The
British dockyard men and sailors were mutinous for
arrears of pay. Many were present as deserters on the
enemy's decks and helped to capture, sink and burn the
British ships in the Medway. But on the means for getting
the lacking cash he was silent.

In the crisis of the Great Fire he showed, as did the
King, the greatest energy, but the populace who remem-

bered it gratefully of Charles did not remember it of James.

His attitude on the Treaty of Dover is the last important point in his political action during this first phase before the Test Act and his open avowal of his religion.

But before dealing with that affair of 1670, let me digress on a transaction of 1669, which has proved of capital interest to English and European history, and on which James's attitude deserves particular attention. It is the more important to deal with it here at some length because it has been so strangely forgotten. I mean the first Divorce Act.

Briefly the circumstances were these.

Lord de Roos had already obtained a *separation* from his wife by the ecclesiastical authority of the Church of England, that is, through the Church Courts. Late in the year 1669 a Bill was brought up in Parliament to allow him to marry again. The occasion is a landmark in the story of our civilization. James strongly opposed the measure. His brother, the King, not so strongly but with some determination, supported it.

We have both to remark the capital interest of the occasion and the motives of the Duke of York in acting as he did: for we are studying the character of a man, and motive in action, not action alone, is the test of character. The Roos Divorce Act is a strong example of the social revolution through which England was passing in the seventeenth century, and its treatment by the Duke of York a critical test of his character.

I have said that the occasion was one of capital interest to the history of England and of Christendom. Let me begin by explaining why this should be so.

Of the few and simple institutions upon which Christian civilization reposes, marriage is one, just as property is another, the conception of civil authority a third, moral responsibility with sanctions in a future life a fourth.

In our own day we have seen the whole of this structure beginning to dissolve in whatever of modern life is separated from the Catholic Church. Property is maintained, though challenged; but is not maintained upon the ground of moral right—it is maintained by arguments of sophistry or of cynical avarice; and, indeed, the negation of property, great monopolies under the direction of a few men, is applauded and is rapidly proceeding to a completion under which the mass of men will cease to be free. The sanction of moral authority through personal immortality is doubted, and more neglected even than it is doubted; it is also more and more widely denied. The moral foundation of civil authority is in equal peril—challenged, or supported for the wrong reasons; so that such authority is coming to mean for most men to-day no more than organized force at the service of injustice.

Now marriage has gone the same road. Since the Reformation, the foundational institution of indissoluble Christian marriage, a sacramental conception, has (outside Catholic society) gradually dissolved. There are still countries in which the principle of terminable marriage during the life of either contracting party is not known to the law. But those countries are few and exceptional. In France, after a hard struggle, the large and powerful anti-Christian minority which has for so long governed that country forced through the principle of divorce in our own time. In every non-Catholic country divorce is the rule and its practice is very rapidly increasing.

It is of the utmost interest to watch the curve along which moves the degradation of any one of our old fundamental institutions. The dissolution of this institution of marriage has, in England, progressed as follows:—

Until the Reformation the principle of indissoluble

marriage (so long as both parties to the marriage were alive) was unquestioned. There are, indeed, modern historians so muddle-headed or so insincere, that they confuse, in good faith or for the purposes of deception, the abuse of nullification with the idea of terminable marriage.

The two principles are utterly distinct, and result in utterly different societies.

Before the Reformation, while our Western civilization was still united, it was, of course, admitted that a supposedly indissoluble marriage might turn out on examination to be no marriage at all. When it had so been discovered by the properly constituted Courts, the marriage was declared null and void. In other words, it was decided that the marriage *had never existed*, and therefore the parties were free to marry again.

In the corruption of the later Middle Ages, and decline of morals in church officials, this obvious and just principle was frequently and grossly abused. But we need not find those scandals only in the corruption of the later Middle Ages: they exist—much more rarely—in the earlier and better part of that period and we have examples long after their end. But no matter what the abuse of the principle, through legal machinery (as, for instance, by letting an undefended suit go by default), no matter how unjust or frivolous or numerous the occasions of scandal, there is an impassable gulf between the principle that marriage is an indissoluble sacrament and the principle that marriage is a terminable contract.

If any man doubt so obvious a proposition—obvious not only in logic but in practice and in its effect upon society—let him consider the corresponding point of property. We all know how in our own time two principles stand opposed: the principle that property is of right, and the principle (at any rate as regards property in means of production and land) that it is not of right. The

128

difference between the two opposing principles is the great quarrel between our traditional society and Communism to-day throughout the world.

Now there is any amount of corruption and abuse to-day in the treatment of property by the Courts of Justice. Big swindlers are confirmed in their ill-doing, small men defrauded, little owners jockeyed out of their rights; politicians take bribes unpunished by the Courts. They help on monopolists and deliver into their hands the small proprietor and the common citizen. Our whole treatment of the business of property to-day is profoundly corrupt, and it is the moral indignation this corruption has aroused which lends its chief force to Communism. Nevertheless, the gulf between the two opposing principles remains as wide as ever: and for constituted authority once to admit that property in itself was immoral would change the whole aspect of our world. Wherever such a principle is adopted Communism reigns and everything is changed.

So with marriage. Whatever abuse in the declarations of nullity, and in whatever number such abuses, there is a difference in quality between these and the admission that either partner to a marriage can, while the other partner is alive, marry again. The one principle declares marriage a sacrament, the other declares marriage a terminable civil contract. To pass from one to the other is a revolution.

It was this social and moral revolution—far more important than the constitutional one, but an accompaniment of it—which began in England in the year 1669, and which, with very slowly gathering effects, has come at last to what we know to-day as increasingly prevalent: what to-morrow will be universal.

There had, indeed, during the turmoil and chaos (at white heat) of religious discussion in the sixteenth century, appeared proposals for terminable marriage not only in England, but in other countries where the Reformers had the ascendant.[1]

But such vargaries attach to a time of confusion; they do not form precedents, though they are ominous symptoms of what is to come.

In this case of 1669 the matter was very different. The thing was done solemnly, formally, and finally, by an Act thoroughly debated, voted upon, acceded to and deliberately set upon record for a specific purpose. It was acted upon as a precedent. It is the parent of our modern anarchy in marriage.

The growth of the innovation was hesitant. One such Act of Parliament upon the average in a decade is all you can find until the great moral change following upon the destruction of the Stuarts, and the entry of the Hanoverian dynasty as a symbol of that change. After 1715 the thing multiplies tenfold. It is not once in a decade, it is once a year upon the average, that some Act of Parliament is then passed permitting a wealthy man or woman to marry again, though the husband or wife is still alive. For a lifetime this rate is continued. After 1775 it is no longer at a tenfold, but at a thirtyfold rate. At last, in 1857, we have the full principle admitted, and divorce becomes a normal part of English law, pronounced by an ordinary civil court, its social effect only restricted by the cost of the proceedings. Since that date, and especially in quite modern times, step after step has been taken to make cheaper, easier, and more general the

---

[1] We all know how Luther gave a permission to his German prince to marry two wives at once, and before the end of Henry VIII's reign, and during that of Edward VI, the proposal of terminable marriage was discussed in England. There was even one case of an irregular marriage permitted by Act of Parliament—in the case of Northampton. In the reign of Elizabeth (in the Foljambe case, in 1576) the English Courts decided definitely against terminable marriage. Laud himself had once married parties of whom one still had a mate alive, but he regarded it as an abominable thing and repented of it the whole of his life.

practice of terminable marriage. We are to-day within sight of its universal application.

The case of Lord de Roos was one of peculiar strength. The man had been grossly injured. It was admitted that the children ascribed to him were not his own. He had obtained, as we shall see, from the ecclesiastical courts a full separation. But the idea that he could marry again was still shocking to the morals of his time—so shocking that it is not repeated for more than twenty years.[1]

The Bill was actively debated in the Lords, and was passed at last by a majority of only two voices. It would not have passed at all if the bench of Bishops had acted as a body. But two, or perhaps three, did not vote with their colleagues, and the thing became law.

Now in this important crisis of our social history the King himself was present in the House of Lords and supported the novel contention. That is the first point to note. Charles acted vigorously in favour of the Bill, and it is mainly due to his action that the Bill passed. James acted as vigorously against it, but of course with less effect. His Catholic leanings were now public knowledge, and such knowledge alone weakened his voice in debate—he had already some months before told his brother that he intended to make sooner or later a profession of Catholicism.

The obvious thing to say with regard to Charles's action was, and is, that he supported this moral revolution in order that he might put an end to the connexion between himself and Catherine of Braganza, might marry again, and have an heir.

I do not think that explanation will hold. In point of fact, although the thing became law, Charles took no advantage of it.

[1] The Private Act for the dissolution of the marriage of the Duke of Norfolk in 1692.

It is more probable that he acted from that general principle of yielding as far as possible to the revolutionary spirit of the time and the morals of its richer men in order to save his throne: that he so yielded is his chief (or only) merit in the eyes of most historians, and his gravest fault.

It is also probable that there was in his attitude an element of opposition to his brother: whose certitude of inheritance, with its consequent effect in the Council, he desired to moderate.

At any rate, he supported the Bill, and helped to get it passed.

Now, why did James oppose?

He was at this moment actively engaged in religious discussion and decision. He was talking these matters of moral theology over with men who were experts therein; we smile when we consider his dissolute life, but he was none the less discussing them sincerely—and the proof of this lies in the great sacrifice he made immediately after; his giving up of the Admiralty. I cannot doubt that the known attitude of the Catholic Church in such matters weighed with him very heavily.

Lastly, there is the obvious motive (which people who know nothing of the Church regard as his only one) that he was heir to the throne and that should Charles obtain a divorce and get a son or a daughter to survive him, James's own position would be lost.

I think it true to say, judging how the mixture of motives would work in this particular mind, that the latter motive was the strongest. I do not believe it was the only motive. He did not look far ahead, and to either side not at all. He wore blinkers. But though he was over-intent upon his legitimate authority, and never sufficiently supple in the exercise of it, there was nothing in him of the ambitious schemer. Indeed, if there had been, he would not have fallen as he did.

I think that the fact of James having for so long been the heir apparent, and having come to regard himself as permanently such, the fact of his having legitimate children born to him, gave him a zeal in the matter which he otherwise would not have shown. But I think that he was supported strongly in his decision by an honest conviction that the innovation of terminable marriage and its permanent appearance in English law was abominable.

I need hardly point out to any intelligent reader that the exceptional looseness of both brothers in their relations with women has nothing to do in either case with their attitude upon this question of principle. As for those who think that a sensual man, backed up in his sensuality by the admitted and as it were consecrated looseness of royalties in his day, has less right to decide upon moral principles than the chaste man, I can only say that their confusion of thought is such as hardly to merit the honour of argument.

One excellent result followed upon this deplorable innovation of divorce through the action of the House of Lords. Charles in his interest over the matter came down personally to the House and presided over its debates. Indeed, if we may believe Burnet (and when that ecclesiastic has no direct motive for lying one may hesitatingly believe him) Lauderdale boasted that he had persuaded Charles to act thus. But even if Lauderdale did say this, I doubt *his* telling the truth. It is much more the kind of thing that Charles would do upon his own account.

He may have been present a little before this particular discussion came on, but it was certainly his interest in that discussion which made him stay in the House of Lords and become habituated to it.

Now this was a first-rate piece of reaction, and if only

it had been long maintained, might have done something to prop up the English Crown. The King *in* Parliament would have ceased to be an empty phrase. His presence would not have saved the power of the English Crown: that was past saving. It would not have restored the old popular monarchy, whose decline had already provoked the successful rebellion of the squires and merchants, and had been clinched by the murder of a king. But the physical presence of the monarch in Parliament during debate might have put some brake on the rapidity of the change, and left a strong memory of kingship—to be revived when peril demanded it.

Accident had kept the King from the House of Lords for more than a century, that is, since the death of Henry VIII in 1547. Edward VI died a child; Mary and Elizabeth were women; by the time James I's accession that foreigner (for so a Scotchman of his time was regarded) inherited a tradition of absence. The monarch was, of course, present as Head of the Council; but in the debates of Parliament, that is, of the Lords, he took no part. With Charles I it was the same.

As it was, the effect of Charles II's presence among the peers must not be exaggerated. He did not sit in state upon a throne, as did the kings of old time: he began, indeed, by taking a chair upon the raised platform where the throne stood, and thus sat apart; but later he saw no harm in standing near the fire in the big room, and round him, as he stood there, the peers would gather, coming and going. He would talk with many of them individually, solicit their votes, present his own arguments. He had no objection at all to people voting against him or refusing to be persuaded by his suggestions. He acted almost as an equal, and even complained of some who were slow in approaching him that they were 'sullen'. It was remarked that the slight stiffness in debate which followed upon his first appearance soon wore off, so that at last he became almost one of themselves in these familiar gatherings. Those who had by temperament a suspicion of monarchy naturally deplored the new custom; they especially deplored the loss of dignity in the peerage, remarking that the Lords no longer sat solemnly in rank for their debates, but had turned with the King's presence into a sort of drawing-room.

Some part of Charles's reason for acting thus was his natural desire to lower the part played by the Duke of York. Before the King came to the Lords, James had all the prestige of royalty in their debates, and, unpopular though he was becoming with the governing class, the prestige of his royal blood still counted. Charles in going down to the Lords in person turned James for the moment into little more than one peer among his fellows. He thus did his brother an ill turn, which perhaps he later regretted—if indeed he fully understood its effects.

Meanwhile there survives one charming and famous sentence of his. He could not help, with his intelligence and detachment and sense of humour, some delight in the pompous absurdity of politicians in bulk, a sight which is surely among the most comic of human affairs. He said, 'It was as good as a play.' He would have felt it still more if he had but looked on it, himself apart; for it is indeed an excellent pastime if it be not too prolonged; and it is no wonder that this man, of whom we are justly told that he found it difficult to fill up his time, took advantage of the puppet show. What fun it must have been for him to listen to some self-sufficient fellow, too wealthy and therefore too much honoured, airing his solemn ineptitude. . . . Or to some man lacking power of expression, and therefore also (if he were wealthy) respected, floundering in speech like a stranded whale. The delights of the farce called parliamentary debate are (to the onlooker, not the actors) innumerable.

There followed, in the next year, 1670, the Secret Treaty of Dover, in which, by his strong action in promoting the triple alliance, Charles brought Louis XIV to the point of offering a subsidy, and so making possible—for a brief period—the due armament of Great Britain which Parliament refused. It promised, as against such subsidy, action side by side with Louis and especially against Holland but in policy also against Spain. It allowed for an extension of English Colonial power by annexation to England of lands in Spanish America. It provided an admirable weapon, though one of sadly brief effect, against the subjection of the Crown to the privileged classes. It was negotiated by Charles himself, but submitted to his cabinet—a group of five men drawn necessarily from that very class. For the Kings of England in the seventeenth century were like men compelled to hunt with wolves instead of hounds.

Of these five one was honest and brave—an astonishing combination in that world—Clifford. Another, Arlington, loyal but timid. The three others were the invariably infamous Buckingham, redeemed somewhat by folly; Lauderdale, unprincipled but redeemed somewhat by a healthy coarseness; and the gifted Ashley, redeemed by no good quality of the soul, on the contrary, made viler by the abuse of great faculties. They all agreed.

The Duke of York was kept out as much as possible from this manœuvre, and when his sister (who had married Louis XIV's brother) came over to Dover to settle it, he was somewhat contemptuously left behind on the road. He saw things in black and white, he would never sacrifice one principle to another. The acceptance of a subsidy, though temporary, though necessary if the fleet were to exist, was odious to his honour. If you had asked him what alternative he had—why, he had none.

The Treaty of Dover contained—before the mention of the subsidy—one strange half clause: the first.[1] It provided that Charles should proclaim his conversion to Catholicism, and that, if this should provoke a rebellion, Louis should lend him troops. On to that is added the subsidy. Who was the author of that clause, and why was it inserted? Louis cannot have been its author with any serious intention, for all his life he urged the Stuarts to an opposite course and not to risk their throne. The Duke of York was capable—barely capable—of suggesting a thing so impolitic at such a time—for he lacked wholly the diplomatic sense, and weighed values ill—but the Duke of York would certainly never have been allowed a say in the matter. Unless it were designed to intimidate Charles later, it can only have been put in at the suggestion of Charles himself.

But why? We shall never know. Perhaps he desired to have written record of a solemn pledge in case, later (he was but 40), the Catholic body should sufficiently increase under toleration (he believed it a feasible and fecund policy) to enable him to follow in age his inclination where it lay. It might mean civil war: for though the bulk of the nation would still support their King, though not of his creed, some might conspire. If so, he may have proposed to reinforce his power. Perhaps it was a sister's caprice. Perhaps (but most improbably) it was the trick I have suggested, to bind him under threat of exposure. There it stands, an unfulfilled, isolated fragment.

Only Clifford and Arlington were present at the signing of those few sterile lines.

With James's conversion and with the resignation of

[1] Nominally the second. The first is but a preamble.

his offices in 1673 the first phase in his public life as heir to the throne comes to an end.

He still had a short respite. His wife, who, for all his amours, had been a stand-by for him, died in the spring of '71: calling to him in her awful suffering, 'Duke! Duke! It is a terrible thing to die!' In the next year he commanded finely in his last battle by sea against the Dutch and the last great fight of the reign. But the war had made further subsidy imperative: the Parliament, prorogued these two years past, was summoned to meet in the spring of '73, and with that the new phase, the phase of active struggle, in James's life began. Those hounding the monarchy had turned him out of the Council and the Admiralty. They now prepared to debar him from the throne.

VI

THE CONFLICT

THE Duke of York's admitted conversion provoking the passing of the Test Act changed the politics of the time, and 1673 is the turning point in the history of the 'Restoration.' From a subtle interplay of various forces which Charles watched and controlled, the struggle between Crown and magnates became more and more of a true battle. This was because two of those forces now emerged into open vigour and were constituted in final form. One was a vivid anti-Catholic feeling, long present in a large and active minority of the nation and supported by a less active but murmuring dislike of Catholicism on the part of many more: the other was a definite and organized faction—of which Ashley (Shaftesbury) from being largely its creator became the captain and director—aiming directly at destroying the surviving parcel of Royal Power and of reducing the last shred of its substance to a shade.

Those who used the feeling against Catholicism as an instrument were themselves at once indifferent to doctrine and contemptuously aware of the monstrous illusions under which their dupes lay. The very rich men who would substitute the power of their class for that of the King had no creed. They had, for the most part, no conclusion on things unseen. For some the fate of man was a matter of interesting speculations, for others not even that. A few of the more dull followed by routine and inheritance ancient dogmas retained by the Establishment (such as Immortality, or even the Incarnation) and were, to that extent, Christian. But few among them were of a calibre to grasp the importance of dogma. Doctrine meant nothing to them.

Yet their motives were not indifferent to Catholicism though they were indifferent to doctrines. The main body of the gentry, the lawyers, the wealthier merchants, felt instinctively that the spirit of Catholicism was a popular spirit making for popular monarchy: that it would combat the idolatry of rules (upon which legal and Parliamentary encroachment depended); and that it made against oligarchy, particularly against oligarchy in its plutocratic form.

Now oligarchy in its plutocratic form was the very essence of the Revolution. The wealthy classes might sincerely divide themselves into Tory and Whig, into supporters of tradition in government and into opponents thereof; but the class as a whole could not but, of its nature, now that it had become so powerful, make for its own aggrandisement at the expense of the mass of Englishmen below it and of the Crown above. The difference between its sections was only the difference between those who saw the opportunity most clearly or felt it most keenly (it was these who made the Revolution), and those who were more confused or more sentimental (it was these who made spasmodic demonstrations of loyalty, who 'abhorred' the Exclusion Bill, who rejoiced in James's suppression of rebels, and who, after the success of the Dutch Invasion, continued to propose expedients which might save the King's title, or at least his son's). But the class as a whole could not but go forward. This class provided every single minister without exception, every officer of the armed forces, all the magistracy. Into it were already digested sundry newcomers from below. It had captured the Universities, it directed and manned the Established Church. In Parliament it was supreme. It held all the county seats, and if, here and there, a man of humbler station crept in as burgess for some small town, yet the great mass of the borough corporations were either controlled by neighbouring great families, or, as a matter of course, returned local landed gentlemen, or sent to Westminster sundry of their own wealthy class whose interests were identical with the territorials.

The best proof of this essential oneness uniting all that body is its economic action, not only in legal decisions against the small man's property or the Crown's, but in the positive laws which it passed in its own favour.

We have seen how the first action of the gentry in this field was to relieve themselves of their old dues to the Crown and to replace them by taxes falling on the mass of the people. But they proceeded to a far more drastic measure. The gentry in their aspect of a Parliament passed a law to which I have already briefly alluded, the effect of which was to deprive of their lands the smaller yeomen in great and increasing numbers.

The trick was played thus. It was enacted that all possessed of a freehold should be required to show title—a demand apparently reasonable. If no title could be presented, the land would naturally be deemed to hold of the manor. In plain English, the ignorant small owner's land was taken from him by the squire. The presumption was that negligence or fraud had permitted or attempted the creation of a false freehold by the tenant, and that his tenure was in reality no freehold at all. If it were, why could he not show the deeds? The more important yeomen were provided with parchments or knew where to seek for them. The smaller men, as might be imagined, were in their thousands caught unprovided: loss of documents in a great lapse of time, the negligence of ignorance and poverty, transfers not recorded, left them without

141

proofs. They were dispossessed and from owners became payers of rent, insecure of their livelihoods. It was a sweeping economic revolution, the successor of that which had so swollen the landlords with the sequestrated clerical wealth, the predecessor of that by which, in the next centuries, the commons were enclosed wholesale and robbed from the poor.

This upper class—or its most active members—had now, with James's conversion, their opportunity. The anti-Catholic card could be played as a trump. Things could be forced to an issue, and the attack could henceforward use against the dynasty a concrete weapon, permanent, formidable, and clearly appreciable by the populace.

The man who had the ability or genius to seize the occasion and, for ten years, to conduct the furious assault was the immensely wealthy Cooper, Lord Ashley, now Earl of Shaftesbury: the man whom Charles had preferred to the chief ministry, the Chancellorship, because he had capacities far surpassing his fellows in the group of five (himself, Clifford, Arlington, Lauderdale, Buckingham) which had hitherto administered the chief departments of Government.

He it was who had supported Charles in the Declaration of Indulgence, and who had passed, in that hostile class from which the King was compelled, in spite of its hostility, to choose his servants, as the chief support of the throne. The more powerful was the effect of his treason.

The cost of the war had made it necessary once more to summon Parliament after a prorogation of two years. The Assemblies were called for the opening of 1673. In the interval James's admission of Catholicism had been made: Louis XIV, the continental champion of that creed, had been checked by Holland—or rather the House of Orange [1]—its opponent, for there it was largely by the young Duke of Orange, the King's nephew, the figurehead of Protestantism across the North Sea, that Dutch policy was represented.

It was the very moment for inflaming religious feeling, especially in London, and launching it at full heat against the monarchy. Shaftesbury had the Duke of York's conversion there to hand for a goad with which to urge his swelling team of remonstrants, and on it he based all the successful actions which he now began to wage, which all but overthrew the monarchy in that decade, the result of which destroyed it in the next. With the opening of the session he went down to the House of Lords, he the King's Chancellor, and denounced the King's Declaration of Indulgence, which he himself had framed, as illegal.

Charles dismissed him. He proceeded to war.

He was but one of that intermarried knot of great families which at last usurped the national executive, and made themselves masters of England, but, as the ablest of those conspirators, let us take him for a specimen and in him examine their type.

He had been born in 1621, and was therefore at this critical moment already over 50 years of age, a little man, but with a strong face and an excellent power both of debate and rhetoric; in morals detestable and in religion nil. Cooper was his name, and, from his mother, Ashley: Anthony Ashley Cooper. He had vast possessions in the south and west of England, and inherited them as a minor. He married three times; the important marriage

[1] When we talk of the 'Dutch' as the Protestant power of that day, we must always remember that even in those few northern provinces of the old Netherlands a very large proportion—more than a third—were Catholic. But that minority, though given far more freedom than their fellows in England, were ruled by the great wealth of the Calvinist merchants and Jewish and Calvinist bankers. In this mass of wealth the largest private fortune was that of the House of Orange.

which put him into the very front rank was his second, that with a Cecil——the sister of Lord Exeter.

During his minority he had been a ward of the Crown, pretending a grievance against the Royal Court of Wards that the King's officials had allowed land of his to be sold below its value. Such control had determined the leading members of the landed classes to be rid of a power above their own. He was in the very heart of that clot which destroyed the popular monarchy of England. He was first cousin to that masterful widow, Southampton's heiress, who managed her weak husband, William Russell. He was close cousin to Halifax (their fathers had married sisters). His life, station, connexions, were the quintessence of all that world.

Thus, with his great fortune, he is begged to accept the freedom of the little town of Tewkesbury. As a matter of course the Mayor and Corporation call him their Member (for that, as we know, is the way in which the Commons were formed), yet oddly enough he did not sit in the Long Parliament. When it was summoned in the latter part of the same year, 1640, he was under age. To wealth on his scale that mattered little, but for some reason there was a double return for Downton, in Wiltshire, the next sham borough which he had picked up. This probably means that he was not wanted at Westminster by the authorities, and that therefore the half-dozen local people who settled these affairs had been told to name some other person. At any rate, the conflicting claims were never arranged: nobody sat for Downton in the Long Parliament; and there was another grievance for so rich a young man to brood over.

He began his career of the Civil War in a fashion most characteristic of that opulent society to which he belonged. He intrigued for this office and that under the King, professing his devotion to royalty. He was given the government of Weymouth—an important maritime post which should not have been entrusted to such doubtful hands, for the King lacked ports, and ports were essential to his supply: it was, as has been said, the Parliamentary possession of the ports which, coupled with the hold on London and on the military stores, decided the rebellion against Charles.

His motive was in part, perhaps, revenge; but also, I think, a certain powerful judgment and prevision in the man when in January, 1644, he betrayed his master. It was his first betrayal: his apprenticeship in villainy. He was only in his twenty-third year, but a character of that kind is able to judge mankind even at 23. He saw which way the cat was jumping, and in following the athletics of the animal was an adept from his youth to his grave.

Having gone over to his fellow squires, with their tail of yeomen and big merchants—what is called by some 'the parliamentary party,' and by others 'the people of England'—he steadfastly served them as long as they looked certain of winning, were actively winning, and had won. His great Cecil marriage was made after his master the King had been put to death; his vast fortune made men on the democratic side pay him a deference he would never have had from a monarch. In some obscure way, perhaps by financial contribution, perhaps through a respect for his judgment in men and affairs, probably through both, he managed to get a considerable hold over Cromwell.

Cromwell allowed him to have back his estates (sequestrated for his former adhesion to the King) and saw to it that no fine was paid—though a fine of £500 had been agreed on. Cromwell next put this man Cooper into one of his little sham Parliaments: he put him in for Wilts, and he continued to serve Cromwell well. Thus on the occasion of Lilburne's imprisonment, he was on the small body which advised that piece of tyranny and carried it out.

Lilburne by his consistent republicanism had offended Oliver. In spite of a great military force gathered by Cromwell to overawe the court, Lilburne was acquitted. These people, who pretended they were fighting against arbitrary power, kept Lilburne in prison in spite of his acquittal, Cromwell specially 'suspending' Habeas Corpus for the occasion.

Cooper was more Cromwellian still. It was he among others, and perhaps he more than any other, who urged Oliver to make himself king.

Then came his second betrayal. He turned against this second master—a much more shaky one than the first— before the end of 1654.

The probable reason of this shift was that he was working (his Cecil wife being dead) to marry one of Cromwell's daughters. It must be remembered that at this moment—and especially after he had urged the bewildered Oliver to seize the crown—that most men would have laid odds on a Cromwell dynasty ruling England. It was therefore natural that a man of the future Shaftesbury's temperament should make his way by alliance with it. At any rate, the marriage, if this astute suitor had intended it, was not allowed; and from that moment Anthony Ashley Cooper became a careful but powerful insistent opponent of the Protector.

Yet the Protector never dared do anything against him. The man must have had some secret power over Oliver, whether of debt, or of exposure, or dread of his abilities. To say that his faculty of speech or his great wealth were enough to account for the position is doubtful. Cromwell could have dealt with them, both. But he dared not deal with Anthony Ashley!

After Cromwell's death he was nominated in the usual way by a few corporation officials to the Parliament of Richard Cromwell in 1659. Then we get his third pirouette. The little man is one of the eight who sign the commission for Monk to be Commander-in-Chief of the Army, and he asks with all his might for the Restoration—another example of his foresight. No one can help admiring the dexterity—in wiliness and tortuous ways—of this wily and tortuous fellow. It is like watching a conjuring man who has turned thief picking pockets with impunity.

After the Restoration it is staggering to note that he helped to try the Regicides! And in 1661 he becomes a peer under the title of Baron Ashley.

On the top of all this multiple betrayal and rebetrayal, he was exceedingly corrupt. He took money from this side and from that; he took it on contracts; he took it whenever and wherever he could get it. It is true he was no exception in this, they all did it. The high-souled or high-phrased Algernon Sydney took money from Louis XIV as freely as did the stern patriot Osborne—of whom Louis's Ambassador reported that he was always asking for more. In the true spirit of your demagogue, and especially of your very wealthy demagogue, Ashley had 'no enemies to the left.' He was all for toleration—by which he meant the following of a popular stream of opinion in favour of a general Protestantism, and for the extirpation of that large minority of the nation which was still professedly Catholic, and that much larger minority which still had sympathies with Catholicism.

But to do him justice, this attitude was not due to any general sympathy with Protestant doctrines, which led so many at that time to desire a sort of coalition against Catholicism without looking pedantically to the political difference between the official Establishment and the various independent Protestant sects. He was himself atheist, or perhaps (for the fashion of the day is a strong influence) a Deist: but it was again, in this crisis of the approaching Popish Plot, an example of his genius for seeing how things were going that he felt in his bones the sympathy with Catholicism to be a sympathy with the authority of the King, a sympathy opposed to the power of the rich and therefore of Parliament. And if there is one thing one may say of him throughout his life, one in which he was consistently sincere, it was his hatred of the Catholic Church.

He was a patron of learning and genius with an excellent power of selection, though used for his own political purposes. He made Locke, for instance; and Locke repaid his creator, not only by spreading a political philosophy exactly suited to the rule of such magnates, but with steadfast praise: indeed, but for the prestige of Locke, the baseness of the man would be more apparent to-day than it is.

Ashley strongly supported the Roos divorce, and by that gained the favour of the King, who was so oddly upon the same side. But Ashley supported it for clearly perceived reasons of his own. If the principle of divorce were introduced into England, the King might marry another wife who would bear him an heir to the exclusion of the immovable James. It is even possible (of this in a moment) that by muddying the waters the divorce might be turned into an engine for making people recognize the Duke of Monmouth as heir; for after all, if the English Parliament could destroy a Christian marriage by one Act, it could equally turn a bastard into a legitimate son by another. Once admit the principle that not the authority of the Church is required for these things, but only the authority of a group of well-to-do men sitting in an assembly, and you can get rid of illegitimacy as easily as you can of the marriage tie. Ashley knew well enough that a Duke of Monmouth as king would be a puppet in the hands of him and his, while a Duke of York meant the menace of a royal master.

He was privy to the Treaty of Dover. It has always been said that he was not made acquainted with the strange half-clause in it (which meant very little, but which at any rate would, had it been publicly known, have created violent opposition) by which Charles proposed at some time to call himself Catholic. The treaty was Charles's own. Officially of the five in Council only Arlington and Clifford were familiar with its whole contents; but it has always seemed to me incredible that Shaftesbury should have been ignorant of that passage. He was in the centre of public things. He was astute. He met every day the two men who had actually signed. For historians to tell us at this time of day, as they repeatedly do, upon the word of most untrustworthy men (whose business it was to apologize for their chief leader), that Ashley was kept ignorant of one subsidiary but, still, striking point in the document, is a little like telling us to-day that a Cabinet Minister had heard nothing of one of our modern Parliamentary scandals. What makes the story still less credible, is that in 1673, at the height of the Test Act agitation, Cooper got his earldom from the King and the title of Shaftesbury to hand down to his distinguished descendants. He was Charles's support and vicegerent. Well, the capital point, which explains the whole nature of the time, is that the King had no choice but to depend upon such servants—who were really his masters—and Shaftesbury's action is the grand example.

It was at the meeting of Parliament in the early weeks of 1673, that Anthony Ashley Cooper, Baron Ashley and Earl of Shaftesbury, determined upon his fourth betrayal. He determined to oppose the Royal Family, and in particular the heir apparent, James. He made up his mind what course it would best pay him at this moment to pursue. From that moment onward he put all the weight of his great ability, his immense fortune, his knowledge of men, his complete lack of morals (the strongest element in intrigue), to the purpose of keeping James from the throne. Nor do I believe that his reason was mainly pique. Men of that calibre (and Shaftesbury was of large calibre) do not act from pique. He had a policy. His unfailing flair told him that the final duel was imminent between the dying principle of popular monarchy and the rising principle of government by the few rich of which he himself, Shaftesbury, was one; that was the motive of his move.

His contemporaries agreed in applying to him the epithet knavish. The epithet is sound in itself but quite insufficient. He had discovered long ago the trend of the tide; he had never failed, in his various treasons against this master and that over a course of thirty years, from his earliest manhood, to smell out which way things were going. Here and now in 1673, he felt himself to have joined the winning side. And he was right.

Such was Anthony Ashley Cooper, first Lord Shaftesbury—eloquent, intelligent in the highest degree, industrious, without morals or honour, immensely wealthy, crapulous, tenacious, looking upon other men from a superior plane, successful, and very probably damned.

His first shot, well aimed and of full effect, was the passing of that Test Act—the reply to the Declaration of Indulgence—to which I briefly alluded in my last chapter.

Since the Crown had used its power during the prorogation of Parliament to relieve Dissenters and Catholics of their civil disabilities and to allow them any employment and the practice of their religion, the Parliament was used to contradict that power flatly and to insist on the exact reversal of what had been done. The Declaration had been cancelled on the news of Shaftesbury's treason to the King in the House of Lords. With his own Chancellor abandoning it, it could not be maintained. The active opposition, the spear-head of the advancing gentry (called 'the Country Party' organized, under cover, by Shaftesbury), pushed through both Houses this law of the Test Act which governed religious policy in England uninterruptedly right up to modern times. It is significant that no one dared oppose its passage. Not even in the Lords where Catholic peers sat of right.

The proposed law laid it down that no one might hold any office, civil or military, who would not take the Oath of Supremacy—that is, admit the King head of the Church—receive the Sacrament after the rite of the Church of England—*and declare against Transubstantiation.*

It was in this last that the core of the manœuvre lay. The Oath of Supremacy it was possible to turn in flank. Certain Catholics had done so for the purpose of sitting in the House of Commons. They could interpret it to mean that no foreign power (even the Pope) had civil jurisdiction in England, and that the King was head of his own Church—which was no concern of theirs. Nonconformists (except Quakers, who abjured all oaths) could, at a pinch, make the same reservation about the King's ecclesiastical power (though many would refuse). They might, the moderate, persuade themselves that a formal reception of the Sacrament (to which no doctrine abhorrent to them was attached), though a humiliation, was not a repudiation of their essential common tenet, which was the right to worship by association rather than under authority. They could enthusiastically repudiate the Pope's right—or any one else's—to exercise any jurisdiction in England. They would reject Transubstantiation with transports: but there the Catholic, *and the Catholic alone*, was necessarily stopped: and was meant to be stopped.

Shaftesbury's Test Act was a weir to catch Catholics, to expose the numbers of them in the public service (nothing like as numerous as their proportion to the whole population warranted, but, still, considerable) and—this was the main thing—to throw a shaft of light upon the Duke of York—to point him out as the villain of the piece: the Heir to the throne an avowed Papist; Protestant England flouted!

It shows Shaftesbury's knowledge of men that he should have foreseen what James would do.

Charles had urged his brother to conform outwardly. It was such an easy thing, and such a little one! It meant nothing. It was but a form. Even if he would not take the Sacrament in the Royal Chapel, let him at least attend its services on occasion. It was but an outward show, it could wound his conscience in nothing and it would help this only surviving son of their murdered father, his King, and one who had given him loyal support, to pass through a grave crisis.

James had replied that he would rather die: and on James's lips phrases of that sort were not rhetoric.

He resigned. All England was advised publicly by his own action not only that he was now a Catholic, but that he thought his religion worth any price and would hold it against any challenger. The Admiralty was his life's work. He had done most excellently there in Administration on command and on active service. It was his interest and, at his time of life, at forty, the routine to which he had formed himself. He was willing to abandon it rather than compromise even in gesture. This iron kind of resolution throws out its friends and is the fortune of its enemies.

At the same time the other resignations which took place in every branch of official service—but especially in the military commands, coming thus all at once, affecting London where the Court and all Government were centred—produced the effect and even more than the effect which the conspirators had expected. William Russell, the son of Bedford (the family most enriched of all, perhaps, by the Reformation), Coventry, Cavendish, the whole group of great landed interests which was at work, felt that a first victory, sharp and determining the future, had been won. And they were right.

The power of the appeal to anti-Catholic feeling lay not in its intensity—it was intense only in a minority, and not even with them save under special excitement by skilful managers—but in the absence of a defence. There was plenty of feeling for the Crown, but how could you get a strong movement in *favour* of the Catholic fraction? A movement to *defend* it? The average man was luke-warm in his hostility to Catholicism, but he was not in favour of it.

The Catholic minority was England no doubt, had strong national traditions, was closely intermixed with the general life, was large—but it was not average. It was peculiar; it was becoming foreign to the bulk of its fellow citizens. Since also, to a very considerable body of the people, a body larger than its own, it was actually hateful, to start a current against it was always easy. With concrete examples to strike the imagination it was possible, at intervals, to light up a flame against it. There could always be aroused at such moments in London a mob which had nothing to lose and would follow the stream. There could be no corresponding force on the other side. And now that the Royal Family was mixed up in the discontent aroused, that discontent had become a permanent and powerful means of indirect attack upon the Court.

The resignations, here, there, upon every side, could be made to seem not only widespread—which they were —but so numerous as to be, in a community Protestant in type, signs of an abnormal Catholic reaction—which they were not. In Holland, for instance, which passed everywhere as the typical Protestant state but where toleration was admitted, the Catholics employed were, in proportion, more numerous than in England even at the moment of their greatest freedom, just before the passing of the Test Act. But the impression was produced, it was profound, it was sufficient for Shaftesbury and his following to build upon.

The first blow had been delivered and it had gone home. The second blow designed by Shaftesbury failed. An agitation was got up against James's proposed marriage with Mary of Modena, because she was a Catholic. The King ordered the Chancellor to prorogue Parliament before the resolution should be voted on. He deliberately disobeyed, thinking in his contempt of the failing Royal Power that even such flagrant flouting of it would be accepted by the King in his determination to survive by concession.

But this time Shaftesbury had gone too far. Charles abruptly dismissed him from his post and its vast revenues. Thenceforward it was open war between Shaftesbury, as the type and head of the Magnates, and the National Dynasty.

The succeeding four and a half years are full of history for the general life of the realm and of Europe. Charles, aided by Danby, moves in a fashion to make Louis XIV, angry at Charles's success in the diplomatic game against him, expose Danby's transaction in a recent subsidy. The patriot statesmen of Parliament take bribes greedily from the King of France. But those years have no public effect upon James. He has been compelled to retire from office.

He is apparently defeated. His determination or obstinacy has permanently embarrassed his brother the King, but he will not modify it. Small or great effects of his resolution are all one in his estimation. He will give way on nothing his faith demands. Such is his temper.

The King had signed the Test Act. He had admitted that defeat. He gave his enemies their head, and at the same time he used the interval to strengthen himself for further negotiation in that see-saw between France and her opponents by the action of which he so well maintained the English power. He leant again towards Holland, and, to strengthen himself against his cousin Louis, as well as to compete with the Country Party and Shaftesbury's aim of weakening him at home, he arranged that fatal marriage between his niece and William of Orange which was to produce—had he known it!—the extinction of his own line. But foreign policy must always be short-sighted. To take long views in it is to fail.

This policy, destestable to Louis, was wounding to James. The Duke of York had affirmed his faith by marrying Mary of Este, the daughter of the Duke of Modena. The Parliament, as we have seen, had protested, and had been put in their place. Here, at least, was ground on which they could not decently intrude, and their leaders felt at heart that they had gone too far. Moreover, their fears of a Catholic heir to James proved, for the moment, groundless; one year and another and another went by and no heir was born to that marriage. Meanwhile Charles saw to it, as I have said, that Mary and Anne, the ultimate heiresses (as things stood) to the throne, should be brought up Protestant. In 1676, when the eldest of these girls, Mary, was 14, he allowed the Bishop of London (Compton: later to be chief conspirator against the throne) to insist on her confirmation, and paid no heed to her father's rights or protests. It was the beginning of her estrangement from him. Anne, still too young for the rite, though brought up like her sister in the Establishment, remained his darling.

In the next year, 1677, Mary was married to the Prince of Orange: it was the climax of Charles's 'swing to the left' in that pendulum of policy whereby he maintained, precariously, the equilibrium of his throne. The little sour, determined man of 27, with his already evil reputation, took off to The Hague and to his singular companions this dull young girl of 15, never to have children by him.

It was the end and the climax of the anti-French move. Immediately after came peace upon the continent—Charles had already refused further aid from France—the Peace of Nimeguen left Holland intact and saved: Louis XIV solidly in possession of conquests made at the expense of Spain. England was free from further expense of war for ten full years, and that, with the continual rise of revenue from the customs, left a barely sufficient revenue for the Crown.

Had the customs revenue and excise grown but slightly more the Government would have had room to act. Even as it was, Charles, in the next storm of attack, was free for the first time to dissolve the Parliament; he was no longer quite under the old dependence on it for grants: he was beginning to gain some economic freedom from its leaders.

It was perhaps on this account, because they saw—particularly because Shaftesbury saw—the danger of losing one of two modes of action against the King, that the other was emphasized: since supply of money at the good-will of the aristocracy was not the immediate necessity it had been to the Crown, the exceptional chance given by the Duke of York's affirmation of Catholicism must now be worked for all it was worth. On that as a foundation the Test Act had arisen. With that as centre, the spectacle of Catholic officers and officials expelled by the score had been afforded. Whatever in huge London was already suspicious had been inflamed; to a less degree the provinces, especially in districts where the evangelical feeling was strong; in many of the country towns, men' had been rendered nervous by the intrigues of Shaftesbury's set, and expectant of some vague coming trouble, when there suddenly broke out the fury of the Popish Plot of 1678.

It is not permissible to affirm that this insanity was the work of Shaftesbury and his crew. The evidence is lacking. It is never permissible to affirm that the sudden corporate ecstasies flaming up in great cities are necessarily the product of intrigue or are originated by deliberate intention. Mafeking in the London of 1900 was spontaneous, so was the raving lunacy of the 'Russians in England' which distinguished 1914.[1] No man of competence or authority was at the origin of the Gordon Riots. No cold speculative genius, still less any political adventurer, created the orgy of the South Sea Bubble; though, it is true, one financial charlatan made it possible. An ardent imaginative race, full of energy, falls at times into these excitements, which are its fevers. The Popish Plot may have arisen from nothing more than the coincidence of sickly mood in thousands and bold adventure in a couple of scoundrels.

On the other hand, it is certain that it was opportune in the highest degree to that immensely wealthy opposition, already half in rebellion, which—now James was set down—was beginning to lack material for attacking the Royal House; and it is equally certain, it is matter of detailed and recorded history, that Shaftesbury and

[1] Many acquaintances have assured me that in this latter case the public insanity was deliberately designed and have given—at second or third hand—chapter and verse. But I am not convinced. It seemed, and seems, to me spontaneous.

Russell, Buckingham, Essex—all the great fortunes which directed rebellion—most industriously circulated and supported stories which they knew to be monstrous lies and rejoiced to see accepted by crowds the suggestion that each Catholic (one man in seven or eight!) was pledged to murder his six or seven neighbours; that Papists were told off to burn all the shipping in the Pool of London—and the city itself while they were about it—for the second time in two years. That in the succeeding desert their chief men had been given each his department in Government (by the Pope—or the General of the Jesuits); and that King Charles of all men (no longer a secret supporter of Papists now, but a martyr to the Protestant cause) was to be stabbed, poisoned, shot: and all this by Jesuits—or perhaps by the poor Queen. A populace can always be roused for its king, and to make the King's peril part of the plot was a shrewd move.

The curious consideration of James Stuart's nobility, narrowness and misfortune has little to do with this frenzy save in so far as it affected his own story. All have read and may read again of Oates, his brazen courage, his huge face, his bandy legs, his fertility of monstrous imaginations. All know how, in the trials, Chief Justice Scroggs raved at and bullied the Catholic prisoners at the bar, shouting at one batch that he was 'satisfied of their guilt' before any proof had been offered, at another, 'You eat your God and you kill your king'; at another 'Much good may their 30,000 Masses do them.' Our point is that the hurricane left James impassive.

Charles bowed to it at the peril of his soul. He signed the warrants for the deaths of innocent men, and once or twice jested as he did so. It was statecraft. But there is a Judge of statecraft also. He could not have resisted without losing his throne? He could have resisted and have lost his throne. For there are other things a man may lose.

Anyhow, his brother, with no responsibility it is true, but in extreme peril, was indifferent. He left for Brussels not because he so desired but because the King ordered it. The chief source of irritation was thus removed, and Charles could breathe more freely, till the tempest should have blown itself out and he could look round the decks and note the wreckage.

He had dissolved that Parliament which had sat since his restoration—eighteen years—he had summoned another which arrived more rabid than the last. He determined on yet another piece of Policy. With London in a frenzy over the Popish Plot he could not openly continue the battle with his opponents. He proposed to compromise with them if only to gain time. He procured from Temple, whom he called back from Holland, a plan for a large body of thirty to sit as Council in place of the few hitherto used as Royal Ministers: it was to include the worst of the opposition. He hoped thus to manage them till the peril created by the Popish Plot agitation should be over. He received all his chief enemies with open arms into this new council—Shaftesbury at its head, his cousin Halifax (a man more sympathetic, detached, of a very high culture, necessarily like all his class an opponent of monarchy, yet—oddly enough—never caught taking money), Russell, Cavendish, Essex, all—the crowd of large estates, the masters of the English people and their king.

In part Charles was successful in this perilous experiment (James, from Brussels, condemned it). Thus the King prevented these magnates from dismissing the loyal judges and packing the Bench in their own favour. But in the long run that experiment broke down, as we shall see, for Charles could not prevent a further move to destroy the regular royal right of succession. That Council sat, that Parliament met, while the courts were full of those trials wherein so many priests and laymen were put to a barbarous death [1] by process of law on the perjuries of Oates and his fellows.

They died innocent. Yet two things must always be remembered in connexion with the murderous extravagance of 1678-9.

The first is that the horror expressed at it by the historians of the last generation is largely hypocritical—they are taking an opportunity to say a number of smooth words preparatory to saying a number of false ones. They condemn the absurd Popish Plot and its blatant perjurers in order to salve their conscience for calling toleration 'the Establishment of Papistry.'

The second is that the frenzy of so many in London at that time had a basis.

I have some sympathy with those moderns who, in reaction against the old humbug, have recently tried to maintain that there was something in the Popish Plot after all. Not that I think them sincere—far from it. I think they are writing to a brief and largely out of irritation against the rapidly increasing power of the Faith in the moral anarchy of their own world to-day. But they have solid ground below their fantasies. There was no plot. But there *was* a new situation in which the Catholic Church was threatening to count for more and more. Enthusiasts like Coleman believed in her triumph at the time or in the near future: a folly. But the highest minds of that day in England were sceptical, the noblest were troubled, and the Church made a strong appeal. Either the

[1] They were hanged till half strangled, then cut down alive and conscious. Then castrated. Then ripped up, their hearts torn out and burnt in front of them. Then cut into quarters, the which (and the head), carted away, were exhibited in public places as a terror to their co-religionists.

Faith must be crushed—as at last it was—or it would spread; for it is a fire. All States discover that sooner or later. There was no danger of Catholicism governing that England. There was danger of its modifying the Protestant tone of that England, of its strengthening Popular Monarchy and weakening Aristocracy, by its permanent presence in a strong minority of all classes.

With which let me return to the new Council, the new Parliament, and the effect of both on James.

There entered the Council at this time another close relative of the magnates' clique, Robert Spencer, Lord Sunderland. If a man were told nothing else about the time than what Sunderland's actions were and how, in spite of them, first Charles and then James were under the necessity of using him and even of leaning upon him, he would be watching under a searchlight the last phases of the dying monarchy of England.

Not that Sunderland's own career and character form an interesting or even a possible subject of study. The whole thing is such a welter of falsity and baseness that there is no connecting thread, not even of strong personal calculation and well-managed campaigns such as you may find in the vile character of his brother-in-law Shaftesbury.

Sunderland played double all his life; perhaps because he was never quite certain what was going to happen next; perhaps simply because he loved playing double for its own sake; perhaps from the very obvious motive of getting double pay by serving both sides. For we must remember what a very great part money played in all the shuffling of that time. The men who were, as a body, eliminating the Crown were struggling as individuals one against the other for coin, salaries and perquisites in the gift of the Crown. Their fortunes were all large, some of them colossal, yet their craving for money was never satisfied. When their modern apologists can find one who (doubtfully) can be acquitted of taking bribes from foreign governments it is made an occasion for enthusiastic praise. The most famous writer-up of the revolution, Macaulay, is moved to his highest flights in assuring us that Russell never received 'a consideration.' Though he spoils his case by adding that this was due to his enormous wealth. The same is, as we have seen, the chief glory of Halifax—and there may have been three or even four others. But a ministry enriched a man of that day very rapidly. Hence the scramble for posts. Legislation enriched them; presents from suitors; land acquired by pressure or through special Acts of Parliament; commercial privilege: all is grist to their mill.[1] So it was with Sunderland. The riddle of his motives other than gain will never be solved, for it could only be solved by getting into the inside of the fellow's mind. But if we make a list of what he did and remember that, in spite of all, both the royal brothers had no choice but to depend upon him, we understand the determining power, in the late seventeenth century in England, of territorial wealth and its easy defeat of the Crown.

Sunderland was a young man of 20 when Charles was restored to the throne. He and his wife (whose love-affairs were innumerable—the most steadfast of them was with her husband's own uncle Sydney) paid assiduous court to the mistresses of the King, especially, at the end of the string, to Louise de Querouaille. It was through this connexion that Sunderland was virtually governing in 1679.

It is Sunderland more than any one else who gets James away to Scotland before the meeting of Parliament

---

[1] Thus Lord Bristol, a Catholic, spoke in favour of the Test Act, and got a large pension out of the taxes from his grateful colleagues as a reward.

in October, 1680; and meanwhile behind the scenes it is
Sunderland who, through his wife's intrigue with his
uncle and that uncle's presence as Ambassador at The
Hague, works up the outrageous Dutch interference with
English affairs when those foreign merchants were good
enough to tell the King of England whom he should
choose as his councillors, and what he should do. While
the violent storm of the Popish Plot was still blowing,
Sunderland ran before the gale, and his voting for the
Bill to exclude James from the throne lost him his place
in the Council. Within two years he was back again, and
as powerful as ever. Then, noting the reaction, he supported James as openly as he had opposed him.

When James comes to the throne, Sunderland is to
be the most zealous of all in the chastisement of Monmouth's rebellion. He had already in the past been an
active supporter of Russell's execution after the Rye
House plot. He is to be present when James sees Monmouth, and it is the most probable conjecture—though
we are not certain of it—that what Monmouth intended
to divulge in order to save his life was Sunderland's
treason—the fact that Sunderland, with all his open zeal
for the repression of the rebellion, had connived at it.
It is equally probable, though also not certain, that Sunderland had promised Monmouth his life if the divulging
of this double dealing were not made—and then saw to
it that the poor dupe was got out of the way by death.

As the crisis of James's reign approached, his action
was of a sort normal to the great territorial lords of the
day, but perhaps in degree excessive. He was taking a
regular pension from Louis XIV of what would be to-day
between ten and fifteen thousand a year. He asked for a
large addition to it as the price of his support; and all the
while he and his wife were carefully informing the Prince
of Orange of all that passed in the English Cabinet. It

was he who at the end persuaded James to refuse the offer of Louis's fleet. It was he who, as we shall see, put in Petre as a foil to draw anger away from himself. It was he who played at religion so assiduously as to deceive his master.

There is the man, one like twenty others of the sort, and a relation to half of them, who enters the Council during the Popish Plot. One contemporary phrase sums the fellow up: 'He disliked women and he hated wine.'

Charles had yielded all that could be yielded—as his policy and custom was. It was a policy which had served him well. In the long run he could boast that it had brought him final success—but perhaps his death was opportune. Had he lived a year or two more the attack would have returned.

His constant method of letting out all the rope in hand was here in full play. At his Council board were the men who had done all in their power to degrade him. At their head he had set Shaftesbury, the man who of all men had most shamefully betrayed and most impudently attacked. But the license had reached its limit— there was no more line to slack.

In the new Parliament, at the instigation of these very men, the proposal was made, the bill introduced, whereby the Duke of York should be debarred from the succession.

There—on the essential point of dynastic right— Charles struck. He went much too far, later, in concession even here. He proposed to maintain his brother's rights under conditions shameful and even puerile: that a Catholic king should not present to benefices was arguable, but that the Parliament should control his armed forces would be the end of monarchy. The suggestion that he should live far from the country and be king in name alone, with an heir directing in his stead, was still more incongruous. But even with such expedients the men who now felt themselves finally triumphant over kingship would have nothing to do. It must be the bill and nothing but the bill, the exclusion of James wholly and utterly.

They used, of course, the fact of his religion. With their followers, still under the excitement of the Popish Plot, it was a genuine motive. Not with *them*. The Russells and Capels, Spencers, Coopers and the rest had not James's religion in mind save as a most valuable tool with which to work. But the work they had set out to accomplish was not so particular a thing as James's exclusion. Their business was to prove once and for all that they gave orders and the Crown obeyed: that they were prince and the Crown their subject. The ceaseless activities of their class, spread over a century, were rewarded. The Exclusion Bill, indeed, did not pass. But within ten years the Monarchy had fallen.

Charles used every expedient. He prorogued and dissolved that short Parliament. He summoned another. It was as hostile. He dissolved this in its turn; but not before, during its anxiety for the measure, the combat had taken an ominous turn. The name of Monmouth had been mentioned. Shaftesbury was playing his last cards.

It is sadly amusing, but a little wearisome in its likeness to our modern politicians and their professions, to read throughout the Duke of Monmouth's career his loud protestations of Protestantism, his peculiar enthusiasm therefore.

They were the product, of course, of the rivalry which he always felt and which evidently succeeded after he had lost his own battle at Sedgemoor: the rivalry of that other champion of the wealthy English faction, William of Orange. But there was this difference between them, very marked indeed. Monmouth cared nothing whatever for the differences in religion; it was mere play-acting, and he knew very little of continental politics; he was but a figure-head put forward. William of Orange, though certainly caring nothing for any positive set of doctrines, had a fine active dislike of the Catholic Church. Moreover, he knew more of European politics than most young men of his time; and he fully understood what the position of the French Monarchy then was, what its claims, what its weakness, and how it might be met. He saw in its final defeat the aggrandizement of himself and his house, and for that defeat he continuously worked. He needed England to use as a pawn in his continental game.

Shaftesbury, then, played both strings. It was both the Duke of Monmouth and William of Orange whom he proposed as successor to the reigning king—when his legitimate heir, James, Duke of York, should on the passing of the Exclusion Bill be 'deemed dead.'

As for the Protestant heiresses of James, his two daughters Mary and Anne, Mary was William's wife, and of Anne there would not be a question unless that should prove impossible, which already seemed unlikely with so strange a husband as William, that Mary should have children.

It must be remembered in this double play of Shaftesbury's that the Duke of Monmouth, though having no right whatever to the throne, was by considerable sections of the people, especially in London, acclaimed as a potential heir, simply because he was a male Stuart and at the same time, by profession, a leader of the Protestant cause.

Thus when later he returned to England at Shaftesbury's bidding in the teeth of the King he made almost royal progress. The Whig cabal of great merchants who still ruled London (he reached the town at midnight from abroad) ordered bonfires and peals of bells. He went up and down England like a young king, touching for the evil. He studied popularity like any modern candidate for Parliament, familiar with all, joining in games and kissing babies. He thought himself universally beloved. It was his undoing within five years, for it brought him to the scaffold.

Shaftesbury is generally credited with the policy of putting forward the bastard as sole candidate for the throne. Macaulay in his simplicity imagines his hero to have been simple. I doubt it. I give Shaftesbury credit for a better brain. He was playing the very familiar double game of putting forward two candidates in order that he might be tied to neither of them—he kept the other up his sleeve: and that other was the young William of Orange, as Mary's husband.

The fact that the Duke of Monmouth's name should have been mentioned at all (and it was mentioned thenceforward at intervals with emphasis until his invasion, and miserable failure, six years later) throws a vivid light upon all the time. Here was a man who had no claim. He was not only the mere bastard of the King (Louis XIV also had thought of making the Duc de Maine capable of succession), but he was a bastard by an ignoble prostitute, born before the Restoration. Against him the legitimate Stuart was a man with heiresses of his own blood born to him and surviving. Monmouth counted not at all. Yet the times were such that it was possible to put Monmouth forward as a candidate for the throne upon the exclusion of a man who was brother to the King, who had won a great victory at sea for England as Admiral, who had again fought with success and splendid courage in command of the Navy, who had been the most powerful man in the Council.

That support of Monmouth would not have been possible unless there had been some large minority of the people fanatically opposed to James's accession (at least, at this moment, just after the Popish Plot). It would not have been possible had the Crown had anything like its old power. Lastly, it would not have been possible if James II had had any of that fascination for the crowd which Monmouth undoubtedly had, and which the legitimate heir wholly lacked. For though the sailors who had seen him at work felt strongly for James—they cheered him as they went to their deaths in the wreck of the *Gloucester*—yet by land he was but a name, and a name in London still associated with the nightmares of Titus Oates's dupes.

The bastard was now (in 1679) 30 years of age; he had been born at Rotterdam in the April after Charles I's death, and while his successor, the young king, was wandering impoverished in exile. The woman Walters, his mother, had had plenty of lovers—if one can use the term for a person in her position. It was a common joke of the times that this particular child was not Charles's, but rather that of a certain colonel; but surely no one who has seen that fine painting of his head after death can doubt his being a Stuart. There is not another of the natural sons of Charles II who bears so strongly stamped upon his features that strange concave shape of face, with its dark, somewhat scanty hairs, and its sad anxieties of expression.

It is a very good example of the way in which the intriguers would say and do anything to achieve their end, that the Duke of Monmouth was being called legitimate! Just as later they lied shamelessly in the matter of James's young heir, making the child supposititious, so in the matter of Monmouth they lied shamelessly upon his bastardy, some even pretending that Lucy Walters, the mother, had married Charles II in his exile.

When the populace is to be deceived its imagination must be fed by concrete things. A story had long been current, and it was now spread on all sides, of a certain *Black Box* containing Lucy Walters's marriage lines—

oh, if only that black box could be found! But in its absence, on the phantasm of it the populace was fed by great gentlemen of culture whose circle include Shaftesbury and Russell, Sydney and Buckingham. The absurd falsehood took root at such a moment with the same rapidity that the lies of Titus Oates had taken root; and by the early summer of 1679 there were whole blocks of the duped middle class in the capital who firmly believed the Duke of Monmouth to be legitimate.

Charles behaved well and with firmness. He made a Declaration, dated 2nd June, 1679 (and repeated in the following January and March), that he had never been married to Lucy Walters, and thus confirmed his own brother in his legitimate position.

The character of James was never better seen than in one detail of this exceedingly difficult passage of his life. It was an episode at the beginning of the struggle for the exclusion of James from the throne.

The Exclusion Bill depended upon the excitement of the Popish Plot.

That excitement was bound to die down. The Exclusion Bill would then seem to the average Englishman in his sober senses an absurdity, and even to the strongly excited Englishmen of the capital it seemed extreme. To defeat the project not very much handling of circumstances was needed: not very great finesse. After all, the Duke's Catholic life was not daily before the public, nor emphasized. The devotion of the plain citizen to the royal line and legitimate monarchy was instinctive and deep-rooted. It needed but one thing to save James from any further trouble, the same action that would have preserved the Admiralty for him six years before would now give him the throne; and that was, once more, the mere simulacrum, I do not say of outward conformity, but of a sort of

negative conformity, such as surely any man may prac-
tise without doing too much violence to his conscience.

The Church of England was still strongly attached,
and remained so attached for nearly ten years, in its
chiefs, to the full royalist position, the duty of obedience
to the Crown, the importance of legitimate descent and
of right title. It was the bishops of the Establishment,
or, rather, certain among them, who now saw what ought
to be done, in their eyes at least, to save the situation.
They approached James and suggested that he should
yield at last, and appear side by side with his brother at
the official services in the Royal Chapel.

Once more, there was nothing that could offend, as it
would seem, a man's honour, let alone his duty to the
Faith. Once more he was asked to renounce nothing, to
take no oath repugnant to a Catholic. He was not asked
to take the Sacrament in the Established rite; he was
not even asked to avoid the Mass, which he might perfectly well hear in his private capacity, though thus officially appearing, now and then at least, at Charles's side
in the Chapel Royal.

There is not one man in a hundred but would have
accepted in such a position and at such a crisis. It was
no longer an office, it was his crown that was at stake.
To have yielded at last, this second time, would have
saved his right to the throne, at the expense of a mere
outward attitude or gesture which involved no direct
inconsistency, no essentially apostate act. It would not
have been much worse morally than what many a Catholic
does daily in the England of our time, that is, condone
in speech and accent and gesture the anti-Catholic hatred
around him: the praise of anti-Catholic history and fiction:
the hatred of Catholic nations, the contempt of the Catholic past.

We can only understand James's character when we

understand why he refused. We have seen how he had
already, years before, asked for information upon a definite point of conduct: whether a man having been baptized into the Catholic Church was justified in hiding his
membership thereof in any fashion. He had been told
that there could be no such justification. He had accepted
the decision with the courage and wholeheartedness which
were his special marks; and acted upon them as auto-
matically as a private soldier acts upon a word of command.

He refused the advice. He advertised his dissent.

He was warned that if he stood out on this one apparently minor point, that if he would not consent to be
present officially in the Chapel Royal, while the service
of the Establishment was being read or intoned, there
could not but follow his own ruin and that of the King;
probably even a revolution. He was further warned by
such of the Anglican prelates as were not without their
private sympathies for the Universal Church that, if he
remained rigorous, the remaining body of the Faith in
England would be crushed out.

They were right in all these warnings except in that
which referred to his brother, King Charles. *He* indeed
was not over-set. He died a king and steered through
successfully. But all the rest came true.

Whether James knew that all the rest would come true
or not, we cannot tell. Probably he did not; he was a
man who never plotted, and therefore never troubled to
look far ahead at the consequence of action: content when
he had decided within his own mind whether action were
right or wrong. At this decisive moment—though not emphasized in histories it was really the pivot of the whole
affair—he answered in these words, which I translate into
English, from the French transcript of what he seems to
have given to a friend: '*My principles do not allow me*

*to dissimulate my religion after this fashion; I cannot
resolve to do evil that good may come of it.'*

The concision of it recalls another phrase of his in a
similar trial. *'By God's grace I will never do so damnable
a thing.'*

This stubbornness raised friction all around.

It gravely disturbed Charles, who, however much he
may have admired it in his heart, must have been irritated
by it intellectually and exasperated by it as a statesman.
It must have seemed to him to be a sort of wantonness,
a deliberate extreme of position with which his brother
had no right to embarrass him.

It perplexed, confused, and even angered his friends
among the English hierarchy. And it took a strong argument away from those who would have defended him in
Parliament, especially in the House of Lords.

But James was persuaded of his duty and did it. He
was consistent with himself at that essential moment as
he was upon nearly every other critical occasion of his
life.

I say 'upon *nearly* every other'; but the phrase is un-
gracious; for on those occasions when he seems inconsistent
or wavering, on the occasion, for instance, of his daughter's fatal marriage, it was not weakening but misapprehension of the situation.

Now, rather than yield he went into exile. At the beginning of March he was in Brussels, and hoped by that
absence, as did his brother, that the impossible situation
would be solved.

The calculation failed. Within two months, by the end
of April, the Gentry of the Commons passed the resolution, that, being heir to the throne and a Catholic, James
had led the Popish Plot. It was upon this manifest falsehood (which no one believed, save perhaps the more yokel
of the squires, the more suburban of the merchants) that

the Exclusion Bill which Shaftesbury had worked up for so long, was read for the first and second time.

Such inhuman steadfastness in James was not without its temporary reward. In the last but one of those short successive Parliaments which Charles desperately summoned—and postponed—to gain time, Halifax (acting hypocritically for the Prince of Orange and to exclude the chances of Monmouth) spoke with such excellence in the Lords that the Bill was thrown out. To their honour, the Bishops voted against it (it would be interesting to know what Compton felt!).

We all know how the last Parliament of the reign was summoned at Oxford—so as to be free of the mob which Shaftesbury could organize in London—how tumultuously it met in arms, with what just contempt it was dissolved. By such Charles was no longer pestered in the short remaining years of his life.

The appeal to the people had come and was for the moment sufficient. They were certainly behind their King. A last desperate plot was foiled, wherein some proposed to murder the royal brothers, others probably, some certainly, to raise rebellion. Its authors perished. Russell (in spite of an abject appeal to the Duke of York) and Sydney on the block: the lesser men hanged.

Monmouth was in exile. Shaftesbury had fled oversea and died. The merchant oligarchies, especially that of London, were broken and loyal corporations succeeded them. The Duke of York returned to the Council, and the long struggle ended—for a brief interlude—in peace.

So far the character of James had been tested, though severely, only in the simple crux of 'Yes' and 'No'. Its morals, not its judgment or constructive faculty, had alone been searched.

There was awaiting him an ordeal of quite another

kind: the ordeal of action over men: of Government. And that he could not meet.

NOTE ON LADY RUSSELL

I have alluded briefly in the text to the use made by Shaftesbury, in his attack on the Crown, of his first cousin, Lady Russell. It is important to emphasize the part played by this woman as Shaftesbury's agent. She was heiress to the great fortune of her father Southampton, which included Bloomsbury. Hence Southampton House in that district of London where the conspiracies against the King were hatched. She was of the iron Huguenot fighting blood through her mother, a Ruvigny. As a widow this masterful millionairess married William Russell, a blameless weak man three years younger than herself and heir, after the death of his witless brother, to the vast territorial wealth of his father, Lord Bedford. That father had put him into Parliament for the family borough of Tavistock. He sat for fourteen years without opening his mouth until his wife's cousin, Shaftesbury, turned against the King. Then he is used to promote the Exclusion Bill, lends to the new policy all the weight of the Bedford interests, ends by getting mixed up in conspiracies and has his head cut off.

VII

THE ORDEAL

CHARLES THE KING lay dying in Whitehall. It was late, long after dark on that cold February day of London brume, 1685; Thursday the 5th.

He had been suffering for but three days. The great bedroom of the Palace was crowded—there were forty or more around the bed and waiting in attendance, Peers, Privy Councillors, five of the Bishops, doctors, servants at the walls. Men went in and out. There was whispering by the main doors; but at the head of the King's bed a little door on the right-hand side, opening on a small back staircase and to the queen's rooms, was kept shut and unnoticed.

For many hours the Duke of York had stood by the bed, watching. Earlier in the day the Bishop of Bath and Wells, Ken, had read the Anglican Office for the Sick, had urged his master to communicate. To that plea the dying man had answered nothing. When it was repeated, he said faintly that 'there was time enough'. When the Elements were brought in and the insistence continued, he would only say again, and more than once, 'I will think of it'. Now, in the dark evening and after so many hours, the moment had come to act otherwise.

Louise de Querouaille, her baby face all tears (for she loved Charles), Barillon, the French Ambassador, knew the King's great desire and were disturbed at the Duke of York's delay. That Prince had been sending orders out upon every side, to the guards, to the city, taking on his office of authority in the perilous moment, but he acted in good time—though what he was about to do was a capital offence in law.

There was in the Palace at that time an English Benedictine, Dom Huddlestone. He had helped to save Charles's life after Worcester, and on that account had been specially protected during all the fury of the late persecutions. He was advised to be ready, and sent another monk, of the Portuguese Embassy, over to St. James's Palace for the Blessed Sacrament. Then (it was between six and seven o'clock of the evening) James, having asked the company to draw off a little to the end of the room, knelt by his brother and asked him in a low tone if he might send for a priest. Charles answered, 'For God's sake, do.'

The Duke of York rose, and in a loud voice called to all in the bedroom to withdraw, by the King's order; all save Feversham, the old French Huguenot soldier, Duras, so long a commander in England, and Bath, Groom of the Stole. These three Protestants remaining seemed guarantee enough even to the Bishops as they filed out into the antechamber. The rest were indifferent.

Chiffinch hurriedly brought in the Benedictine through the Queen's rooms by the little door, and James said, 'Sir, this good man once saved your body. He comes now to save your soul.' Charles whispered faintly, 'He is welcome.' He was received into the Faith, repentant—especially that he had delayed so long. He was anointed and annealed, the Absolution given. When the Blessed Sacrament was held up he made some poor effort to kneel, but was dissuaded, for it was not in him; he could hardly even swallow and had to be helped with a glass of water. Then as his head sunk back he saw the Crucifix held before his eyes and heard the adjuration to depend upon the sufferings of Jesus Christ. The little door opened again, and the priest was gone. It was something later than eight o'clock. The company was recalled and came back numerous into that changed room. They watched all night as he sank, blessing his children, recommending his women lest they should suffer, and, at times, groaning in great pain. At the turn of the night, lethargy eased him. At dawn he was failing, but could still ask for the curtains to be drawn that he might look for the last time upon the morning light. A little later his speech failed; then he fell blessedly unconscious of pain or anything. At noon he very quietly died.

James desired to be alone. He commended with himself—perhaps praying for his brother's soul—for about a quarter of an hour in a room apart. Then he issued and met the Council. He made a speech to them which was printed and distributed, saying in this that he would support the Church and State as he found them, and immediately summoned a Parliament to meet in three months; on the 19th May. He had inherited Laurance Hyde (Lord Rochester), his brother-in-law, from Charles's administration, and he put him at the head of his Government—a strong Protestant and supporter of the Church of England. He kept Lord Sunderland as Secretary to the Council.

Two problems of very different magnitude met him at the outset of his new responsibilities and demanded solution: one a question of revenue, the other of religious practice. He took in each steps not extravagant nor unwise, but already, by a shade, on the blunt side.

The Duties at the Ports continued to be levied, of course, day by day; as in the last week of Charles's life, so in the first of James's reign. Thus had it been for centuries and it was, by this time, a mere necessity of the routine in the greatly increased commerce and revenue of London.

One cannot imagine the Port of London in 1685 held up and all its goods in bond pending an assembly of county gentlemen at Westminster; or, alternatively, a anarchic rush for free import during the *interregnum*.

There was further a very strong feeling loudly expressed by the London merchants that it would be grossly unfair to allow the competition of goods entered free against goods already brought under the customs. James was not only right in collecting, but compelled of necessity to collect. Guildford, experienced in Treasury matters, but timid and of doubtful loyalty, proposed an impossible scheme for holding the money till Parliament met—which would have meant, in practice, opening the reign with a quarter's burden of debt and incurring high interest as well.[1] James was careful himself to proclaim the fact that technically the only legal foundation for the customs lay in a vote by Parliament, and he emphasized this by summoning that assembly more immediately than any previous king had done.

Charles had died on February the 6th, the Friday. James had been proclaimed and called his first regular Council on the Saturday; at the very first opportunity after the intervening Sunday, Monday morning, the 9th of February, the writs were ordered and the summons for a new Parliament issued. Not till this had been done was the proclamation for continuing the regular customs, pending the meeting of the Houses, issued. When they met they heard his claim with satisfaction and their first act was to confirm the revenue for life.

Nevertheless, James might have done one thing which he did not do and which would have been of excellent effect for the future. He might have emphasized the deplorable necessity and the strong need of early confir-

---

[1] The Bankers—already powerful—charged the Crown eight and even ten per cent.

mation by the House of Commons. He might have made the whole thing an occasion for throwing into high relief his vast respect for the now fixed rights of Parliament in the provision of revenue and his own misery at being driven through necessity of doing justice by the Merchants of London, even to so brief a technical breach of what had been law for nearly sixty years. Such a protestation would have been humbug, of course, and that was why James would not stoop to it: but it is just that sort of humbug which is essential to the government of men.

The matter of his private worship was of greater moment. Those of James's subjects who objected to his having accepted the Catholic faith were reconciled by this time to his domestic practice of a minority religion, though most of them probably wondered why he would not publicly attend the State Service while privately hearing Mass. But *public* expression of Catholicism—even within the Palace—was a different matter. It bore the character of a challenge. That instinct for using the unpopularity of Catholicism as an instrument against the Crown was as strong as ever in the territorial class, and though its most daring members had lately been scattered and punished, new intriguers could always arise. James compromised by agreeing that when he went to Mass it should be in the Queen's chapel, and as an individual, not as a monarch. But he insisted on some of the ceremony which he thought due to a monarch, and therein, again, he erred. As in the case of the customs, he should—for policy at least—have beslavered his critics: he should have emphasized the wholly private character of his worship. But here, again, he refused to cringe. On the contrary, he had himself accompanied to the very doors of the chapel by the great officers of his Court, the guards lined his way, and though it was understood that no one need follow him farther than the doors, the doors stood wide open. This ceremony, and the fact that Mass could be seen and followed half publicly in the Palace, gave rise to violent anti-Catholic sermons in the City of London—whose bishop, be it remembered, was that Compton of the best birth on the bench, and a ceaseless intriguer against the Crown.

It was sincerely feared by many that James intended by such acts to make the full public worship of his religion familiar, and through that familiarity to spread its influence. Probably he did. But that was not the way to set about it. It gave a handle to the more calculating of his enemies who were spreading the falsehood (already!) that the King was making an attack upon the State religion.

In the matter of toleration, he did nothing unwise. He released the thousands of Catholics who were still in prison for nothing but their Faith and also the great number of Nonconformists so persecuted. But he went no further; except to warn the lawyers that the Government discouraged prosecutions on grounds of religion. Any further action towards toleration of Catholics and Nonconformists alike he put off to the assembly of Parliament.

On St. George's Day, the 23rd of April, he was crowned and anointed in Westminster Abbey by the officials, and according to all the rites (saving the Communion) of the Church of England. He took the Coronation Oath to support that Church as by law established.

There followed the trial of Titus Oates, which was already in process and which only the death of Charles II had postponed. His guilt was clearly established and the judges in condemning him to a heavy fine, flogging and the pillory, expressed regret that they could not hang him.

Here again nothing clashed with popular humour. Oates had been over in Holland hobnobbing with Shaftesbury before that worthy's death, but no one could use his sufferings now as an excitement against the throne. Oates was found out, and most men in London had grown ashamed of their past madness. Since he could not legally be put to death, he lived on to receive a handsome pension for his perjuries from the grateful Prince of Orange, when he became King of England.

On the 19th of May the Parliament met. By way of opening speech James re-read the declaration he had made to the Council on his accession, promising to support Church and State as he found them. He asked of them the regular revenue of half excise and all customs for life, which his brother had had, and some further special vote to meet Charles II's debts and the expenses of putting down a rebellion which Argyll had begun and of which more in a moment.

The Parliament were enthusiastic in his support, they cheered the speech continually, willingly granted the revenue for life and gave him as special revenue for the moment more than he had asked. A motion to persecute dissenters was rejected unanimously on account of the King's desire for tolerance.

So far as the Commons and the people and merchants of London were concerned, the support of the King on his coming difficulty with the Rebellions was strong, sincere and united. These Rebellions we have not to follow in detail save as illustrations to the King's character and position. They were also invasions and were planned for Scotland and for the South, by Argyll and Monmouth in Holland. The Dutch connived at their departure.

Argyll sailed from Holland (financed by a rich widow of that country) on May the 2nd, and after touching at the Orkneys landed on the west coast of Scotland, where he raised his own retainers and issued a proclamation against King James. He had little following and the whole affair was over in six weeks, Argyll himself being captured on June the 17th and his last hundred men dispersed.

He was executed on the 30th at Edinburgh, showing great firmness to the end. But in the matter of that execution the King was guilty of a false attitude directly due to his ill understanding of men.

Scotland was led by its nobles. The small governing class had very high moral power in the lowlands; in the highlands the clans followed their chiefs like devoted families. These nobles were in high feud, fed with blood. The lineage of Argyll had judicially murdered, and would gladly murder again, their opponents. When the turn of these opponents came they exercised the same ferocity.

Now James had been appointed to the Government of Scotland five years before (1680) during his brother's reign when, after the excitement of the Popish Plot, it was advisable to keep him away from London. A subtler and more far-seeing man would have imposed peace upon the Scottish factions (so far as was possible) and would certainly have prevented what followed in the case of Argyll. That great Highland Chief had taken the Oath under the Test Act in order to maintain his numerous jurisdictions—he was a sort of king in his own western lands. In taking the Oath he had explained the sense in which he took it. His enemies on this ground eagerly condemned him as a traitor (1681). It was a monstrous verdict and it was a piece of folly in James to have permitted it. He did so because, of the two factions, the dominant one of the moment supported the official establishment in Church and State: because the fanaticism of the persecuted Calvinist enthusiasts had led them to murder and to the open profession of armed rebellion. But the motive was worthless. It had no place in a judicial record.

Argyll escaped from prison and fled oversea. Now, upon his invasion, failure and capture, he was put to death *not* on the ground of his present armed action against his

King—which was clearly treason—but (in order to emphasize the triumph of his enemies) upon the old iniquitous sentence of 1681. It was a permission on James's part lamentable and inexcusable. Because he had heard that one must satisfy opinion, and because the ruling opinion in Scotland was thus inclined, he gave it its head. Because he knew that statesmanship should be wary in going counter to the powerful, he supported the powerful just when it was an error to do so; yet later he offended them just when he might usefully have yielded. Because, in this case, one violent body called itself the friend of the Throne, he connived at its excesses out of season. When, later, he might have curbed the Scottish nobles by relying on their inferiors, he missed his chance.

In the much graver matter of Monmouth's invasion the King showed more balance.

Monmouth had not struck coincidentally with Argyll. He had delayed. He could only scrape together a force of eighty in one ship, but he rightly counted on some measure of popular support in the West and he carried arms for five thousand. He landed at Lyme Regis, at the boundary of Dorset and Devon, on June the 11th. He issued a proclamation that he was come to defend the Protestant Religion, laws and liberties of England; denounced James (whom he called 'Duke of York') as a usurper, idiotically accused him of poisoning his brother the late King *and* of setting fire to London. He declared war on him, such a monster.[1] Monmouth was so well received at Taunton that it turned his head. He declared himself King (under the title of James II), ordered the

---

[1] Argyll's proclamation made the same asinine accusation of murder. But we must remember, in that rebel's favour, that he respected immemorial tradition, and when he sent round the Fiery Cross to his clan saw to it that it was (*a*) made for yew, (*b*) duly fired, and (*c*) extinguished in goat's blood.

dissolution of Parliament and set a price on the real James II's head!

Monmouth, after the rout (pompously called 'the Battle') of Sedgemoor, was caught near Ringwood, in flight. Thence he wrote a piteous appeal for his life to the King. On his arrival in London a week later James consented on his earnest appeal to see him, but was disgusted by his cowardice: for Monmouth knelt before him and then crawled on the floor imploring mercy and denouncing all his comrades in arms. In the carriage on his way to the Tower he continued his supplications. Next day he still stormed the King, the Queen, the Queen Dowager Catherine of Braganza, and others at Court with letters imploring pardon. When all that failed and he knew he was to die he rallied to a sort of indifference in which he showed an equal carelessness to the agony of his legitimate wife (upon whose great fortune he had kept his state) and to the religious talk of the bishops. At ten o'clock on June the 15th he was beheaded, with shocking indecision, on Tower Hill. His last words affirmed the rights of his mistress (as against his wife) and his assurance of Heaven.

Of the rebels found in arms a small minority were given over to military execution at the hands of one Kirke, formerly in command at Tangiers: a man whose vileness is sufficiently proved by his desertion from the flag a few years later, his treasonable relations with William of Orange and his horrible cruelties in Ireland. His action here, in the West, did not exceed the severities common to the time, but they disgusted the King sufficiently for him to call a halt and to submit the authors, aiders and participators in the Rebellion to the Civil Courts. Five judges were sent into the West to try the great number of criminals presented; at their head was Jeffreys, an able, very handsome lawyer, time-serving as the rest, whom Charles II had picked out to be Lord Chief Justice. They first sat at Winchester, where the old widow of one of Cromwell's regicides was condemned by the jury, in spite of her own very ardent lying, on overwhelming evidence of harbouring fugitive rebels in arms; but James used his royal power to commute her sentence, from burning, the legal course, to beheading.[1] The court proceeded through the West as far as Exeter and back to Wells. Of the many thousand presented most were acquitted; of the rest some were pardoned; the remainder received a short sentence of flogging or imprisonment. Between 1,100 and 1,200 were more severely dealt with, principally as being guilty of rebellion in arms. Of these only just over a quarter[2] actually suffered the full penalty; the remaining three-quarters were given sentences of ten years' transportation to labour in the plantations.

And here the next point arises in the examination of James's character. Was the repression of Monmouth's rebellion excessive? Was the severity exercised due to him? Did he strengthen or weaken the Throne by its severity?

Of his right to use such severity no one of the time could make any question. The conception that such punishments are intolerable is a modern one, which we are justified in holding, but which was unknown to that day. The victims loudly complained. They would have acted in exactly the same fashion towards armed rebellion against *their* power, had their faction been uppermost. The question does not turn upon the character of what was perfectly legal in the circumstances, moral in the eyes of contemporaries and normal in the forms of punishment enforced. It turns upon the policy of such action.

[1] James has been blamed for the clemency as 'an example of his arbitrary government' interfering with the due course of the law!

[2] 331. We have a sample in the case of Dorchester: 292 condemned to death; only 74 executed.

I think, upon the whole, the verdict must be in James's favour—but somewhat doubtfully. A very great measure of severity was certainly necessary. For now a long lifetime England had been in a recurrent state of actual or potential civil war; the whole mind of society was distracted by that mood, in spite of its rapid advance in commerce and discovery. War had devastated the country during one set of active campaigns; it had led to the murder of a king, to the attempted murder of the King's two sons. Men—the men of average sense in England—were intolerant of renewing all this chaos and violence. Moreover, the assault on Monarchy had been merciless. It was win or lose all the time. Charles II had said with admirable conciseness and truth of the Rye House conspirator, William Russell, Bedford's son, the weak victim of his wife, 'If I do not have his life he will have mine'—and that was still more true as between James and his bastard nephew. As for the 300 odd executions, the number is nothing startling. Europe had seen—and has seen—infinitely greater holocausts and was—and is—accustomed to them, from the Irish coasts of the Atlantic to Poland.

Compared with the irresponsible abominations of Cromwell and the more legal but sanguinary vengeance of Elizabeth in the North of England, the example made of the rebels in Monmouth's rebellion was mild. When James II had been driven from power by the faction opposing him a legend arose which enormously magnified the character of the legal repression exercised, and invented a thousand tales against the infamous Kirke and the more regular Jeffreys. History must not be confused with legend, but legend serves a useful purpose in guiding history. This legend, though it would not have arisen but for James's fall so soon after, is evidence of:—

(1) The strong support throughout the country of the

faction opposing James: a small minority in action but probably a considerable minority in vague sentiment.

(2) Of the change in custom by which severities normal a hundred years before, and even thirty years before, would now, in 1685, be criticized. True, they were criticized by interested parties. But these parties appealed to neutrals and even to opponents. They would not have done so had not opinion been upon the change.

It is such considerations as these which make me say— though with hesitation—that James might have more wisely reduced, if not the capital executions, at any rate the large number of transportations. The action came late in his time—more than thirty years after the worst offences of Cromwell. The world was slowly changing, and the Assizes under Jeffreys were allowed to become a myth damaging, in some degree, to the Throne.

We must not allow our natural disgust with the vulgarity and falsehood of official Whig history, made current by the Revolution, to blind us to reality. James, though not a cruel man—he had never been guilty of a single act of cruelty in his life—was a fixed one. And he was a man to whom no mercy had been shown or would be shown if he yielded. Yet some relaxation of sternness half-way through the business might have profited him. As it was he expressed his condemnation of the lengths to which his justice proceeded. But he expressed it too late. Moreover, he specially promoted Jeffreys—and himself later acknowledged that error. He did it because in the midst of powerful enemies he wanted sure friends. But it was an error.

Anyhow, the rebellion was crushed, and whether too severely or not made no very great difference to the power of the Throne at the time, though a great deal to the later myth against James himself. What was next toward was of far greater moment. After the summer of

1685, when the Rebellions were over and done and the Crown assured, he proceeded to his main effort, which cost him all—Toleration.

With the end of the summer the Rebellions had been crushed and punished and the adjourned Parliament met again in November.

It was the prime object of James II to obtain, with its aid, *not* an increase of the Catholic party (though he hoped for that) but an England in which the various forces of the nation should combine in support of the Government and in a general tranquillity under a popular Monarchy.

James, in making the chief aim of his life and reign the solid founding of Toleration in England, was but carrying out a policy which had been the central idea of the Stuarts since Charles at the end of his exile had made his declaration at Breda. Over and over again had Charles II returned to it. He had attempted from the first days of his reign to the last to enforce it by personal action. He had always been foiled both by his Parliament and by his own too constant policy of preserving his Throne by yielding to the powerful. James proposed now at last to reap the fruit of such persistent effort, to take advantage of the recent defeat all opposition had suffered, from Shaftesbury's to the last rebellions, and to set up the policy of general religious Toleration finally, firmly and for good.

But what do we mean by Toleration?

To-day the word has acquired a vague sentimental atmosphere of Justice. With uneducated people it is even used as though it meant a sort of virtue. Even with those accustomed to think and acquainted with the past of Europe, the modern fashion is very strong. Therefore to say that James was working for Toleration might sound like a sort of slight praise; indeed, those moderns who desire to blacken him in history, are eager to tell us that his real aim cannot have been Toleration at all, because he was too stupid, too wicked, and withal too obstinate a man to entertain so noble an ideal.

Certainly James's admission of other than Catholics to similar equality with the members of the Established Church was but a consequence of his own Catholic sympathies. Certainly his action did not proceed from any general principle that all philosophies (and therefore all the actions consequent upon them) are equally to be admitted in the State. That is what your average modern historian, or, what is much worse, politician, means by the word Toleration. No man in a period of clear thinking could be stupid enough to entertain the idea for a moment—and the vigorous, though constrained, mind of James, least of all. The real position was something more like this:—

No society will willingly admit among its membership a body alien to its own principle of life, for such a body will always remain potentially destructive of the rest. Thus treason is punished. The spreading of counsels subversive of human society is punished. The practice (or even publication) of ideas regarded as subversive to any particular society is also punished. For instance, polygamy of a particular kind was punished by the United States in the nineteenth century, and Toleration was forbidden to the Mormons. Again, advocacy of surrender during a national war is punished everywhere. But when, of two kinds of unity, one is regarded as the more essential to the life of that society than the other, then, in order to preserve the life of society, the less important difference is (reluctantly) allowed to exist: that is, *Tolerated*.

In the seventeenth century the principle of social unity was not a devotion to the nation, such as we presuppose to-day, but obedience to one's lawful Prince.

The argument behind religious toleration was the argument that subjects of this lawful Prince, having been reduced to the common acceptation of one government, yet being hopelessly divided in religion, their division in this should be recognized so long as they obeyed that common head. To preserve this good of political unity, the other good of religious unity must be sacrificed. That was the argument for Toleration in 1660-88.

It was not a principle of *universal* application: Toleration can never be such. To say 'I will tolerate anything' is a contradiction in terms; you tolerate only what is tolerable. It was a particular policy relative to a particular problem. It is perfectly conceivable that some one other than James, ruling seventeenth-century England, might have strongly supported the principle of Toleration merely for the sake of order, though himself equally contemptuous of the original Catholic faith and of its various Protestant derivatives. James's policy had for its personal motive, without a doubt, his strong sympathy with the Catholic Church, of which he was now a member. But that policy remained, none the less, a policy of Toleration alone, and of Toleration with the political object of internal peace.

Is it then true that those who opposed James's policy of Toleration, and who said that he was by it attempting to impose his own faith upon the nation, were mere liars or fanatics accusing him of absurdities and impossibilities?

No, it is not true.

In the first place there was, and had always been, in a certain small proportion of the Established Church parsons and Bishops (and laymen too), a tradition vaguely in favour of reunion with the Universal Church of the West. They would have it that in doctrine the Church of England was not pledged to anything un-Catholic: that only points of discipline and organization separated her from the older Communion. They thought for themselves alone. They would never have moved the great corporation of which they were so small a part. England was then mainly made up of agricultural parishes. The actual communicants of the Church of England were then certainly a very large majority of the people, and that people was profoundly opposed to the prime doctrine of the Real Presence and all the atmosphere of Catholicism. James himself overestimated the possibilities of the tendency, and it is perhaps this which accounts for his blunder in the case of Massey.

But the second ground for fear of Catholicism was much the stronger and more universal. It was this: that if the Catholic Church were once given free play in the England of 1685, its very numerous adherents admitted to every profession, appearing in both Houses of Parliament, on the Bench, in the Commons, as officers of the Army and Navy, its practice openly performed and its facilities for education completely enfranchised, there would necessarily have been (in that time) a large accession in numbers to the Catholic body, and, over the State in general, a large accession of Catholic influence. This was what opponents of Toleration dreaded. They dreaded it so much, that some—even many—thought Toleration might make Catholicism triumphant.

In that they were quite wrong. The opposition to Catholicism was—by 1660-88—so widespread throughout the bulk of the nation, and so intense within a very large fraction of it, so connected with its organized wealth, and indeed with almost everything corporate in England (University, Bar, Borough), that no matter what scope were allowed to its argument and persuasion, the Catholic Church would never have achieved any other position than that of a perhaps larger but still unpopular minority.

England as a whole would have remained a Protestant State.

That is what would presumably have happened, even had James had his way and had his effort endured. We might have had England something like what Holland is to-day—a country with a good deal more than a third of its people Catholic, though its central tradition and ethics were Protestant. But there would have been this difference beween the case of England and the case of Holland: in the Northern Netherlands, as in Scotland, the Reformation had come in the shape of a very violent movement, full of intense emotion, Calvinistic in form, combative, and determined upon victory. Whereas in England the Reformation had been worked by a dominant unpopular governing group against the grain of the people, very slowly, confusedly, and, as it were, without vitality, because that very governing group were concerned, not with Protestantism so much as with keeping their newly-gotten millions of church spoils. All the development of true Protestantism in England had been arrested or diverted by an Official Establishment which preserved many Catholic terms and not a few Catholic forms. Further, in England there was no territorial division as in Holland. There was not in England, as there was in Holland, a whole Catholic district; though here and there (as in Lancashire) the Catholic proportion might be somewhat larger than elsewhere.

This and the religious tradition of many of the older families, might have made Catholicism in modern England, had James II succeeded, a stronger force even than it is in modern Holland.

One thing is certain: had he succeeded, English literature would have had its large proportion of overt Catholic spirit. As it is, whether in Dryden, or in Pope, or in Swift (who, beneath the surface, was more than half sympathetic), the Catholic force in English literature is not overt. English literature, at once the expression and the moulding of the English people, has been (and is), from the time when Shakespeare ceased writing, definitely Protestant.

Toleration being the 'great idea' of James's reign, let us see what forces opposed and what supported his effort.

Against James's main object of Toleration stood the following forces:—

(1) (Much the strongest.) The wealthy as a whole, including the great merchants, especially those of London. The form of government was still in the King's hands. The real power, ultimately, lay in the newly rich class, which had steadily increased in strength since the Reformation, especially since Cecil's working of the Gunpowder Plot. Their persistent policy was to weaken the formal Government of the Crown till they could completely capture it: which they did, in 1688.

(2) Supporting this, against a Catholic King, was the anti-Catholic feeling of the nation. This feeling had grown steadily in the eighty years since the Gunpowder Plot. Much the larger part of England in numbers was now Protestant in life and anti-Catholic in tone. A large minority—perhaps nearly half—was definitely anti-Catholic. A lesser minority—but still a large one, perhaps a quarter—desired to extirpate the Catholic religion by whatever means, wherever it was found, but especially in England. Only a small minority, an eighth to a seventh we say, was actively Catholic; but numbers varied very much with persecution, and the Catholics who would sacrifice all to maintain their religion and hand it on to their children were perhaps not one in twenty of the whole people. But as much as a fifth to a quarter of the adult English may—as late as this date—have been Catholic

more or less—counting in those of vague Catholic tradition. Much the most of these last were by now indifferent.

(3) The National feeling, covering nearly all the nation and including many active Catholics, was irritated by the great strength of Louis XIV and the French nation, for the moment much the strongest power in the West of Europe. Now this national rival (*a*) Stood for Catholicism (though at some issue with the Pope); (*b*) Stood for Popular Monarchy against the wealthier classes everywhere. Therefore, in reaction against it, the National feeling in England tended to suspect Popular Monarchy, to support the growing power of the wealthier classes here, and even, in part, to sympathize with the similar power of Merchant Government by the rich in Holland, at whose head was William of Orange; the opponent of Louis XIV.

(4) A further cause of weakness was the fact that, while James's main object was general toleration and peace under the active rule of his house, he himself was a convinced Catholic, so that (*a*) He necessarily thought first of his co-religionists in trying to secure freedom of worship; (*b*) All his acts would be interpreted as part of a plot in favour not of unity but of Catholicism alone.

In support of James II's attempt to establish a tranquil and tolerant society under a Popular Monarchy, only one main force was in action: the devotion of the English to their traditions and therefore to the reigning house, and the remaining power of Kingship. But to this we must add two lesser forces—which were in contradistinction one to the other, but which both helped to make the attempt possible: (*a*) The effect of time. James was a man of only 52 years. If he lived to carry on his policy for, say, twenty years, it might well take root, and England become a united country still essentially Protestant but with a considerable and contented Catholic minority, probably destined to increase; (b) The inheritance of the Crown lay in two young women of 23 and 21, his daughters Mary and Anne: both strong Protestants and married to Protestant husbands: Mary to William of Orange the Dutchman, head of the opposition to Louis XIV abroad, and Anne to Prince George of Denmark. As James, after a marriage of thirteen years, had had no son by his present, second, Catholic wife, Mary of Modena, it seemed certain that the Crown would fall ultimately to a Protestant succession, and this helped to modify the forces acting against James.

As we shall see, it was the upsetting of this last expectation, by the birth of a son, which turned the scale against James and led to his defeat.

Under such conditions did James II begin his great experiment of religious toleration.

His policy had three parts.

(1) (The essential.) To repeal the Test Act and Acts, which, it will be remembered, prevented any one from holding a post, civil or military, or voting in Parliament, unless he took communion as a member of the Church of England and swore an oath denying the presence of Our Lord in the Blessed Sacrament.

(2) The forming of a small army—some fifteen thousand men—to act in defence of the Government. His existing forces were but a handful of 5,000 men for all garrison purposes as well as for action in the field, and the recent rebellions were a warning of its insufficiency. Apart from these there was only the militia under command of the local squires; that is, of the rich class which stood, in the main, against Popular Monarchy.

(3) (Much the least important.) The modification [1]

---

[1] The falsehood is continually repeated that he desired its *repeal*. It is one of many score such traditional falsehoods in connexion with this reign.

of the Habeas Corpus Act. This Act still survives as an historical curiosity, but is now of no effect, because a modern government can suspend it at will, and can secure, even without its suspension, the imprisonment of any one it chooses; since the Courts are now part of the executive. But in Charles II's and James II's time the Habeas Corpus Act was a weapon for powerful men against the Government, and was intended to be used as such. For though the King could usually rely on some judges he could never be certain of all—as a modern government is. The legal body in general had become, in the seventeenth century, part of that wealthy class which was, on the whole, in opposition to the Government, that is, to the King. Any judge was free, under the new Act, to say that a prisoner should no longer be detained pending trial, under the pretence that the Government's plea for delay did not satisfy him, and thus limit the time for the collection of evidence by the King against conspiracy.

Even before the Parliament met, James was opposed in his own Council by Halifax (whom he dismissed), and, less clearly, by Rochester: both supported the Test Act against Catholics, and the former tried to confuse the modification of Habeas Corpus with its abolition. The Test Act was the real battle-ground, and support of it was increased by the news, in October, that the King of France had abolished the makeshift Edict of Nantes, which had, in its origin, been hurriedly put forward to patch up peace after a disastrous civil war which threatened to destroy the French, but which had lingered on, and in effect created a separate privileged and hostile Nation in the midst of France. For it must never be forgotten that the Edict of Nantes was not a mere declaration of Toleration. It was the granting of special territories and governmental powers to the small but wealthy Huguenot minority which was so intensely bitter against the mass of the French people. Over 400,000 Huguenots emigrated—one-tenth of these came to England and greatly inflamed public feeling.

Parliament met on the 9th November. It opposed Toleration. It supported the Test Act in the House of Commons, refusing to continue the commissions given to certain Catholic officers who had acted against the late rebels; and the House of Lords—the Bishops unanimous through their aristocratic spokesman Compton of London —were equally determined to maintain the civic disabilities and persecution of all Catholic subjects.

The King prorogued the Parliament and determined to act in favour of Toleration through the *Dispensing Power*. The Dispensing Power was the right of the King to relieve *particular cases* from the action of a general law: a larger application of the principle by which he can pardon even a convicted felon. There had never been any doubt of this old national principle: it was immemorial and taken for granted. But because the relief now offered would give civic rights to a Catholic, dissension arose, even among the Judges. It is characteristic of the time that, just as the great Lords specially chosen by the King for his Council were divided in their allegiance, the Judges, whose support of any form of Government is essential, began to waver.

It will be remembered that Shaftesbury, Russell and the rest had proposed a few years before to dismiss the Judges who supported the legitimate Government and to appoint in their place lawyers favourable to the new revolutionary claims. It will also be remembered that Charles successfully maintained the immemorial right of the King to appoint and dismiss his magistrates. But he could not prevent the legal corporation from being part of the new upper-class oligarchy which was undermining the Crown; and in *any* body of Judges at this date most would sympathize with their class. Some would even help a revolutionary change in favour of the Parliament and gentry, against the King. So it was on this occasion of the Hales Judgment.

A minority of four Judges—two of great weight—astonished James by putting forward (in private) the novel doctrine that the King could not give a particular dispensation. This—though private—manifesto of revolutionary opinion on the part of such important members of the new oligarchy was a signal of all that was to follow. Just as the wavering of the Judges between the rich and their King in Charles I's day on the matter of revenue had been a sign that the aristocratic House of Commons was already winning against the old Popular Monarchy, so the wavering of the Judges now on the fundamental points of royal right showed that the last remnant of power in Kingship was in danger of being lost to his son.

The four revolutionary Judges were removed, and a test case was tried. Sir Edward Hales was a Colonel in the Army; could he remain in that office, accepting the Crown's ambiguous 'supremacy', but without publicly and solemnly denying the real Presence of Our Lord in the Blessed Sacrament (the essence of the Test Act)?

The Lord Chief Justice, Herbert, the most respected figure on the Bench, held that he could remain an officer without such apostasy, as the King had given a special dispensation. But he urged the gravity of the case and called in all his colleagues. All save one concurred.

This instrument in favour of Toleration was thus henceforward legal and James would and did use it in strict conformity with law and custom. But the Hales case was unpopular, especially in London and wherever the hatred of Catholicism was strong, both because it emphasized the claim of the minority to civic rights and because Hales was a recent convert; he seemed to give a lead to that large number of indifferent or curious men, or men with some vague memories of the older religion, who were approaching the Church.

It also tempted those many men without religion who will always try to please whatever power can advance them; in this case, the King. In general, Toleration favoured the growth of the Catholic body. To the wealthy class—who counted much more than the populace, but who used popular feeling—the Hales case was alarming because it emphasized and fixed one of the few remaining powers of the Crown.

The effect on the gentry showed itself at once. Compton, whom we so perpetually come across in this reign, a member of the Reformation aristocracy, had been made Bishop of London by James's special favour during Charles's reign. Yet he had been specially prominent in attacking the King in the House of Lords. James had to bear this ingratitude, for it was legal; but now, things went further and threatened disorder. Sermons of a violent kind were preached in London inciting the Protestant majority to the hatred of the Catholics in their midst. One case, that of Sharp preaching in St. Giles', was particularly flagrant, and Compton was asked to restrain him. He demurred. James, though head of the Church, rightly decided that his abnormal position as a Catholic forbade him to act directly in the discipline of the Church of England. Only a fool could have decided otherwise. Yet he exceeded, not his right indeed, but sound policy, in the *indirect* action of his which followed. He nominated an Ecclesiastical Commission to deal with Compton's insurgence. It was framed according to both Statute and Precedent; all its members were Protestant and Churchmen; the Primate (who excused himself on account of age) was put first, the Bishop of Durham (a man of great weight and strongly in favour of religious peace) and the Bishop of Rochester, three Lords of Council, and the Chief Justice of Common Pleas. On the 6th of September, 1686, they suspended Compton.

In the same year, earlier, James had allowed Sclater, Curate of Putney, to keep his emoluments after conversion on condition of paying for a substitute. The action is comprehensible on the plea that conversion should not ruin a man. Still, it was allocating an Ecclesiastical income away from the Establishment in that one isolated case, and therefore seemed as unjust as it was certainly unwise. Also, characteristically, James quite misjudged his man. Sclater was a low parasite who in the subsequent persecution ratted in the most abject manner.

Meanwhile the Universities, essential parts and supports of the New Aristocracy and the Church of England, were most resolute against Toleration. James was as resolute in imposing that policy upon them. It was perhaps too much to hope that the Catholics (and Nonconformists) should have places in Oxford and Cambridge in proportion to their numbers, but the King was determined that *complete* exclusion should cease. He maintained in their posts and fellowships Walker the Master of University College, who had become Catholic, and three others—a tiny proportion out of the whole body of the University, but a test of toleration. This was in the spring of 1686. But by December he took a further and most ill-judged step. He appointed another convert Catholic, Fellow of Merton, Massey, to be Dean of Christ Church. I say the step was most ill-judged; but it must not be imagined that James had no reasons. The Dean of Christ Church is head of a college: and two heads of colleges, Catholic, was no excessive proportion. Moreover, as with Sclater, James imposed on Massey the duty of providing a substitute, out of his own salary, for the services of the Church of England. But the Deanery of Christ Church is not only the headship of an Oxford college. It is also a high ecclesiastical Dignity in the Church of England, and James's choice of *such* a college on which to put a Catholic head was a direct (though his only) interference with that great national organ which he was pledged to maintain intact. Early in the next year, 1687, he failed in a more important point: Cambridge refused (in spite of the King's orders) to grant a Catholic his degree (one Francis, a Benedictine) unless he apostatized and repudiated the real presence of Our Lord in the Sacrament of the Altar. James in this case admitted defeat, and the right of the University to make its own rules.

So far the policy, even in the matter of the Ecclesiastical Commission, had—with the exception of the bad Massey case—been consistent and possible—though it would have required a very skilful hand to maintain it. But James, who was as unskilful as he was straightforward and sincere, also blundered very badly on a capital point: the distinction between his religion as an individual and his office as a king.

He published, as King, arguments in favour of Catholicism found among Charles II's papers in Charles's own hand; he added to the Council a quite disproportionate number of Catholic peers (four); he attempted the conversion of his chief Minister and brother-in-law, Laurence Hyde, Lord Rochester, and on that peer's refusal he dismissed him—with a large income out of the Royal Purse, it is true, and with more from the forfeit lands of the rebel Lord Grey, but still he dismissed him; an act which at once appeared not neutral and tolerant, but active and propagandist.

Two men had fought for supremacy in the Council which directly ruled England, Rochester and Sunderland (Spencer), both of the new oligarchy. When Rochester fell, Sunderland was supreme. We have seen his charac-

ter. Partly through a love of intrigue and power, partly
to shield himself in case of disaster, he gave James advice
unfailingly bad and ultimately ruinous. It was he who
insisted on Father Petre, a Jesuit, being taken secretly
into the Council. He foisted this additional member on
to the governing committee to shield himself, so that any
outbreak of popular anger could be deflected on to this
priest. So James in his exile sadly admits. But how blind
to allow himself to be bamboozled! Sunderland supported
the most extreme, the most unwise of measures: he ultimately professed himself a convert—of doubtful sincerity.
He probably thought that James would succeed in his
policy of toleration, and he wanted to fill his pockets as
Minister; but he hedged by keeping in secret touch with
James's enemies, the exiles in Holland; he and his wife
regularly betrayed James to William, and his judgment
in domestic affairs was wild. It is a signal example of
James's lack of perception that he increasingly relied on
such a man.

So far we have seen James in a sort of preliminary
action against the strong forces which he proposed to
meet and to overcome. He had proposed to himself to
accomplish what Charles had not achieved, but had at any
rate kept successfully in the balance. He proposed to
do what seemed possible through Charles's final (apparent) victory over the aristocratic opposition of great
Merchant and Territorial Magnates. But Charles—as I
have said—had won his battle, not his campaign. He was
like a commander besieged who, after heavy battery of
his defences, has compelled the foe to retire for a while
and refit. But the long bombardment has left his defences
half ruined, and a return of the enemy may easily over-
throw them.

In such a situation James, when the struggle grew general and warm, should have used every element of concession, of division, of delay. We are about to see him do the opposite; to make a frontal attack upon far superior forces and to find himself enveloped and undone. He is to be discovered in this last and conclusive phase of his ordeal incapable of manœuvre.

We have completed the first two years of the reign. Rochester had been dismissed at the very end of 1686. By the turn of the year, in early 1687, James was definitely opposed by a growing National feeling. It was the moment to draw back and temporize: he went forward: and all his acts, even those many of which in themselves were just and suited to a full tolerance, fell on a public opinion inflamed by his excess.

Thus it was consistent and just that he should allow Catholics to worship in public—but the Mass 'flaunted' was intolerable to the large minority of fanatics and irritating even to the general Protestant majority of London. If Catholicism was to be tolerated it was just that the Religious Orders should have their houses in London, their schools, their chapels; but, at such a moment, it was a violent provocation to sustain them with a special favour. The King's attempt to impose a President of his own choosing (not a Catholic) on Magdalen College in Oxford led to another failure after a prolonged and undignified quarrel, and its effect was worsened by filling the College with outsiders—many of them Catholics. Later, on the President's death, a Catholic Head was appointed and something like *one* Catholic College in the University there created.

He was well within his rights when he burnt a libel by one Claude (a French refugee) on Louis XIV; but he did it at a moment when the false idea of his subservience to France [1] (the one thing he was trying to avoid!) was widely received and when Louis himself was adverse to the prosecution. He had raised a regular force of more than 13,000, less than 16,000 men—more than a third but less than a half the largest of his brother's armies in the past—quartered in a camp on Hounslow Heath. In this he acted as any Government must act if it is to exist in face of potential rebellion; but he had a greater object, which was to provide England with a standing force in a Europe where large armies were now normal. It made him independent of France. [2] It was admirably drilled, as might be expected of so industrious an organizer, but he exaggerated its parades and his visits to it. He also favoured a public Mass in Lord Castlemaine's tent; and he most severely punished a Minister of the Church of England, one Johnson (formerly a Chaplain of the Russells) for circulating a tract inciting the army to mutiny.

In all this, logic was not offended. Policy was. If you are to have toleration certain privileges are the logical result of it. But they should be allowed to grow rather than be suddenly thrust upon an inflamed opposition. Incitement to mutiny must be punished. But there, again, is policy in degree. James acted as though the positions and strength of his opponents were indifferent to him. To a strategist they are everything. He acted without 'feeling' his enemy: without discovering where resistance would be solid, where shaken. In other words, his tactics were null.

All the forces against him had thus been given their opportunity when he proceeded to the main act of his

[1] He had consistently followed his original protests against the use of subsidy from France. He had claimed a sum due on his accession, but refused—to his ruin—all further aids in money or men.

[2] James's own words were: 'Vassal! Vassal to France? Had my Parliament allowed it I would have made this realm more powerful than in the days of the kings my fathers!'

reign, excellent and just—and he proceeded to it just at that critical date when it was certain to arouse the maximum of resistance.

On April the 4th, 1687, James II published his famous Proclamation establishing the equality of all before the law irrespective of creed. This, the most serious of those many Stuart efforts at Toleration, was the last: '*The Declaration of Indulgence*'.

By this order, modelled on a parallel already established in Scotland,[1] all offices were thrown open to Dissenter and Catholic alike, all persecution of opinion under the old Criminal Statutes was forbidden.

The active Dissenters—a minority of the Protestants—were delighted and hastened to express their gratitude. But the stumbling-block was the proposed freedom of the old Religion. Such a proposal raised a monstrous image. Popular imagination will construct any monster in moments of exasperation, and the wild idea took root of a plot to compel by force a change in the new Religion of the English. We can afford to smile at the folly, but its effect was very real—and in many textbooks still endures. It was believed that, in some magic way, a now Protestant country was to be compelled immediately by force to Catholicism—and henceforward every attempt to confirm the policy of Toleration took on the simple aspect of Tyranny. To this James's own fatal confusion between his person and his office contributed at every step: his surroundings were Catholic, his public actions, his Council, in the midst of an alien air.

An Order in Council, a Proclamation, had been for centuries a legitimate instrument of government. But however prolonged, it remained provisional. To be perma-

---

[1] But in Scotland, where the extremists had committed murder, levied war, and openly preached the death of the King, their gatherings in the open were forbidden.

nent it must be confirmed in a Statute; that is, an act of the King in Parliament assembled.

James had said as much in his Declaration and proceeded to the summoning of a Parliament which should make law what was certainly a righteous and (as he thought) an acceptable piece of justice. He argued that the safeguards were ample: that only Protestants could sit in the House of Commons; that even from the Lords the Catholics had been excluded: that a Catholic minority in the realm could never be a menace to the overwhelming majority; that their freedom was of right and was common sense. He sent round to see whether the gentry in a new House of Commons would agree to social peace. He was disappointed. His inquiries discovered[1] that while most of the independent borough votes would accept religious freedom—for they were strongholds of dissent—yet the Squires small and great were by at least two-thirds opposed. They knew they could now once more raise the cry of a Papist peril. And this class was much more than the country representatives. They dominated half the boroughs, so many of which were but villages or less. Half the peers who, as Lords-Lieutenant of Counties, had been asked to give a list of Catholics and Dissenters fit to represent the Shires, resigned. It was clear that no new House of Commons would make Toleration law.

Things were at a deadlock. Without the gentry no law could be passed. Without a fixed law Toleration could not be permanent.

At this point, in the summer of 1687, we come on the first important forgery in favour of William. It was presented by the Dutch Ambassador, Van Citters, and called 'The Remonstrance'. It pretended to be a solemn

[1] I append in a note at the end of this book an analysis of this inquiry partly preserved in the Bodleian and privately published. I owe it to the kindness of Mr. Douglas Woodruff.

declaration of the Council offering the Crown to Louis XIV as successor to James. Clumsy nonsense—but the impudence of the thing is significant.

What James, in his sanguine misjudgment, had thought a self-evident piece of justice, which all would approve, the territorial aristocracy used to the destruction of his House. Active, though secret, intrigue by them had begun to bring in his son-in-law and nephew, the Prince of Orange. Yet the feeling for the Throne and the reigning house was as much a part of the main English feeling— as distinguished from the wealthy directing class—as was Protestantism. And if it be asked why in such an atmosphere of disaffection, James could still carry on, the answer is this: The succession to the Crown was clearly Protestant. James was elderly. He had reached the age at which his brother had died. Of his two daughters, Mary, the elder, was married to William of Orange, the Protestant champion. When her turn came all would be well. She was childless; but her sister Anne, married to the Prince of Denmark, was not barren nor her husband vicious. She was, in spite of efforts to convert her, as Protestant as Mary. The future seemed secure to a Protestant succession; for James had no son by his Catholic wife—whom most believed to be incapable of bearing children, especially since a recent illness. The discontented could afford to wait. So things stood, when, in December, 1687, it was rumoured, then confirmed, that the Queen was with child.

All things changed. The child that was to be born might be a boy, and if he were, the immediate succession of Mary, with William of Orange at her side, would be certainly long deferred and most probably debarred altogether. Had James understood government, he would have been warned, as the Cecils had been during their long reign from 1559 to 1612, as Oliver had been during his brief one, as even Charles had imperfectly been, by an organization of secret service: in plain English, Spies. Had he conceived what the wickedness of men could be, he would at least have been prepared for the intrigues now woven all around him. But he was wholly simple in intention as in vision, and it was his downfall.

A campaign of falsehood began at once, malign and utterly unscrupulous. The Queen's pregnancy was denied in pamphlet and story; the people were filled with an absurd lie that the whole thing was a plot to prepare in due time for the substitution of some other man's son as the King's. It is good proof of the impotence into which the ancient Monarchy of England had fallen that such demonstrable lies could not be checked or their authors punished.

From that moment onward bursts and blooms such a foison of forgery, treachery and falsehood as perhaps no country had ever seen before and as certainly England had never known—with the King as the bewildered victim of these lies and false documents. Its atmosphere seems to have poisoned posterity itself, so that those who have written on this brief turmoil have lied upon it with a grand assurance astonishing even in academic historians. They are still at it.

James was not even aware of how sharp a change the expectation of an heir to the exclusion of Mary and William had made. It is incredible, but it is true. He chose the moment when the peril was rising highest to fall into the chief trap laid for him.

The great Edict of Toleration had been out a year. It was wise and just, and grossly inopportune. It was at this juncture doubly so.

He republished it on the 25th April, 1688, with an admirable preamble in defence of civic appeasement and religious liberty for all; telling the people what they

might make of a united England, and adding that it would
certainly be confirmed and made law by Parliament when
it should meet in the autumn. But ten days later he took
one step further which opened his guard, and at once the
enemy took advantage.

On Friday, the 4th of May, he and the Council issued
an order to the Bishops that the arguments and Edict
for Toleration should be read from the pulpit of every
church in London upon the next Sunday fortnight (Sunday, the 20th), and at every country church on the following Sunday, the 27th, and the two following.

James's object was both plain and sincere. It was but
the thorough publication of the Document to all, a thing
only to be effected in those days by reading in all the
churches: but this effect was a direct challenge to the
Clergy of the Church of England as individuals. For most
of them rejected the whole idea of Toleration, thinking
Unity in Religion the chief guarantee of society, and a
large minority of that clergy (in London certainly a
majority) hated the idea of freedom for Catholics as
strongly as they hated Catholicism itself. The two ideas
were identical in their minds.

The political opportunity this blunder afforded was
immediately seized, and used with great skill. What followed was a plot against James which can best be called
Compton's Plot. For, in the lack of documents (when all
was done secretly by words alone), we have the moral
certitude that in the small gathering about to be described
and its action, only Compton, Bishop of London, can
have been the active agent and the good old Archbishop
no more than a puppet.

The order to read the Edict from the pulpit was, we
have seen, given on May the 4th. Nine days were allowed
to pass without protest, as though obedience was to follow
as a matter of course. On the evening of Sunday, May the

13th, after a dinner at Lambeth Palace (when the un-initiated had departed), the energetic aristocrat Compton, Bishop of London and James's personal enemy, was secretly closeted with old Sancroft, the Primate, Turner of Ely, and White of Peterborough. They drew up a secret resolution against obeying the order. Not a word of this was allowed to reach the King.

Next, seven others judged favourable were summoned to join them; only four came: St. Asaph, Bath and Wells, Chichester, and Bristol. Some Bishops, we know, favoured Toleration and were therefore not consulted. The seven agreed to, and signed a Memorial, nominally drawn up by Sancroft, as head of the Church, asking to be excused on the political (and false) ground that the dispensing power was illegal. The thing was carefully kept back till the last in order to deceive James with a false security. He took it for granted, after so long a silence without protest, that he was to be obeyed. They did not present it to the King till late on Friday night, May the 18th, as an ultimatum, calculating that it would then be too late for the King to compromise—as the order was for the following Sunday morning—and that James would have to refuse point-blank, or capitulate. In point of fact, late as was the hour, the King had, for once, the wisdom to negotiate. He bade them return next day, Saturday, when he would have considered his answer. But the snare devised for him was more cunningly laid than he knew. *The Bishop's Memorial had been secretly set up in type and printed in very large numbers, and was ready organized for delivery everywhere.*

By way of forcing his hand the confidential document on which he was deliberating was, to his amazement and disgust, published broadcast throughout London early on the Saturday *before* the time arranged for his private conference with the Bishops. On that day, which he had probably designed for a reconciliation, was he thus check-mated. Therefore did the Saturday pass without negotiation, while every clergyman in London and thousands of the laity had read what the King had been led to believe was a private memorandum! The Declaration of Indulgence was read in very few London churches the next morning!

The Council, thus caught suddenly in the noose, were divided as to what should be done. Sunderland, and even Petre, thought it wiser to accept the successful ruse and insult rather than to provoke a conflict. Other Bishops meanwhile signed the original Memorial now that it seemed accepted. The original seven signatories were summoned to appear before the Council on Friday, the 8th of June. On the day before, the 7th, it was urged by the venerable Sancroft that, to avoid embittering the quarrel, they should not suffer imprisonment awaiting trial but should give their own recognizances for coming up for trial. The others agreed, Compton presumably with reluctance. But when they came before the Council, where they were received with dignity, even Sancroft (who had been got at in the meanwhile by the politicians manoeuvring in the background against the King) broke his word and all refused recognizances. There was thus no choice, since they refused to be at liberty, but to make martyrs of them by keeping them in custody till their offence was tried. That was the second move, and it was a most effective one. Their confinement was of a most honourable sort; they were given complete freedom in the Tower, and that very evening met at Evensong; but Compton had had the satisfaction of seeing a vast popular gathering acclaiming these fathers in God on the way to the horrid dungeons of a Tyrant.

Such was the second step in the successful manoeuvre against poor bewildered James. Thousands, I say, had read the protest, published prematurely to force James's hand. Tens of thousands had watched from the river banks the Via Dolorosa of the Martyrs from Westminster to the Tower.

By this time half London was at fever height and the Bishops were its heroes. No one troubled about the exact point at issue: the broad division was between Toleration of the Catholics and their suppression; and the seven Bishops stood as a symbol for their suppression. That was enough.

All this was on Friday, the 8th of June. On Sunday, June the 10th, the royal child was born, and it was a son.

William of Orange had been informed that the Queen's child would be born in July. Such had been the Queen's own judgment, and it was reiterated by all those in her confidence. From the moment a child was expected he had determined to await the issue and, if it were a son, to try his fortunes at war. His plans were thrown into complete disorder by the antedating of the birth a full month. He sent his Dutchman Zuyleistein to James to convey his most emphatic congratulations on the birth of an heir—and began his new preparations to supplant that child. I have said that perhaps no group of men in history were so steeped in falsehood as the conspirators against James II, and William in this, as in other vices, was easily the master of them all.

Zuyleistein, after he had left William's false message with James on June the 23rd, made visits to the greater gentry who had determined on destroying the Monarchy. These had met in every sort of secret gathering here and there since the Prince of Wales's birth. On June the 30th, just a week after Zuyleistein's leaving the Court, he met seven of the boldest—probably at his instigation but with Compton an ardent second—they signed a cipher letter to William inviting him to come over. The thing was done at the house of Shrewsbury; there, with their host, and Compton, Danby and Devonshire, the renegade Turnley, Sydney (in whose handwriting the document was drawn up) and Admiral Herbert set their names.

The letter was based on the undoubted truth that James was generally unpopular and distrusted personally as an opponent of Protestantism, and, as King, the determined author of Toleration. It absurdly exaggerated the numbers who would join the foreign invasion, and contradicted itself by warning the Dutch leader to do all in great secrecy and to bring over an ample force lest the English Monarch should secure himself by victory—for they knew how the mass of Englishmen were torn between their objections to the Catholic Church and their love of the National reigning house.

But where the conspirators could speak with authority (and were indeed right) was in their affirmation that, at the first proof of the invader's strength, the gentry—of which they were examples—would desert what was left of the Monarchy. Herbert took the letters over to Holland, and then joined that foreign Government at a substantial salary as naval commander over the Dutch sailors who were to effect the invasion of England.

Meanwhile the pitch to which the Anti-Catholic feeling had risen in London was shown by the popular outburst over the Trial of the Seven Bishops. James had been forced, by the intentional delay in the private protest, by its wide, instant and organized publication behind his back, into a position where his wealthy opponents, now so much stronger than the Monarchy, held all the trumps. Either he must accept the rebellion of the plotters and thus admit the new revolutionary doctrine against the Crown, or he must bring them to trial. Once brought to trial either acquittal or condemnation was fatal to him, the former through popular rejoicing that the enemies of Toleration had won, the latter through popular anger against their failure. The trial began on June the 29th and occupied two days, ending on the 30th. It was made to turn on the dispensing power of the Crown. The Judges were divided. The Jury acquitted; and a vast popular demonstration, spreading to the Army, acclaimed the verdict. The Plot had thoroughly succeeded.

What we have now to follow is the series of treasons which ended with the Dutch invasion and the capture of the Palace by foreign troops.

William of Orange had prepared to interfere at the birth of the child if it should prove a son, which, as we have seen, he expected in July. We have seen also how his plans were confused by the birth of the Prince of Wales taking place a month earlier, on June the 10th. The letter inviting him to invade in due season, written by the plotters under their ringleader Compton, the Bishop of London, was before him within a week of its writing. To bring his foreign army into England, William had now to consider the situation on the Continent and to manœuvre for success in spite of various (and mutually conflicting) obstacles. He had already formed two years before, in 1686, the League of Augsburg against the great power of Louis XIV of France. It was not a Protestant Alliance; it was an Anti-French alliance, originally including the Catholic King of Spain and the Catholic Emperor and including Venice and the Pope, Innocent XI, who feared the Gallicanism of Louis and who cordially supported William.

William did not *chiefly* now—June 1688—desire to reduce Louis' power, much as he desired that end. He *chiefly* desired to usurp the Throne of England where he could further attack that power. His legitimate reversion to that throne, at least as consort to his wife, was now lost through the birth of a prince. He had to deceive (1) His Catholic Allies against Louis, (2) The people of England, most of whom, though divided on James's policy of religious toleration, loathed the idea of a Dutch monarch. He had also to get the Dutch Government (of which he was not master—though its most important subject) to lend him ships, men and money for the enterprise. Now the Dutch were chiefly concerned with preventing an attack on their territory by Louis XIV. They put 20,000 men on their borders and would certainly divert nobody for William's invasion so long as Louis' great force stood ready to move *either* against them *or* against the Rhine: no one knew which direction it would take—though the Dutch were nominally at peace, so far, with the French.

All that summer, July and August, Louis kept warning James of William's duplicity and intended invasion, and he offered the support of the French Fleet. James did not believe him, and his pride was hurt at what he thought patronage. For James's great idea was by toleration at home and a strong fleet, avoiding all entanglements with France, to make England as strong and independent as possible.

William told his Catholic allies the falsehood that he had no intention of dethroning the Catholic King of England. His agents repeated that falsehood to their English agents. But so long as Louis' movements were uncertain, William could be lent neither money, ships nor men: he was hung up.

On September the 1st Louis declared to the Dutch that if a move were made against James, the Dutch must expect attack from himself. The declaration checkmated William and nearly saved James. But James repudiated the proffered aid. It made the Crown of England seem dependent; it made him look, in the eyes of his Protestant subjects, the hanger-on of a Catholic Power, and he would have none of it. He publicly repudiated Louis' friendship, said he could trust to the solemn promises of the Dutch Government. He recalled his Ambassador in Paris (Skelton) to mark his disapproval of so anti-national a policy as that diplomat had advised. James's decision to stand alone was patriotic, sincere and proud—but against such forces as were then massed against him it was fatal. It was the act of a truthful and open man incapable of following a conspiracy, and it was the end of his chances.

Louis gave him up as hopeless, promised the Dutch that he would not attack them and turned his great armies off towards the Rhine.

That was September the 24th, and from that moment James was lost. The Dutch Government, the pressure on their frontiers thus removed, consented to William's secret scheme.

Meanwhile yet another forgery appeared. It was fabricated in Holland by Burnet, made Bishop of Salisbury later by William. It was a document purporting to come from England and to disprove the legitimacy of the Prince of Wales. William had an enormous edition of it printed: 80,000 copies (corresponding to a million to-day).

James woke up, too late, to his danger. And thereupon performed the last acts of a man quite separate from his world: a man who saw things through the wrong end of a telescope.

If there was one thing he ought to have done in this crisis it was to stiffen. *Now* was the time for that immovable resolution which he had shown out of season for so long.

He was doomed. But to maintain his principles to the last, to go down fighting, would have given him back in all men's eyes the prestige his chivalry had cost him. He would still have lost the battle, for the gentry, the supports of society, were abandoning him; but he would have

left a great name—and might (who knows?) have returned. But his ignorance of men left him bewildered.
He lost his head. He took the very opposite of the course
that would have been the moral salvation of his legend.
He prepared to compromise with the great conspiracy
against him.

He did not go so far as to forbid religious freedom or,
as the Bishops amazingly suggested (to such a man!),
abandon the Faith. But he reversed his former action at
the Universities, he restored the old town franchises—
the old corrupt corporations with their dependence on
wealth. He offered the Dutch a formal alliance. He was
still in part deceived. The peers who were most deeply
intriguing with William swore the most vividly to their
loyalty: the Bishops—three of whom were now strictly
bound to William—prayed publicly and loudly for James.

On October the 14th William renewed his affirmations
to his Catholic allies against Louis that he had no intention of dethroning his father-in-law. Nothing was farther
from his thoughts! On the contrary, he would, on reaching England, *do all he could for the freedom of the
Catholics*. The Dutch Government solemnly confirmed
the falsehood, and on October the 19th William sailed.

A gale blew him back and held the great Dutch fleet
and the Dutch and mercenary troops in the transports
wind-bound for a fortnight. On November the 1st the
wind went easterly and he sailed again. Making northward, as though for Yorkshire, he went round in the
night, passed the Straits of Dover on the 2nd (the British
Fleet at the mouth of the Thames could not beat up
against the strong breeze to attack), and, after passing
the Start in a mist, turned, and on November the 5th
landed at Torbay with his 16,000 men and moved inland.
He was ill received. The populace saw the strange host
go through, German, Swiss, Huguenot mercenaries of

every kind, solemn Dutch Guards—a large and powerful
corps, the six British regiments in Dutch pay, and—
officering more than half the force—the French Huguenot gentry as cadres. They received the vile pamphlets
which Bishop Burnet had drawn up denying the royal
parentage of the Prince of Wales—they heard the protestations and read the banners proclaiming 'Religion
and Liberty'; but, much as most in Devon might mislike
Catholicism, they hated invading foreigners more, and
they stood aside. William, sullen, disappointed and
alarmed, proposed to abandon the attempt within the first
week. What saved him was Churchill's treason. On the
eve of William's landing the plotters in London still
carried on their deceit. The Bishops especially lied boldly,
still vowing and protesting their deep loyalty to the King.
Sanscroft assured him no Bishop had arranged with
William!—perhaps he was deceived. But Compton sur-
passed himself. He affirmed that he was as innocent as his
colleagues! Thus James, duped, as ever, still hoped.

The King had a larger army than William. It was
very well trained, and, though irritated by the presence
of a few Irish units and though (many of them) sharing
the popular disgust with the King's religion, loyal to
the national dynasty and to the King's person—as was
the great mass of the common people. But, more powerful
than the people and far more powerful than the poor
remnant of monarchy, was the wealthy class now in full
political power. From these, of necessity, the officers were
chosen, and that class, those officers, were determined to
rule and to destroy the King.

Churchill, with the rank of Lieutenant-General, was
the chief traitor.

On November the 16th he swore a special and peculiar
loyalty to James and went off to organize the betrayal.
He sent to Salisbury, as though to oppose the Dutch,

three regiments of cavalry whose commanders were in the plot. They deserted and tried to bring over the rank and file, who to their honour, in a great majority, refused: less than 200 followed their leaders into William's camp. Churchill next, on November the 22nd, tried to keep James right at the front in Warminster, with the object, perhaps, of having him killed, certainly of putting him bodily into William's power. James decided to fall back on London, Churchill pressed him hard to remain; finding him determined, Churchill went over to the enemy on November the 23rd. It is some slight relief in the almost uniform baseness of William's character that on such an enormity he expressed a measure of disgust.

With Churchill's desertion it was clear that the gentry as a whole were lost to James: they began to desert *en masse*, and with them the framework of the army was broken up.

Indeed, the remarkable feature in this revolution of an Aristocracy against a King is the purely aristocratic quality of it in the army. The gentry betrayed, the rank and file in the main stood loyal. It is what one knows to be the truth with regard to the nation as a whole, but it is important to emphasize it in the case of the military forces. That army is spoken of vaguely by historians under the title of 'disaffected,' even as being what, let us hope, no army ever was, 'constitutional.' In point of fact, the mass of the men were, as one might have expected, with their king. The contemporary account is clear enough: and it is difficult to say which was most surprising—the desertion of the officers from their prince, or the ineffective loyalty of the poor private soldiers at a few pence a day, dissolving into a dust without cadres.

It was on November the 21st that the King decided thus to fall back. The army was bidden to take up its place at Reading, Windsor, and the villages round about.

The royal party halted for that night at Andover. James had with him that stupid glutton, his son-in-law, Anne's husband, Prince George of Denmark, whose perpetual bleat, '*Est-il possible?*' has given him his nickname in history—for as each new desertion came in, that was his comment. He waited till his father-in-law had gone to bed, and then stole off to the first Dutch outposts (the situation of which he already had in his pocket). He left behind him one of those letters which all he and his kind had been instructed to leave, full of a pretended sorrowful devotion, torn between love and duty—its terms dictated by we know not certainly whom, but most probably by Churchill through Churchill's wife, Anne's masterful mistress.

James made no great case of the fellow's treachery. He simply gave him his nickname, and said that apart from the foulness of the affair, the loss to the army was less than that of a single trooper. And he was quite right.

The action of his wife, Anne, was a more serious matter. It is a good example of the way in which the rich men who were working this revolution had organized its every detail, that though her husband, the Prince of Denmark, had not abandoned the cause (in which he had been called 'the foremost volunteer') twenty-four hours, yet she, nearly seventy miles away, was acquainted with it the very next day. She got the news post-haste. Who brought it? In the day and night between the 26th and 27th she and her master-mistress, Churchill's wife, got away by the back stairs to the street door of the Cockpit. The man who was conducting the whole nasty business was still that same Compton, Bishop of London—the greatest by birth on the Bench of Bishops—who had persistently, regularly, and industriously betrayed his master —it was to James that he owed his position. He had a coach and six waiting for the Princess, and himself, mounted, with sword and pistols, conducted the armed guard which he had gathered together as escort: he took Anne away from her father's palace, to the North, by the Nottingham road.

Anne also had to leave a letter behind. For it was part of the organization. And she also had to tell the lie which had been appointed to her particular rôle. She pretended that she also was sadly torn between two affections and had but gone away under the impossibility of determining her duty on hearing of her husband's departure—to her 'unexpected.' She hoped—she looked forward to—a reconciliation.

The King himself arrived at Whitehall that morning, while everything was in a turmoil of discovery, and it is both comic to remember, and illuminating upon the hysteria of the time, that Anne's old nurse, finding her mistress's bed unslept in, roared through the corridors that the Papists had murdered the Princess.

James had always loved this particular child more than the rest; more than those little ones whom he had lost, and more than her peevish, weak but offensive elder sister. There had been something more buoyant and gay about the stupid Anne than about the other, though Heaven knows that neither was a daughter for a man to be proud of. All the memories of the years in which she had been his little child and in which he had been so devoted to her struck him at once at this moment, and it has been said by those who were witnesses that he seemed at the moment so distraught in his manner, that it looked as though the sudden, the unexpected thing had deranged him. What he said through his tears was simple enough: 'God help me! My own children have forsaken me!'

It would be worth a reasonable historian's while, engaged upon understanding the past, to ask himself why this woman acted in this fashion. What were the ingredients of the vileness? Had she been her sister Mary, there would be nothing to explain. But Anne was not her sister Mary. And there is the very powerful testimony in her favour of Swift, one of the very few men in that generation who told the truth. Swift, writing in a private paper for no eye but his own, said of Anne, when she was Queen, that she was 'the only good woman he had ever met in his life.' That she had, like her sister, in youth been troubled by vices, is well known; something of the taint followed her through her life; but that has nothing to do with this particular black action.

When I think of her character as a whole, her amiability, her passivity, her stupidity, I can put it down to nothing more than a yielding like a jelly to the strongest push, and particularly to the masterful Sarah. All her world was moving for treason, it would have wanted a little touch of heroism in Anne to have remained; and heroism she certainly had not. She was conducted away, by the most intelligent and most unscrupulous of the conspirators, the Bishop of London; and hanging to her arm, dragging her forth, as it were, was the wife of the most unscrupulous and the most treacherous of the officers, John Churchill. Between them both, she left that hypocritical letter behind, and went her way. But how hypocritical it was we may judge by that phrase, 'unexpected departure,' applied to her husband. Remember, that phrase was written in a letter left for her father on Sunday, November the 26th. Just over a week before, on Saturday, the 18th, she had written herself to William of Orange that he 'had her wishes for his good success in his just undertaking; that she hoped her husband would soon be with him.' She added that he (George of Denmark) had gone the day before, the 17th, with the King towards Salisbury, *'but intends to go from thence to you as soon as his friends think proper.'*

What was James in this moment of despair? What should we have seen if we had met this man, now 55 years old, in his fall?

There remained to him something of the vigour which had inspired fine episodes in arms by sea and land: the man who had been thought as a youth, under the great Turenne, the bravest of the brave; the lad who had challenged all he met; the young sailor who had shown such superb courage in the battles of the North Sea. He still retained determination; but something physical in him was weakened. He had aged.

Any man finding himself, unprepared, jostled against one appalling situation after another, is physically struck; especially if he be elderly.

James's judgment is to be blamed without limit for not having appreciated against what forces he was pitted, and it was this lack of judgment which had brought him to such a depth of disappointment. But even so, he might have met them with some of the rapidity of new resolutions, grasping the change in the situation even though that change should be developing before him so rapidly—had he not been under physical disability. It betrayed itself in some hesitation of speech; he stammered a little. He had very heavy bleedings at the nose, which would not be stanched; and it was already noted that in conversation he would sometimes remain in a sort of lethargy.

In such a state of body, active through the persistence of his will, dull through the recent ageing of his senses and substance, you have two men, as it were, struggling one against the other: the younger man surviving by memory, by the persistent strength of his right, by an unalterable standard of honour which he maintained till his last breath, and by a powerful conviction of religious truth in the face of men who had no care for the things of the

soul, or who were fanatics contemptibly inferior to him.
In all these things James was a figure worthy of the
occasion.

But with all these things he would none the less have
failed. He would have failed perhaps after a fashion
more consistent, or at the lowest, more dramatic, had he
not now suffered the fatigue of body, the lessening of
physical activities, the beginnings of the weakness of age
—which yet took twelve years to kill his spare, tall and
nervous frame.

*　　*　　*　　*　　*

It was the Monday, December the 17th, and evening.
Those in the houses on the extreme west of London, new
built (where are now Albermarle and Dover Streets),
heard through the raw and foggy air a regular tramp of
armed men coming up Piccadilly Lane from the west.
Under the rare lights their blue uniforms could be dis-
cerned; the loud noise of their drums reverberated from
the brick walls, and they bore their colours before them.
The lighted matches (for they were ready to fire, and
shoot down the Englishmen who were still defending
their king) glowed through the murk in little points of
red.

The Hollanders put out a detachment down the hill
to hold St. James's Palace, the Dutch words of command
ringing through the December night; then the mass of
them marched on towards Whitehall. They fell from
column into line in front of those fine windows, standing
on the earth that had drunk Charles's blood, and at the
gate where the British Guards still stood they shouted
their summons.

The British Guards were commanded by Lord Craven,
a man now 80 years old, long a soldier. He refused the
summons: and his command in their turn fell into line,
drawn up with loaded arms to meet the invaders.

224

It would have been a fine incident in the history of this country if the English Guards had been permitted to lay down their lives, as they were willing to do, for their king, and to have fallen under the fire of that superior force of foreign invaders. It would have been a symbolic action only, but it would have been something stamping history honourably for posterity to remember. Yet James must not be blamed for his refusal to shed blood. He had fought so often, and was so accustomed to the affair of arms, that he could not think of these things as a mere king, still less with an idea of the future. To resist under hopeless conditions he thought not military: and he was perfectly right.

He gave the order to withdraw. And the Guards, their lips full of oaths against their shame, retired. The Dutch sentries were placed at the very doors of the Palace, and beneath its windows; the uncouth Dutch syllables, at the changes, went up through the foggy air. James was a prisoner within.

The enemy had calculated that to wake the King from his sleep would add to his disarray. It was after the turn of the night, between twelve and one o'clock, and nearer twelve than one, that the messengers from William of Orange (including Halifax, who had been compelled to this ignominy in just retribution for his dirty work) demanded to see the King. James was asleep. Lord Middleton woke him, and Halifax announced in as brutal a fashion as he could—avenging by his rudeness the indignity thrust upon him by William his master—that James must leave London before ten o'clock next morning, and go off to Ham, as the Prince and his foreigners would be in Westminster by noon.

James refused Ham, as ill suited to that season, and said that he would move to Rochester; but (and this is particularly to be noticed) Halifax had orders to insist that he should go by water, lest his passage through the town should excite once more the loyalty of the populace for their king.

Somewhat before noon next day the tide served. Whether William had been told this and so advised in fixing the hour of his arrival, we do not know. It is probable. It was at eleven that James said good-bye to the Ambassadors and such of the peers as were faithful to him, and went on to his barge. The rain was falling pitilessly, and it was very cold. All about the barge were twelve boats filled with Dutchmen who were his escort and his goalers. A great mass of his subjects, miserable at the sight, watched through the misty rain the craft drop down the tide. Not many hours before they had acclaimed with enthusiasm his return to the City. And such men under arms as James still had, Englishmen, not Dutch, murmured. Clarendon, who would not exaggerate on that side, tells us how 'it was not to be imagined what a damp there was on all sorts of men.'

So the last king left England.

An hour later William was in St. James's with six thousand of his best troops, Dutch, French, German, and the rest, and another thousand in the Tower. And that same night Anne, his sister-in-law, with her master-mistress, Lady Churchill, at her side, went off to the play in a splendid carriage. It was her father's.

VIII

DERRY AND THE BOYNE

JAMES was in St. Germans. A year and more had passed since his landing from a small ill-found boat off a stormy sea in the cold and furious gusts of rain on that Christmas evening in Ambleteuse. His wife and the child had safely preceded him, though in the same miseries, under the guardianship of Lauzun.

Louis had received the King, in this his second exile, very nobly. He had met him with all the Court in splendour from Versailles. He had lodged him royally in the Palace of St. Germans where it stood on Le Nôtre's high terrace looking over the miles of wood below, to Paris and St. Denis, a dim broken line of roofs and spires upon the eastern horizon. There—until the strain of the wars led to embarrassment—they received from Louis' strong generosity an income for their dwindled and impoverished court. Thence James could proceed, when the moment should seem arrived, to the re-conquest of his throne.

Not many weeks after William's usurpation, in March of the following year, that moment had come. The clique which had betrayed the English Crown was at issue with itself, as men who act from avarice and ambition may well be. If leaders could be found for the English people, the King of England would return. But his enemy was established over the organization of England. The blow should be delivered in flank; and the flank presented was Ireland. Ireland was still held for James. It appeared—at that distance—to afford an ample recruiting field, and upon

227

Ireland was the effort directed. Thither should James proceed, to that front should William be drawn, leaving Great Britain uncertainly grasped in his absence. Then, with a broad sea interrupting his communication, might he be entangled, delayed and perhaps defeated; while the populace in England, already murmuring against an alien and degraded court, might discover the necessary chiefs and rise for the restoration of the natural line.

The military advice and decision to attack by way of Ireland proceeded from Vauban. We are about to follow the actions of James II in a campaign which Vauban counselled and for that purpose we will concentrate upon its two chief episodes—Derry and the Boyne.

Vauban is not the subject of this book—he might be the subject of libraries. That very great man, that very strong brain (the maker of the defensive for two centuries, the strong middle-class character which imposed itself upon all that shining court and army of Louis XIV) determined the Irish expedition.

Was he right?

The event went against his judgment, and when the event goes against the judgment of soldier or statesman, he has been proved wrong. Vauban was wrong for the same reason that Napoleon was wrong in undertaking the campaign of 1812. He did not understand the local conditions.

The local conditions in Ireland were such that, short of an effort far greater than the French monarch could spare in that one direction out of so many, the expedition was certain to be defeated. The reason for this was that there was complete lack of material.

A man receives the report that there are so many stands of arms, so many guns, such and such a recruiting field. He presumes that the ammunition for the guns will be present, he thinks of the guns in terms of his own army, he is particularly impressed by the numbers of men available.

Now in the case of Ireland the numbers were there; what is more, the material for recruitment was the finest in the world. Louis' civilian envoy wrote buoyantly at the beginning of the compaign in admiration of the young men coming in to serve—tall, eager, serviceable; and the numbers were large. There would be no difficulty in getting twenty, thirty, forty, fifty thousand if one needed them. The loyalty of that recruitment was undoubted; its enthusiasm was universal.

A man acquainted with this sort of outline, these rough elements of the situation, might well misunderstand the position. The Allies misunderstood the Russian position in 1914 in much the same fashion. But numbers of available recruits, their physical powers, their rude health, their devotion to the cause, are all worthless unless you can make of them an army. Now to make an army of them, especially for the particular purposes of this campaign, you needed at least a sufficient *material*. It was the material that was lacking.

It was lacking in a degree which astonishes us who read of it to-day. We find it difficult to understand how under such conditions any prospect of success could have been held out. We should be less astonished if we understood how difficult it was to obtain at short notice, with regard to a country of which so little was known, and from envoys who were ill acquainted with the details of military equipment, what a modern well-organized intelligence department would demand—and God knows that even modern well-organized intelligence departments learn little enough!

In the first training of the recruits few had anything to handle but staves; some tipped with iron, most of them of the bare wood. The stands of arms available were reported at 20,000. That is how they stood on paper. In reality they were in such a condition that only one in twenty could be used. The trouble had been going on for a long time, and the decay was at its worst at that moment.

The paucity of artillery was shocking. In the first march northward something like 5,000 men on foot and 800 or 900 horse were accompanied by exactly *two* guns. Under the walls of Derry, when the siege began, there were, in a force of some ten thousand men, but three field pieces, two small mortars, and two cannon firing shots of not more than twelve pounds weight apiece: these to attack walls twenty-four foot high and eight or nine foot thick and defended by thirty pieces of ordnance!

But there is something more. Of the muskets present in the host, the proportion that could be securely and constantly used, even out of those which had been passed as serviceable, was insignificant. 'Out of every ten muskets,' says Hamilton (speaking of the infantry in front of the walls of Derry), 'one might be counted upon to shoot.'

Here, again, is a letter from the French envoy writing to Louis XIV's Minister of War and giving a report of the Colonel of a regiment at the siege. The Colonel says, that 'in all his regiment there are only seven muskets; the others have little sticks three foot long; a few have pikes, but without iron upon them.' Then he goes on to say that there is no organization of hospitals, of medicines or provisions.

What was perhaps even worse than the ridiculous lack of artillery, was the lack of gunners, or perhaps (for we cannot decide in the absence of evidence) the bad state of the pieces themselves. They could not make certain of a mark. It is particularly noted that at about half-extreme range the single mortar at work fired almost at random. 'They could never say what house they were going to hit.'

Here is a typical detail. In the absence of firearms an attempt was made to rush up over the vile roads, and in abominable weather, a certain number of sabres for the cavalry. The sabres arrived, but they were without belts —so that (as the contemporary account goes) 'the soldier had, all the time, to carry his sword drawn in his hand.'

But even so the sabres were few enough at a time when cavalry was the decisive arm in the field. One little anecdote quoted in the MacPherson original papers, is sufficiently illuminating, not only as to the material condition of the army but as to its discipline. A captain in O'Neill's regiment happened to die, whereupon twenty-five of the dragoons immediately deserted taking their horses with them, and such of the Captain's command as remained argued that they need no longer serve, since they had engaged themselves personally to their officer, and to no one else.

It is to be advanced in their excuse that not only regiments but troops and companies were throughout the Europe of that day, as a rule levied personally, and that there was still a strong personal tie between the local followers and their officer. How much stronger this tie was in Ireland with its still tribal memories, need not be emphasized. But the point is that it made cohesion very difficult, and the full discipline necessary to a force which was in reality but a forlorn hope (and therefore needed a specially strong bond of union) was quite unattainable.

Anyhow, these mutineers were tried by Court Martial, and condemned to draw lots that one of them might be shot. But when the unlucky man had drawn his lot, it was found that there was not a firearm in the command which would go off. The officers dared neither borrow their muskets, nor even perhaps their firing party, from other troops of their own regiment. They had to beg them of another unit, Lord Mayoe's. And note that these men were dragoons; that is, mounted infantry supposed to be specially detailed for fighting on foot with firearms.

The truth is that the expedition could not conceivably succeed against the force which an organized English Government would certainly sooner or later send against it, and could not even succeed against the small walled town, Derry, with which it had first to deal.

There was a total of thirty-five thousand men enrolled, of whom in the infantry, not one-sixth were fully trained soldiers. There were three regiments of horse, and one of dragoons, partly armed (say three thousand five hundred), and of artillery, on the first parade when James reached Dublin, exactly eight small field guns—there were some few other pieces laid by but not yet mounted. Of course, certain relief came in from France in the course of the campaign, but nothing like enough. And here it is essential to understand what part Louis XIV could play; what extent of aid he could afford. Louis XIV could not make it his *main object* in his wide European policy, nor even a principal object, that James should succeed. It could only be with him a quite subsidiary part in a general plan: the plan of a French king defending, in the turn of his fortunes, three frontiers against a gathering of ever more numerous and more powerful enemies. The situation of his armies, the campaigns as a whole, compared with the Irish episode, stood as ten to one.

Louis did what he could for the legitimate King of England: he lent him what aid was in his power. But it was impossible for that Crown to support the Irish expedition with any substantial weight of men, money, or army. There were twenty other things to be done.

The instrument, then, at the disposal of the Royal cause in Ireland was lamentably insufficient. It is remarkable rather what, in such pitiable conditions, was done. Thus the bridge at Caldy in the advance northward was forced against a very much larger body with less than a thousand men, of whom only one-third were infantry: yet the rebels broke before them, running all the way to Derry and leaving 400 killed and wounded behind; and generally, before Newton Butler, the forces of the legitimate king had the better in the open field. But what destroyed the campaign at its outset (the final issue, I say, was never in doubt) was the attempt to lay siege to Derry.

Derry was the capital point. It was the chief port of the north (Belfast in those days was not yet a town: the only Williamite place of consequence besides Derry was Inniskillen). Derry was the critical port in the North. It could afford a rallying point to all the disaffected: it was a gate of entry from the sea for munitions and men. It must be occupied.

The story of the so-called 'Siege of Derry' is sufficient to explain all the breakdown of those operations.

The city of Derry stood—and its nucleus still stands—upon a striking site. It is a rather narrow oblong hill, more than 100 feet in height, overlooking the River Foyle at some four miles distant from its mouth in the bay or lough of the same name. This hill lies to the west of the river which is here about three hundred yards broad. It had (and they are preserved) strong walls twenty-four feet high and from eight to nine feet thick, with a good ditch outside: these walls flanked by nine bastions and two half bastions. There were four gates to the four points of the compass. At the river-mouth where the stream considerably narrows—four miles, as I have said, below the town—there juts out a point of land, called Culmore, upon which a fort stood; and here, for the purpose of what follows, it is important to explain the rôle of land batteries against vessels at this time.

It was now more than forty years since Blake had proved that, with the gun power of the day, the ships of

war of the seventeenth century could pass in front of, return the fire of, and escape destruction from, land batteries. Of course, things would depend upon the strength
of armament on either side, on the range, on the conditions of wind and tide. But the point to remember is that a
land battery did not close a passage to men-of-war, save
where the battery was very strong and the passage very
narrow. Land batteries could inflict heavy loss, but they
could hardly hope as a rule to destroy an enemy fleet. The
risk of heavy loss prevented ships approaching them save
under necessity; but when necessity arose ships could in
those days approach them. That, put very generally, was
the balance between the two; and we have to remember it
in the story of what follows.

The town had recently been thoroughly well munitioned and provided. There were eight regiments there,
counting well over seven thousand men; and a certain
body of volunteers were available—less than one might
expect from the political and religious enthusiasm of the
place and time, but still numerous. It mounted thirty
guns upon its walls, and had ample provision of gunpowder and stock. This garrison and munitionment had
recently arrived (upon the 25th March, 1689), so there
was plenty wherewith to meet any enemy coming up in
April, when the forces of James were due. The only
weak point in the situation of the Williamite side was that
considerable numbers of refugees from the country had
taken refuge behind the walls, and a really prolonged
blockade might lead to difficulties in feeding the whole
of that swollen population.

Why such a blockade was ever allowed to be established
by so weak a hostile body, why so large a number of
trained and well-armed men with such a superiority of
guns should have submitted to be contained by an insufficient force is still a mystery. But contained they did

234

allow themselves to be and therefore in the long run pressed for food. Still they always had plenty of powder and shot.

The inception of the attempted siege was due to a blunder. James was advised that if he appeared in person the presence of the legitimate king would be enough to make the authorities of the town admit his forces. His illegitimate son, the Duke of Berwick, who was with the army advancing upon the place, had written to him to that effect. It was an error: and what James did upon receiving this advice (he ought to have remained in Dublin and never to have gone north at all) is characteristic.

In the first place, he took what he believed to be every precaution; riding thirty miles across the country to see the Commander-in-Chief of his army (Rosen—of whom more in a moment) at Newtown Stewart. In the second place he imagined that the very confused situation in England (where the mass of the nation, though Protestant, were certainly in favour of the Stuart line, and where the large Catholic minority still had great social standing) was repeated in this corner of northern Ireland. Here also were Protestants indeed, and (so James imagined!) they would be divided in the matter of allegiance, as were their English co-religionists. Many would hesitate to attack their lawful king. Many would loyally support him. He did not appreciate the truth that the Protestant in Ireland had convinced himself for a lifetime past that he belonged to a superior race and was of right the master of the place, and that the Catholic native population were a menace only as animals may be a menace; he did not know that he was dealing with frenzy and illusion raised to that degree.

There are three excuses for him. One was that no English authority (since the Lancastrian usurpation of the English throne in the Middle Ages) had ever attempted to understand Irish conditions. The Lancastrians let Ireland go. The Tudors returned to it as to another world. James knew vaguely more about the Irish than do our professional politicians to-day, for he was of great birth and European experience; still, he misunderstood them; and we have all seen how the ignorance of those modern politicians of ours, even today, with Ireland at twelve hours from London for transport, at a few seconds for information, with overwhelming superiority in wealth and power, has managed to lose Ireland.

The second excuse for James is that he had had recent experience of the enthusiasm for his claim in the South, at Dublin, where the considerable Protestant body with its organized English Church and great endowments seemed to have accepted him readily enough.

The third is that, as we shall see in a moment, the man originally commanding in Derry had prepared to yield, and that the town only resisted because a strong popular movement insisted that it should do so.

At any rate, on April the 18th, 1690, James rode out to summon Derry, and to present himself before its walls.

Here appears one of the defects of James in his later years. He had always been prodigiously industrious. He had always from youth attended to detail with masterly industry. But these habits seem, after his fiftieth year, to have hardened into meticulousness and the losing of judgment under a mass of petty things: into a loss of a sense of proportion, even in matters which he was daily handling and which were before his eyes.

We have a very clear sentence upon that new defect in him, passed by a contemporary who was with him— himself a great diplomatist trained to judge a situation. He says of the King at this moment: 'he is perpetually attending to unimportant matters, passing by the essentials, and he accumulates such a load of small particulars in his head as, when it comes to taking a broad judgment, completely impedes the action of his mind.'

It was obvious that James ought to have consulted not only the Commander-in-Chief, Rosen, thirty miles away, but the man in local command of the force actually in front of Derry—Hamilton. Now Hamilton had already summoned the city, and the authorities so summoned (that is, in practice, the well-to-do merchants of the place —for the Corporations were always that) had already virtually capitulated. They said they were ready to treat, and, as essential to that transaction, stipulated that King James's forces should not advance within a certain distance of the city.[1]

It is only just to them to point out that their military adviser, the Governor, Lundy, who absurdly exaggerated James's military resources, had called the place untenable, advised capitulation, and prevented the landing of two further English regiments which were lying ready to disembark in Lough Foyle. The mass of the people[2] who had less to lose, were discontented with the policy of Lundy and the Corporation. They were all for defending the place. They knew nothing of military affairs, but by a piece of luck their military judgment happened to be perfectly sound. James had nothing serious to bring against them, yet would they not have had their way but for another blunder on James's part. The King may have had some vague knowledge of negotiations going on between Hamilton and the Corporation; but without considering what the effect of advancing soldiers beyond the agreed limits would be, he appeared on Windmill Hill, southwards of the town, and rode on towards its gates— and round him was an escort of dragoons.

---

[1] They were not to go beyond St. Johnstown.
[2] In that day Derry was in the main Protestant. The modern town is almost exactly half Catholic.

The rumour at once flew round the town-mob that they were betrayed: that the stipulation of keeping the King's army at a distance had been treacherously broken: that they were all to have their throats cut by the murderous papishes marching against them. The mob took charge, shut the gates, manned the walls, and when the royal trumpets rang out to give the summons, they answered by firing a piece which killed an officer at James's side.

I will not say that the ignorance and enthusiasm of the Derry mob saved the Crown for William. William would have defeated the royal forces in Ireland in any case; he had overwhelmingly superior strength, and nothing could have withstood it in the long run. But the resistance of Derry put heart into the Williamite cause, and affected the legitimists with a memory of failure.

James went back to Dublin, taking his Commander-in-Chief, Von Rosen, with him, and left, for what was now to be called the 'siege' of Derry, de Maumont in command, Richard Hamilton second, the Duke of Berwick and that able French officer de Pusignan as the two Major-Generals below the Commander-in-Chief and Hamilton.

Of a true siege there was none. The conditions were quite unsuitable for a siege: indeed, they were so unsuitable even for a blockade that it is to the credit of James's commanders—or to the shame of their opponents—that they could establish even that.

The total royal force available for the North was on paper under thirteen thousand men. Of these the number that could be spared for Derry was only six thousand. There had been days of incessant rain, through which these raw troops had marched; there was no proper surgical or hospital equipment, nor doctors, nor medicines, nor surgeons; and the active force seems never to have been more than two-thirds or at the best three-quarters of the nominal total. Inniskillen lay on the flank and occupied the other moiety of the troops available.

Within Derry there was actually a larger force of men and a very much better provision of artillery and firearms, and a larger amount of ammunition, than in the lines outside the town. If we try to put the thing in military terms, it is almost farcical: a larger, a better-equipped force contained behind its walls by a smaller and worse-equipped one, a formidable defensive attacked with inferior weapons that could not affect it: the besiegers working at a great distance from their ultimate base over very bad roads, the besieged handicapped by no distance over which to convey their munitions and arms: the besieged with ample housing, living under conditions of comfort so long as the provisions lasted, the besiegers in the open field under what was, at the beginning of the operations, abominable weather.

I have said that it is a mystery how, under these conditions, the men of Derry allowed themselves to be shut up at all. If the mystery can be solved, it can doubtfully be so from the difference of command on the two sides. The King's army was led by officers experienced in European warfare; the regular commanders on the rebel side had abandoned action and the men of Derry were led by amateurs, of whom the most famous was Mr. Walker, a clergyman, a rector from County Tyrone, whose account of the siege, lively, inaccurate, and in some places deliberately false, makes very good reading. He at least had no doubts that the war was a war of religion! He did two great services to the besieged: he provided them with a head in the first moment when they were but a mob or rabble acting against the constituted authorities; he restored order and put discipline into the people he had to manage.

We ought to remember in this brief account of the

operations, that the trained professional officers left to their own judgment would not have attempted the reduction of Derry. The man in chief command, that big gormandizing German, of excellent military capacity, called Von Rosen, knew very well that the idea of a siege was nonsense and objected to it from the beginning.

Theoretically the person who ordered the operation to be undertaken was James himself; but James acted on the advice of Melfort, and Melfort was thinking of Scotland rather than Ireland. As for poor Richard Hamilton, who was in active command in front of the place, he had to tell his Government in Dublin that there were but six battalions, heavily under strength (the best of six hundred men, others of less than four hundred), and that about one musket in ten might be expected to work properly. It sounds ridiculous, but I believe it to be historically true, that for effective purposes the Royal Infantry in front of Derry in the first weeks of siege would not have counted at the most much more than three thousand men in actual line, and that the useful firearms at their disposal were certainly less than four hundred.[1]

In such conditions it was obvious that the so-called besiegers must dig themselves in, or they would have been at the mercy of a surprise sally by the very numerous besieged. Even against entrenchment such a sally should have succeeded. It was never made. If the reader desires to know how many shovels there were for the purpose of rapid entrenchment in the hands of some three thousand odd men, he will be interested to learn that there were thirty.

So the situation stood for not quite two months, when with the early part of June, the lack of provisionment

---

[1] As late as the end of June the French Ambassador quotes a letter from one of the Commanders who had been sent up *as reinforcement to Derry*. The unfortunate Colonel takes the roll of the muskets at his disposal in the whole regiment. He finds that there are seven!

began to be felt for the first time by the men of Derry, who had thus allowed themselves, in spite of their superior numbers and far superior armament, to be contained within their walls. If the situation could be maintained long enough, something might after all be done for the King's cause, and an army ridiculously insufficient for a true siege might effect its purpose by a blockade and hunger.

On June the 15th three sail from England despatched by William's Government appeared in Lough Foyle, and they bore ample provisionment for Derry. For some little time, southerly winds blowing straight down the Lough forbade any approach, and meanwhile the royal troops had thrown a strong boom across the river somewhat below the town. They were compelled also, in order to meet the threat of the Williamite shipping, to move down the banks of the stream to the point called Fort Charles, with a few big guns which had by this time reached them as reinforcements—for, five weeks earlier, a French fleet in Bantry Bay had beaten off the English vessels under Admiral Herbert and had landed stores.

There is in connexion with that action a very pretty anecdote. When the French Ambassador came, overjoyed, to tell James of the French successes, James, whose patriotism had the intensity of a religion, and for whom the British Navy was the darling of his own creation (how admirably he had commanded it!), answered: 'You have defeated us? It's the first time!'

It was always so with him. We shall find him later on the Norman cliffs watching the British fleet destroy his last hopes, but pointing, even as they did so, with admiration to their gunnery and seamanship, to their intrepidity in boarding.

Mainly on account of the adverse winds, then, this Williamite fleet in Lough Foyle with two regiments of trained veterans on board, well officered and munitioned, and with provisions for the town as well, lay useless so far as the men of Derry were concerned. They could signal to the town, and town to them, and an individual could get through—as one did by swimming; but there could be no reinforcement or provisioning.

The two Commanders of this fleet were Rooke and Kirke, the first destined fifteen years later to occupy Gibraltar, the second, a very strange person, to find himself on the quarter-deck. He was that Kirke whose reputation for murderous brutality had been laid in Tanger, whose 'Lambs' made themselves famous for the same brutality after Sedgemoor, and who was now more congenially joined to the Usurper's party. The whole of that generation was full of soldiers of fortune, but not one other so unscrupulous, so daring, so free from morals, as this worthy.

He had strategy in him too. When he found that there was no getting up the river to Derry, he profited by the adverse wind to go up west round the land and reinforce Inniskillen and its already strong, well-equipped body of Protestants who, lying on the west flank of the Derry operations, had reduced to the slight proportions we know the forces available for the 'siege.'

Meanwhile the hunger of Derry increased, and the position within the walls became serious as the end of June approached.

Rosen, knowing very well that he had not the wherewithal to attack the town, proposed to make war in our modern fashion, and to sacrifice the civilian population at large. He wrote a letter to James telling him that the 'conditions had induced him to determine to exterminate all the rebels throughout the country.' He told those within Derry that if they did not surrender the place by July the 1st, he would gather the rebels from all over the countryside and drive them under the walls where they would starve.

He was as good as his word, and on July the 2nd a great drove of all sexes and ages, including little children, appeared driven in front of the Royalist lines towards the city. Derry held twenty prisoners, and the besieged replied to Von Rosen's German tactic by putting up a great gallows in sight of the Royalist army, and threatening to hang thereon the twenty gentlemen, who very naturally wrote, not to Von Rosen indeed, but to Hamilton, begging him to give way.

It was James who saved the situation. The moment he received Von Rosen's letter he ordered the manœuvre to be stopped. A circular was sent round at once to all his officers telling them to 'refuse obedience to any order of this nature from our Field-Marshal-General.' Indeed, of all those concerned, James seems to have been the most indignant at the cruelty and the most effectually so. There is a contemptuous tone in the letters of those about him as though blaming him for too great softness of heart. But a very fine phrase should be sufficient for us. He said that 'his honour as a king and the keeping of his word was to be preferred to the preservation of his throne'; and he added that if Von Rosen had been his own subject he would have hanged him.

As July ran out it became more and more evident that attack would never be possible. It was a race between hunger and relief. How bad the situation was we know from the prices fetched by horse-flesh and by dog-flesh 'fattened' (as we are told by the amiable clergyman who commanded the Hosts of the Lord) on the bodies of James's dead soldiers. The besieged tried to get meat by stampeding cattle from the enemy's camp. With that object they tied up their own last cow to a stake near the walls and set the animal on fire, in the hope that its career in agony, breaking loose, would carry confusion into its fellows. But the stratagem failed. Relief came on the 105th day of the siege (July the 30th, 1689). Kirke had the north wind he wanted and enough of it. The few guns on Culmore Point could do nothing against the advance of his ships. The first struck the boom and recoiled. The second, the *Dartmouth*, a frigate, or perhaps the *Mountjoy*, broke the obstacle, and rather over half an hour later, bowling up the river before the strong breeze, three ships and their provisionment lay at the quays of the town.

On the next day, the last of the month, Rosen, with his men, turned south and marched away.

There intervened, between Derry and the Boyne, a year. It was passed in a precarious but seemingly assured administration sufficiently solid. A kingdom was attached to its king, and Dublin was a capital. The ancient dispossessed nobility and gentry of Ireland had resumed the lands which a swarm of adventurers had seized less than forty years before. There was a Court. A renewed world lived. But Ireland is not England. It was King of England (of Scotland only after that of Ireland) that James would be. He disapproved—in silence—the restoration of the Irish lands. His religion taught him nothing as regarded Ireland. It was England which he must recover. All those who saw Europe as a whole told him to be patient. With Ireland secure, England would come at last. But James was perhaps not so out of perspective as usual in still hankering after a direct appeal to England and a landing there. Ireland he was to lose. Action from Ireland the English would resent. England itself might yet rally to him.

At the moment when James was entering the rapids, in 1687, there had appeared at The Hague an aged Commander, who might properly be called the veteran of all Europe: Schomberg.

He was a man already 72 years of age. He had come after a stormy voyage (necessitating a landing in a British port) from Portugal. He saw the Prince of Orange. What they said to each other will not be known. It is possible or probable that they talked over Orange's approaching treason to his father-in-law. But Schomberg had nothing to do with that. His sword was at the service of whoever would have it. He was worth a brigade to any man—his name alone.

He was a great noble of the Rhine (his mother was an English woman—Dudley's daughter) who had fought in all wars. It was his father who had arranged for James I the Palatinate marriage. Before he was 20 he had been in the field side by side with that Von Rosen, a similar soldier of fortune, whom we have just seen at Derry and who was destined to face him, opposed, when Schomberg himself came over to fight against James in Ireland.

He had steeped himself in arms during the struggle between the Protestant princes and the Empire—what is called the Thirty Years' War. Though Protestant by birth, and, it may fairly be said, by conviction (for he was tempted at one moment to join the flowing Catholic tide in France and would not), he went over to the service of the French King before he was 40 years of age, by which time he was among the most renowned captains in the west. He was given a command in the French Scots Guards and for seven years was perpetually fighting in the service of the French Crown. Indeed, upon the approach of his fiftieth year, he naturalized himself and his sons subjects of Louis. Five years later he married into one of the great Huguenot families (as they then were) of the French nobility, the Aumales of Harcourt.

When Louis, with Charles of England, was fighting the

Dutch, his service was lent to the English King. He prepared that invasion of Holland which the battle of the
Texel perhaps prevented and (it is important to note this)
he devised the details for a large standing army to support Charles II against the rich men of his Parliament.
He had raised German regiments for the French; he was
in the grandest way a soldier and nothing else, appearing
in this field and that, under this master and that indifferently; and now in his old age his name alone was
a military fortune to whoever might command it, for
wherever he went a refusal of his advice led to disaster,
and acceptance of it to victory. He knew admirably how
to form, to command, to restrain, to launch any armed
force of whatever material, and already ten years before
he had out-generaled Orange before Maestricht. He had
already been a Marshal of France (the last Huguenot
Marshal) in 1675.

It is one of the strong arguments against the revocation
of the Edict of Nantes by Louis XIV (and the weight of
political opinion is against it) that it lost to the French
service so many admirable Commanders, but in particular
this Captain.

Not that he was exiled; he was honourably sent off as
Ambassador, but he would no longer stay; for he felt
that the taking away of privileges from men of his rank
on the plea of religion made it incumbent on him to leave
the service of the French King.

Even at this great age of his, he sat a horse as well as
any man in Europe, he inspired men's confidence in any
troops under his command, and, as we shall see, he died
gloriously enough, his face slashed with the sabres of the
cavalry charge of the Boyne—but the mortal blow was
struck by some bullet from behind him: from his own
side; a bullet aimed by some discontented trooper of the

French brigade, or perhaps some random wasted missile. We shall never know.

At any rate, he died well and has left a great name. They buried him (after William had entered Dublin) in St. Patrick's Cathedral. His relatives for more than half a lifetime after that glorious death of his refused the money for his monument. Swift with his creative indignation put up the thing we know; but its original and very fine inscription was not allowed to stand. There he lies. I was at the pains of paying reverence to his tomb some few weeks before writing this. Soldiers of his calibre are not so common.

This man led the vanguard of the Williamite force, landed at Carrickfergus in the late summer of 1689 which had seen the failure at Derry. Through the winter of 1689-90 his command, and the royal army opposed to it, lay inactive. Schomberg's force, waning with disease, ill-found, was yet on a front protected by ground which forbade attack. The opposing armies could only watch each other. Neither had a hope of victory in attack. With the next season, the summer of 1690, William himself had landed with heavy reinforcement and a powerful park of artillery. The odds were turned; all the strength was now on William's side, and James's troops with their few pieces and insufficient numbers awaited them to fight a defensive action behind the line of the River Boyne.

In the world of politics and religion the Battle of the Boyne is a date, or a symbol, or a turning-point, or anything you will. In the world of legend it is a thick growth of nonsense, beautiful or ugly according to one's taste in gods and men. There is a sort of ghostly Battle of the Boyne up in the air, where kingdoms are won and lost, heroes perform incredible feats, and a complete decision is arrived at in a doubtful struggle between two mighty armies—one of Papists, the other Orangemen victorious.

But in the interesting field of military history the Boyne is nothing of all this.

It appears (to those who care for reality) as a conflict in which under 25,000 men, of whom a quarter to one-third had sufficient training, possessing six field guns, fought a rearguard action to allow the retirement of the army, resisted, in a bad defensive position, for some hours the attack of between 42,000 and 45,000 men—a good three-quarters of them of long training, and supported by fifty guns; and allowed the force to retire with safety.

There was no decision. The defensive so maintained by the much weaker force was successful in permitting it to effect its retreat; the superior force failed, or was too badly hammered, to follow up; their far inferior opponents, who might have been destroyed, remained an army in being, and were able, in spite of the overwhelming odds against them, to continue the war. The covering action of the Boyne allowed James's army to get away with less than six per cent losses in men and the abandonment of only one gun.

First as to the position.

The River Boyne runs eastwards into the sea thirty miles north of Dublin. At the first bridge across it, one and a half miles from the bar, stands the maritime town of Drogheda, approachable at high water by vessels of moderate draught. The time of high water, at the full and change of the moon, is about half-past ten (this detail is important in the story of the battle). At the quarter moon, low water is at about that hour.

Above Drogheda there is no bridge until you come to Slane, eight miles away. A couple of miles from Drogheda Bridge up-stream (rather less, of course, from the last houses of the town), some six miles therefore from the

Bridge of Slane, stands, on the southern side of the river, a slight open elevation known as Dronore, round which the Boyne curls in a half-circle. The slope of Dronore—it is only 300 feet high—lies open to view from the opposite or northern bank in its whole extent. Where

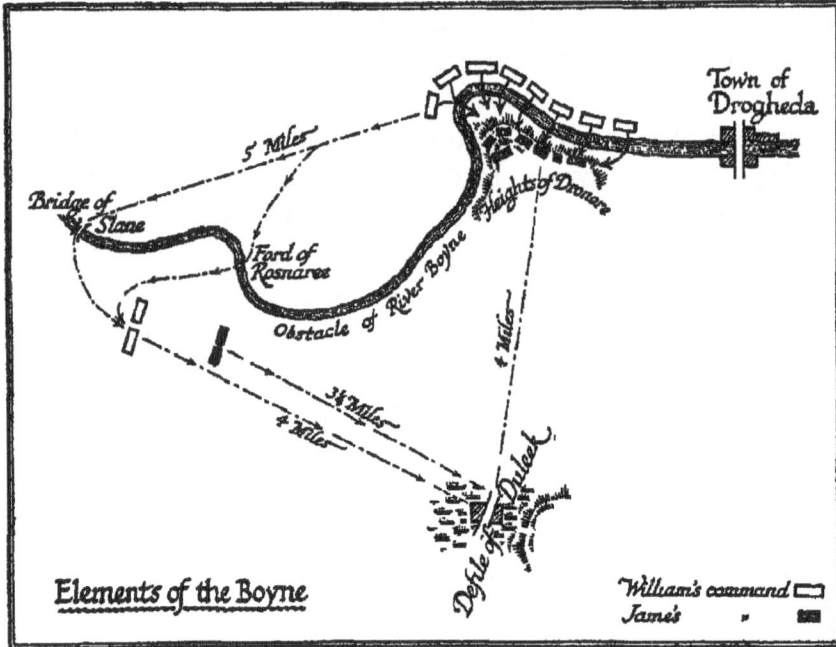

Elements of the Boyne

it falls on the left in the direction of Slane the ground becomes rather more difficult, and in places was marshy, or at any rate intersected with wet ditches, at the time of the battle. At the other, the Drogheda end, the ground sinks to a lower elevation and is dry. The River Boyne, as it curls round this half-circle jutting northward, is at that point on an average 150 yards wide, growing slightly wider as it descends, to a full 250 or 300 yards by the time it approaches Drogheda town. The river is fordable at low tide; easily fordable at springs, and still fordable at neaps.[1]

[1] The term 'spring tides' means the very high and low tides just after full and new moons. The neap tides are the tides of the quarter moons in between, where the water rises less and also falls less.

On the day the battle was fought, July the 1st, 1690, the moon was five and a half days old: the tides were far from their extremes; the neaps were already beginning; but they were sufficiently low to make the river fordable in several places before the end of the ebb. But a little below the bend the fords became unpleasantly deep even at the end of the ebb. Further, let it be remarked that when troops have to ford a tidal river, they have not an un-limited time in which to do it; if only a certain number get across in time before the water rises the operation is dis-astrous, because it leaves a section of your force cut off and at the mercy of their opponents, without the possibility of being relieved and supported by their own men. On the day of the Boyne the lowest moment of the water was between 9.30 and 10 a.m. The day was not chosen to fit the tides; battle fell on the date it did independently of that factor: but the fording of the river by William's attack had to wait for the tide. The depth of water differs with recent weather, rainfall and wind; but probably at the fords the men had less than three feet to wade through at the lowest water; by one in the afternoon their depth would be increased by a foot to eighteen inches or more, and the deeper would be impassable.

Again, though the position of Dronore could be turned by the Bridge of Slane, that bridge was a couple of hours' march away, and by the time the enemy had got to it and crossed it, and doubled back again to the defensive position on Dronore, a morning would have been ex-pended, fatigue would have been incurred, and warning given to the defence to retire in time to prevent en-circlement, and the cutting off of their line of retire-ment. That line of retirement passed through Duleek —the only road: a point where all the retreating army must pass as there was marsh on either side.

Again, the town of Drogheda, in the streets of which

no army would engage itself on the offensive, was something the right of the defensive could repose upon: it was unlikely to be turned from that direction.

On the whole, therefore, the position of the Boyne was not so very bad, as it is sometimes described to be. Still, it was weak. The troops occupying it were in full view of an enemy on the northern bank; it was approachable on many points at low tide; it contained little opportunity for cover behind which to gather reserves; it could be turned on the left by a superior force, and behind it was the narrow defile of Duleek.

The northern bank, on the other hand, was excellently suited for the preparation of an offensive. It contained deep ravines opposite either end of the defended position across the water, depressions so shaped that it was possible to gather very large bodies of men in them and prepare for the attack without being observed from the southern side, or molested by its fire.

Now as to the composition of the opposing forces. The Williamites had for their best troops the Dutch Blue Guards under Solms, which were veteran and of first-class quality, in three battalions; two French Huguenot regiments, so called,[1] and a further Dutch force under Nassau; there was a brigade of English under Hanmer, and a Danish body under Cutts. There were two Inniskillen regiments present also. The Reverend Walker, 'bombarded General' for the occasion, was on the field—and fell there. Which moved William to comment what the devil was he doing in an army.

This force, so diverse in composition, but Dutch and French for its main professional body, was to undertake the direct frontal attack across the river.

[1] The rank and file were not picked for religion. All the officers were. Thus a private in one of the Huguenot regiments dying pulled out a rosary to tell his beads on it. A Dane, moved by the sight, shot him dead.

The first line, the spear-head of the attack, was designed for the French and Dutch, the greater part of the small English force was to come up in second line, and (it is here that the reality differs most from the legend) the Orangemen played on the whole the least part in the battle. This is no derogation of their valour; it is merely an account of the part which their general gave them to play.

So much for the Williamite attack. One-fifth or rather less of William's army was detached far off to his right or west to cross the river at Slane; the infantry by the bridge, the cavalry by the ford called Rosnaree.

As to the 'general idea' on both sides, that also is misrepresented in legend, though more accurately appreciated in our histories as regards William's side than James's.

Neither James nor his commanders intended to hold the line of the Boyne and to risk a decision there. Any one could see that it could not be permanently held, and that only incredible luck on James's side or incredible blundering on the other could prevent the obstacle being crossed by such superior numbers, and the position being turned on its left towards Slane as well.

The 'general idea' on William's side was simple enough: to make a strong frontal attack across the river at low tide upon the defensive position at Dronore, previously cannonaded, and meanwhile, with the extra fifth of the army, which could easily be spared out of such large numbers, to cross higher up at Slane and make straight for the road leading to Duleek. If this outflanking party got to the Duleek road in time it would cut off the chances of retirement from James's men, envelop them, and so achieve a decision by the destruction of the whole force.

The 'general idea' on James's side was to fight a delaying action only, in order to give the main army time to get away, in the hope of its fighting again under better conditions with reinforcements. Perhaps the opportunity might come with the exhaustion of William's much larger command. There was the possibility of William's having to recall troops to England if the French effort against him by sea, or if the English disaffection against him at home, compelled him to do so. The delaying action must also be fought to cover the capital, an error to which I refer in Note III at the end of this book. A retreat was intended from the first, and was successfully carried out. The army was saved.

Now this idea of a covering action involved the absence of even the very few guns which James's force had at its disposal. They were, as I have said, twelve; and, of these, six were sent back with the baggage in preparation for the retreat that had been planned: the remaining six were withdrawn before the attack on the fords began. William's attack was made therefore with the support of fifty pieces and against the defence of none.

This withdrawal of the guns was not (as has been represented) an elementary blunder: it was a choice of two evils: either certainly losing the few guns of the force, for the advantage of possibly gaining some delay; or suffering more rapid pressure for the advantage of saving them, so that the army in its retreat should not be entirely deprived of artillery. On the whole the withdrawal of the twelve guns was such a choice as most commanders of the day would probably have made.

Let it be remembered that in any case William's artillery was overwhelmingly stronger than James's—more than four to one—that guns in those days had not regular teams and were very slow-moving affairs, drawn by cart-horses pressed for the service immediately before they were needed. Had James's twelve guns been used on the banks of the Boyne during the heat of the action they would have been lost. Nor were they sufficiently numerous to have defended the many places over which the enemy could get across at low water. It might have been worth while to risk the loss of the guns for the sake of checking the passage of the fords; but so few would have done little more than check, and perhaps they would have been pounded to silence by the immensely superior fire of their opponents before the advance was undertaken. Guns could not be moved rapidly at will in 1690; they had very little mobility, their rate of fire was slow. At any rate, withdrawn the guns were; first half of them—six—before a shot was fired; then the remaining half-dozen before the heat of the action developed.

The task of covering the retreat on Duleek, which had been designed, was to be left to the cavalry, and very well did they fulfil the task allotted to them. Tyrconnel had grown fat, and his health was gone; but he showed vigour enough throughout the day; and Berwick behaved admirably, charging over and over again and, taking it all in all, effecting the purpose which he and his father had desired.

Now, as a last point before briefly recounting the action, let us appreciate the importance of Duleek. Duleek, lying four miles back from the centre of the position at Dronore, was a 'defile,' a word which means a 'narrow' through which an army must pass in single column. Upon it the roads of the neighbourhood converged; it was the only gate to the only avenue of retirement; for an army with its train is tied to roads, and, as I have said, the sodden ground on either side forced all the troops to pass in single column through the place. The retreat, if it could be accomplished, would have to go through Duleek, and so, too, would the advance following upon that retreat should the attack not prove decisive.

For the retreat to get to Duleek first, therefore, before

William's 8,000, who had been sent to outflank (round by Slane), could cut them off, was the essential point of the Jacobite plan. It was achieved. As for the commanders upon William's side, the detachment going round by Slane was under Douglas (whose treachery to James we may regard as comic or tragic, according to our mood, but which has nothing to do with the military movement)[1]; the cavalry of this flanking detachment was under the command of the younger Schomberg. The elder, that famous white-haired veteran of fight after fight throughout Western Europe, the whilom Marshal of France, the true professional soldier of the day, was with the main attacking party, where he met his death—a man respected by every soldier, and by many beloved. William himself was nominally, as King, conducting the main movement, the frontal attack, under the real guidance of the elder Schomberg. Solms and his Dutch Guards we have already mentioned, also Cutts leading the Danes; while of the Huguenot French force the best regiment was commanded by de Ruvigny, a very gallant cavalryman in his thirty-eighth year, known by the courtesy title of Caillemotte. He also was to fall on that field.

Those who desire to visualize the conflict must not forget this thing about it—that the cries of encouragement to attack and resistance which proceeded from the leaders on either side were for the main part given in the French language. This was not due to the presence of a French Huguenot brigade on the one side or French regular royal horse upon the other: it was because French was the language of the higher gentry there engaged on either

---

[1] He had always avowed a tender attachment to James (who had made his career), and only fifteen months before, on the eve of the Dutch invasion, had been drinking that monarch's health upon his knees, coupled with the toast of 'damnation to whoever should be so base as to draw sword against him.' Let us hope that the curse did not take effect. But one never can tell.

side; for these were all either bilingual or wholly French-speaking: William, Schomberg, Berwick, Hamilton, James himself (for all his ill accent and English contempt of the French tongue).

The day—Tuesday, July the 1st, 1690—broke in a fine clear dawn over the neighbouring sea; and the sun rising just before four o'clock into an unclouded heaven showed the Irish dispositions clear to William and to his gunners upon the northern bank.

It was the moment of high water, or, rather, the last of the flood. The mixed detachment sent by William towards Slane went off, apparently, about six o'clock upon its flanking errand; too late. Schomberg had urged its despatch the night before—it would then have appeared on James's flank suddenly, at the beginning of the action. William delayed it. Probably he thought, in some dull way, a flanking force ought not even to be close to its final point of attack till the front was engaged. He seems to have mistaken that for 'synchrony'—it lost him his decision. But, then, William was no General. If James were a doubtful commander for a large force, William was a much worse one.

The main frontal attack waited for the fall of the water, but during the morning William's fifty guns pounded away across the river upon the exposed Irish lines and their raw troops. We may conjecture that it was somewhere about nine o'clock, the last two hours of the ebb now running furiously, and the river rapidly lowering, that a galloper brought in news from William's extreme right by Slane, that the infantry under Douglas had crossed by the bridge: with more difficulty the mounted force under the younger Schomberg by the ford of Rosnaree.

Here also the command of a king nearly spoilt the affair. James did not understand the capital importance of the

Slane turning movement. He suggested that a few mounted men sent out westward 'to observe' would suffice. He was frightened of weakening his main front. Luckily he was overruled, or, rather, overpersuaded. A whole regiment, O'Neill's, was detailed for the purpose of guarding James's left flank, and was drawn up that morning facing, and checking, across a belt of difficult wet land, the Williamite flanking force when it appeared.

At this moment it is probable—not certain—that a blunder was committed by Douglas. Under the conditions of those days especially (and, indeed, until the advent of quite modern inventions for rapidly communicating orders) a flanking party sent out from the main body and separated from it had, while it was in such a position, all the responsibility of an independent command. If Douglas with his infantry, and Schomberg's cavalry as well, had, with part of his force, engaged O'Neill over the obstacle of wet ground, and pushed the rest on at once for Duleek, the battle that was about to be engaged in might have been decisive, for they might have cut off James's line of retreat.

But one cannot fight in column. Douglas noted that body of his opponent's, O'Neill's, drawn up as a flank guard and halted. Meanwhile Lauzun brought up in support of O'Neill on this extreme left or western flank a column of French, and gradually advanced further Irish troops to threaten Douglas's flank movement. But though Douglas, thus halted, hesitated to hold the Irish and French against him with part of his force and with the rest press on up the Duleek Road, his movement had been already sufficiently menacing to determine the pressing of James's retreat, and it was at this juncture, in the mid-morning, that the six guns still remaining in the defensive position on Dronore were withdrawn to take part in the retirement.

James, having seen to that withdrawal of the guns, went off to Lauzun upon the Slane flank, taking with him further foot and horse and leaving orders that yet more reinforcements should be drawn from his main body to protect the vital road to Duleek. As yet not a man had moved from William's side of the river to cross the stream. The state of the water did not permit them to begin this attack till 9.30 to 10 o'clock, and by that time not a gun was present on the side of the defence to check the Williamite crossing.

In infantry, the defence on Dronore in the frontal position was now reduced to eight battalions under Richard Hamilton, and to the horse on the right under the command of the Duke of Berwick: both Generals were nominally under the orders of Tyrconnel, but really each was responsible for his own action.

William's guns, which had already thrown disorder into the Irish troops on the open slope, redoubled the pressure of the cannonade; the fifty drums of Solms' Blue Dutch Guards matched their noise as the column to which they were attached, debouched from the ravine where they had been hidden and took the water upon a front of ten men. These veterans achieved in this first stroke all they had intended.

Though the Irish had held their fire until the approaching Blues were at the deepest of the water, that fire was ineffectual in the hands of raw men against soldiers of long training. The Dutch made the southern bank with but small losses, broke down the resistance of the much lesser force opposed to them, and forced it to fall back in some disorder upon the fields sloping up from the river.

Thus was the Boyne first crossed and the first point on the southern bank held.

A little later as to the head of its column—but with many of their men crossing simultaneously with the later part of the Dutch Guards—came the two Orange regiments, Inniskillen and Londonderry, just below downstream. A hundred yards again to their left, farther down the slackening current, the Brigade of French Huguenots took the water. Beyond them again the English regiments under Hanmer, and to the left of these, on the extreme left of William, opposite the horse of the Irish right, the Danes under Cutts and the Dutch body under Nassau. The total number which had surmounted the obstacle and were now on dry land was something like 10,000 men.

But this stage of the battle, in which the attack was only beginning to make good its hold of the farther shore, was propitious to cavalry work, and to that checking of William's pressure which had been left to James's horse in the original plan.

The Dutch Guards were charged by Tyrconnel before they could completely form, and though the Irish infantry failed to check the French Huguenots, the Irish cavalry broke in among them as they were with difficulty making their landing upon the southern bank. Their leader, Caillemotte, was mortally wounded in the sabre strokes, but still had the strength to cry to his men, 'A la Gloire!'

So it was all along the river-bank: King James's horse charging and charging again at the Dutch, the French, the Danish, the Orange, the English units, as these painfully made good their formation on the farther shore and thereby acquired an increasing power of fire to beat off the sabres.

The Jacobite horse obtained local successes, not sufficient to check the general attack. The Danes in particular were thrown back by yet another charge of Berwick's, who had already struck hard, but unsuccessfully, at the English brigade under Hanmer.

It was in the midst of this pell-mell of Williamite infantry slowly and partially forming, of Jacobite horse furiously charging to prevent such formation and to drive the invaders back into the tide, that the great Schomberg met his death in the strange fashion to which I have alluded—for it was not an enemy's bullet that killed him. The old man had seen Caillemotte fall, a man bound to him by strong personal ties; he took that commander's place at the head of the Huguenot brigade, crying out to them in French that they should recall their courage and their indignation against their persecutors. Tyrconnel's horse charged, and in that charge Schomberg received a sabre wound or two in the face; but what felled him was a bullet coming (no one knows who fired it) from behind his own position. He was hit in the back of the neck, and fell.

Now, as the last stage of the action approached, the advantage of numbers told heavily. William himself, upon the extreme left near Drogheda (he had been slightly grazed by a cannon-ball while still on the far side of the river, the day before, while James's guns were still in line), found very few at first to resist him. He gathered his horse, Dutch, Danish, and French, but containing also a certain proportion of the Orangemen; and, there being hardly anyone to oppose at this point, he easily held the Meath shore of the stream.[1]

From the security of this virtually undefended place William led his whole column forward against the Irish retreat. He was unexpectedly charged by Berwick. William's Inniskillen men broke, when the Williamite French under Belcastel came up just in time to prevent the rout of the Orange cavalry; but the still steady fire of the few remaining Irish foot at the side of Berwick's Horse forced Belcastel slowly back. There was still one fresh

[1] It was marshy ground; William's horse got bogged. He was forced to dismount, and had there been enough men on James's side to do any execution at that point, his enemy might have fallen.

body of cavalry, of those thus commanded by William on the Drogheda or east wing of the battle. It was under the Dutchman Ginkel. The Irish forced it back as it appeared; but a body of English troops shot into them, and so confused them that only one last charge by Berwick could extricate his friends.

The mêlée died down; the full retreat had begun. It had been impossible to prevent the complete forcing of the river; but Berwick and Tyrconnel's cavalry had so far saved the situation that the King's forces could retire in order.

Douglas on the flank by Slane with more than ten thousand men still stood impotently facing Lauzun, James, and the considerable force which had been brought up in rapidly succeeding detachments from the centre: he had proved hesitating and sluggish, but at any moment he might move.

There was no time now to be lost upon either side. Douglas, seeing the main Jacobite force in full retreat, now marched straight and rapidly for Duleek. Lauzun marched parallel with him on the other side of the low ground between them, making for the same point.

It was the defensive which won in that critical race. It was at this hour that the one gun, which I have already mentioned, was caught in the mud of the main road and could not be saved.

A few stragglers fell out from James's retiring force, but the main body covered the four miles to Duleek in a steady column, and even as they reached it Berwick and his horse back from Dronore drew up behind them as a rearguard. The defile was saved, and the retreat continued with that screen of cavalry facing the now cautious and perhaps exhausted bodies of William's cavalry which headed the enemy advance.

At the end of the long July day the royal army was

saved; it had lost some 1,500 men, over 21,000 were in column and secure. It was not attacked in the night. William had lost some 2,000 men, and the defence had been so damaged that his large force was exhausted.

The legitimist army fell back upon the capital during the following day, still in good order, and remained intact for the furthering of the war.

The capital was lost, and James withdrew from it. It was for him to decide whether he would remain in Ireland with the army there left to meet its increasingly superior foe, to assist at its last struggles and to fall with it, or to pursue what he had always desired and had been reluctantly compelled to postpone, an appeal to England.

He had long ago decided. He had a ship waiting for him at Waterford, and he sailed for France from Kinsale to prepare what he still thought the main affair: a crossing of the Channel and a rising summoned for him in his own realm of England.

Tourville and a French fleet had cleared the Channel. The Dutch, allied with their Prince, had sent their ships against him and had been defeated off Beachy Head. The English Fleet under Russell had not engaged. It had retired to the Thames, left the Dutch in the lurch and in inferior numbers and so secured their defeat.

While the Irish armies still maintained the losing game and held their enemy with decreasing power, James planned what he believed would be the decisive movement. Of the great men who had driven him from the Throne by their treason, many were changing again, in a new treason to their new master—or servant—the Prince of Orange. Russell, the Admiral, was engaged in that conspiracy; Churchill promised James support. Shrewsbury—in whose house the final plot against James had

been devised—was entirely engaged in turning his coat;
Godolphin corresponded with the Queen.

When the large body of Irish soldiers in their last
defeat had obtained honourable terms and so many had
retired overseas, James believed that these, with a French
contingent, would form a nucleus for him sufficient to
turn the tide and to rally a rising to his side. To the number of 8,000—with their allies a force of 12,000—they
were gathered in the Contentin, and Louis XIV lent his
fleet to secure their passage. One half of the French naval
force was to come up from the Mediterranean and join
the other half in the Channel.

It was then that the last blow fell and that the King's
untiring efforts were ended for ever.

Those who watched called it 'the finger of God', and
indeed so complete a set of coincidences one may rarely
meet in the human story. In full summer, heavy gales
from the west held half of Louis' fleet in the Mediterranean. No junction could be effected. In the narrow seas
Tourville, with but half the total force, had orders to
attack the Dutch Fleet before the English could effect a
junction with it. He was just their match. Hardly had he
started when news came to hand that the English Fleet
under Russell—who now betrayed for the third time—
had joined the Dutch. Corvettes were sent out in desperate
haste to recall Tourville; they did not find him.

Pursuing his original orders, or perhaps because he
remembered the blame given him for not following up
his victory the year before, Tourville engaged under odds
of two to one, off Barfleur. A mist prevented his destruction on the first day. He kept the desperate action
up through a second and a third. On the night of the
third most of his ships fell off and escaped to St. Malo
through the race of Alderney, where their enemies dared
not follow. The remaining thirteen, anchored under the

insufficient batteries of The Hogue, right inshore, were boarded and burnt by the British sailors under James's eyes. The loss in ships was of little effect on Louis' fortunes; it was not a tenth of his fleet in numbers, not an eighth in fire-powder. It was soon replaced.

But the defeat was the conclusion of James's active life. He could hope no more. His throne was lost for ever.

There are two points to be curiously examined even in this moment, when all is over.

Why did Russell—who had promised to support James —fail to do so? Why did not the fleet which he commanded act as it had acted at Beachy Head and weaken the Usurper? Russell was but a distant connexion of the great family whose name he bore, and even had he been its very head, most of these families were hesitating for a restoration. Why did he betray?

Next: Was James's proclamation issued before his intended crossing a cause of failure?

As to Russell, historians have attempted to reconcile his declarations with his actions, his double treason with his quite straightforward fighting of the fleet at the head of which he found himself. But a simple consideration of what he did and said would seem to solve the difficulty.

Russell was playing the familiar game which nearly all traitors have played throughout the ages, of keeping open two doors for escape. He was not particularly concerned with his professional pride as a sailor, but he was very much concerned with being on the victor's side, whoever should turn out to be the victor. In a conversation of which we have record, and which has every mark of being authentic, he conveyed to an intimate what his real position was. He would keep out of the way of James as much as possible. He would give the French Fleet the opportunity for escorting James's expedition and seeing it safely landed on the English shores. He knew very well that if it were so landed, the reaction in favour of James after those brief months of Dutch rule would be explosive—and he, Russell, would find himself on the right side.

But he also knew that if he had orders to join the Dutch Fleet, and if that junction was effected and action were joined, no mortal could prevent in that case a plain hammer-and-tongs fight. When the shots had begun, one side or the other must conquer. There was no opportunity for betraying in the midst of the battle, and apart from that, it would have been the worst of policy to attempt it.

Perhaps up to the very moment when the fleets engaged Russell was still prepared to take James's side. But his captains would not have followed him; they were professional men; when an enemy was to be fought, they fought him. What decided Russell's final attitude was the preponderance of strength which appeared upon the day of the action. If Tourville had not engaged, he might have shilly-shallied long enough to give James a second chance. But Tourville chose to engage, against odds of two to one, and having so engaged, it was impossible to prevent the superior fleet from carrying out the action to its inevitable conclusion.

As to James's declaration, after The Hogue, it made no difference one way or the other. But to a student of his character it is important. Was it one more injudicious act, or was it justified?

This is what happened.

While making his preparations for the counter-invasion, James issued a declaration which was of great length, but the gist of which lay in three brief and simple passages. He was still determined upon toleration for the Catholic and the Nonconformist; on that point he would not budge. He knew, of course, what a risk it was to maintain his principles intact; he preferred to maintain them.

Next he offered a general pardon for the rebellion, without looking too closely into the motives of the worst actors therein. To this pardon he marked certain exceptions. He put down twenty-seven names of the more prominent of the traitors; he added three of the seamen who had outrageously misused him at Sheppey in his misfortunes, and a general phrase reserving to himself the right of bringing the rest of that lot to the punishment which they richly deserved.

Thirdly, he announced it to be the duty of magistrates and gaolers to release those who might be ordered to prison by the usurping government and said, in effect, that he would not pardon continued treason upon their part in support of the clique who had seized his throne.

Of these three points of the declaration by far the most important was the renewed affirmation of tolerance. It was *this* which aroused the strongest antagonism in those members of the governing classes who were now turning again towards the support of the legitimate king. It was because he would not budge in *this* matter that the declaration did have a certain adverse effect when it appeared in England.

As to the exceptions from pardon, many of them were set in with the object of covering those who were really working in aid of him; for instance, he exempts from pardon Churchill, by name, yet at that very moment he is depending upon Churchill as his chief support against William. The list is not entirely composed of men whom he would thus conceal from the vengeance of the new masters they had given themselves, but it is more than half composed of such names.

As for the assertion that it was the duty of magistrates

and of the officials of the law to support the legitimate cause, it was so obvious that it hardly needed reiterating.

James in this declaration (which was drawn up by Herbert, not by Melfort) acted as he had acted throughout his whole life—far too straightforwardly for the management of men. He desired that when he should be victorious, when the double traitors who had promised him their aid should have brought him back again, when the English people had welcomed him as they certainly would have welcomed him in a second Restoration, no one could accuse him of having laid traps and having punished men unwarned, however wicked. The contrast is absolute here between what James did in preparation for his counter-invasion to recover his legitimate rights and what William had done in his first Dutch invasion to cozen and to oust the true king. William, it will be remembered (and his advisers), lied and forged steadily from the first declaration in Holland that they had no intention of seizing the English Crown to the final repudiation of their pledge in the Treaty of Limerick. You cannot, perhaps, put your finger on one single declaration that these men or their leader made which did not deceive its victims and was not intended to deceive its victims. James, by the form of his declaration, as Herbert has drawn it up, clearly showed that he repudiated such methods, and adopted their opposite: that he would give fair warning, saying the most he intended to do, and keeping his honour clean.

And yet he was wrong, if we are considering the governance of men. For without duplicity the governance of men in great bodies and in moments of conflicting opinions is impossible. But if he was considering not so much the governance of men or even his material success as the maintenance of his own honour and the salvation of his soul, then he was right.

IX

THE END

THE loss of the thirteen ships at The Hogue, the flight of the rest, was the end of James's active effort to recover the throne. He was just on 60, had nine more years to live.

During five of these the ultimate political chance still lay in the balance, though very doubtfully. They were marked by little that could affect James's mind.

Two years after The Hogue his daughter Mary died. With his love of his children he may have felt a pang; but there was little to mourn. It may be doubted if any human being felt a void at her passing, unless it were William. She had been a sort of cold companion to his morose, barren, and perverted life; and it is touching to read that his unpleasing indifference to women did not prevent his keeping a memorial of her: a locket with her hair. After all, through her he had achieved that ambition in the pursuit of which he had passed through every moral degradation of falsehood, forging, and hypocrisy. Moreover, with Mary dead, he was alone among the great nobles who had set him up and made him feel at every turn the ignominy of his false title:—alone, save for the too close companionship of his minions, the elderly Bentinck, inherited from a long dead youth: the young Keppel, more pleasing to age. Yet even in that companionship there was a flaw, for the two were jealous one of the other: the now elderly Dutchman of good birth, still serviceable but no longer of the same attraction; the young Dutch beauty of no birth at all, loaded with the spoils of the loyal and the defeated.

Three years after Mary's death, in 1697, her father's claim, in practice long lost, was ended in a formal document. The general peace whereby Louis XIV concluded the last long phase but one of his continued wars included, as regarding his negotiations with William, the Treaty of Ryswick.

The loss or gain to France or to the Dutch (for the English had no lot in the affair, and were merely used as pawns by their new King) do not concern us. All that concerns us in the settlement which Boufflers and Bentinck arrived at is the manner in which it affected James II: and that turns upon three matters, all in the much-contested opening clause.

(1) The recognition of William III as King of England.

(2) The payment of her jointure, hitherto pocketed by William and his favourites (50,000 crowns a year), to the Queen of England, James's wife, Mary of Modena.

(3) The recognition of James's son as William's heir.

I will take these in order.

1. All that Louis XIV consented to in the matter of recognizing William, was an open promise that he would not abet any effort in the future to deprive William of his acquired position.

The thing was gone into in great detail: every word weighed; that was the final result. Louis did not recognize William III as legitimate King of England, but he promised for the future not to enter into alliance with those, nor to aid those, who were trying to prevent the continuance of William's being King *de facto*: King *de jure* he could never be, either in Louis XIV's mind, or in his own, or in anybody else's.

2. On the second point we have one of the worst

examples in that great series of betrayals, falsehoods, and thefts, which make up the story of the Dutch invasion and of the Revolution.

William was anxious—intensely anxious—to get the Treaty through. He and those about him knew that one necessary condition of success was that the robbery of James II's Queen, Mary of Modena, should not continue. This annual income of fifty thousand was her own private property: nothing could excuse the theft of it. Had William or his emissary boldly refused to pay this money, had they kept it without excuse or apology, for their own advantage, they would have cut a less sorry figure with posterity. But to act thus straightforwardly was not in the man's nature. It was still less in the nature of those who had betrayed their last king to let him in, and then done their best to betray him in turn. Further, with that clique money was the chief consideration of life, and almost the only one; whereas it is only fair to William to admit that his hatreds, his ambition, and his peculiar ideas of pleasure, were more to him than financial profit.

The Treaty had to be got through: it was urgent, it was pressing. The terms were far better for William than, in their hearts, he and his intimate and negotiator had expected; *therefore the promise was given to pay back her money to the Queen.* But mark in what form that promise was made! The promise was to pay that 'to which she was legally entitled'. The word 'legally' was specially used to bamboozle the more honourable negotiators. And it succeeded. No one can doubt that if by the word 'legally' we mean 'of right' or 'lawfully', the money was simply Mary of Modena's property, and to keep it back from her for the advantage of the usurper and his friends, native and foreign, was plain theft. But the word 'legally' might also mean 'by the decision of a court of justice' or of a lawyer, without specifying what court of justice or what lawyer. They knew very well what the decision of their own lawyers would be. The money was never paid.

3. There is no doubt that William III, being childless and with no prospect of having a child (for in his case indeed could be affirmed what was a falsehood in the case of his rival, and any child purporting to be his would certainly be suppositious),—admitted the principle that James II's boy (he was now 9 years of age) should succeed him upon the English throne. But he only admitted it upon the condition that the child should be brought up a Protestant. It was sound policy upon the part of the Prince of Orange.

For the student of James II's character the interest of this third point lies, of course, in the fact that he would not for one moment have accepted the turning of his son into renegade, nor would the boy's mother. He had given up everything for the Faith. It was not in him in these last days, when he had nothing more to lose, to exchange the eternal for the temporal.

The Treaty as a whole James met with a fine dignity. He showed both justice and gratitude when he said that the King of France had first of all to consider the good of his own people and of his realm. He might have added that if this realm were so exhausted and this people so drained in blood and wealth that further war would have been a crime, then peace even at great sacrifice was necessary. It may be debated how great the sacrifice was. Vauban in his famous letter to Racine was most indignant. But then Vauban was a soldier and an engineer —a very great one; but not a statesman.

At any rate, the Treaty, whether wise or unwise, from the point of view of Louis XIV, a success or a failure from the point of view of William III and his intimates, matters not to our subject. James saw it quite rightly as the foreign act of a prince not responsible for the rights of England or her national dynasty, and of the many proofs in his career of sound discrimination in close moral points, of distinction between justice and advantage, this admission of his was perhaps the noblest.

He said also in connexion with it a very fine thing: that one more necessary disappointment of his hopes meant little to him because Fate had from his earliest years 'inured him to contradiction'.

With the Treaty of Ryswick his hope or opportunity of any reversal in this world's evil fortunes was at an end. But in his own heart it had been at an end long since. He had engaged himself long since upon matters of greater moment than the Crowns of England, Scotland and Ireland.

For those last years of James were occupied in a spiritual contemplation so noble, so profound, that it is no wonder it is ignored or ridiculed. His whole being burnt and was purified in repentance and in the love of God, in sacrifice willingly made, in self-abasement before the Divine, in humility and therefore (unperceived as yet by himself) in glory.

He has left of that last passage memorials[1] in his own hand that are among the most moving in the great assembly of worship and praise with which the story of Christendom is filled. He was—though he knew it not —reaping the reward: the reward of a constancy to the Faith which had begun with none to help or persuade him, in that isolation of soul which was his bitter doom, of a loyalty in service which was so strangely maintained through years of sensual licence and vagary with women neither loving nor loved, through continuous unbridling

---

[1] They have been privately reprinted for the Roxburghe Club by Lord Derby, from which text I quote, and to whom I must tender my thanks for giving me the book.

of the flesh, relieving the body, never relieving that soul from its dreadful loneliness. It was a reward for that temper in which he had written,[1] during the most fiery of his trials, in the midst of the Popish Plot, with his greatness seemingly ruined: 'If occasion were, I hope that God would give me grace to suffer death for the true Catholic Religion, as well as Banishment'.

I know not where to begin in that fine body of secret, sincere expression to God from that soul.

'I abhor and detest myself for having so often offended so gracious and merciful a God, and having lived so many years in almost a perpetual course of sin, not only in my youth when I was carried away with the heat of it, and ill example, but even after when I was come to years of more discretion, and that thou hadst been pleased to have called me from the Pit of Heresy, to have opened my eyes to have known and entered thy true religion, to have covered my head so often in the day of Battle, delivered me so many times from the dangers of the Sea and noise of its waves.'

'The noise of its waves. . . .' He had braved them all of every kind.

Then again, there was found in the fragments of his papers this touching thing, a writing out of the words of Our Lord from the memory of a French Gospel Book—and how pathetic is the misspelling!

'Si quel cu'um veut venir apres moy, qu'il renonce a soy mesme, qu'il porte sa croix, et qu'il me suive.'

Let me, even in so brief a study, quote one more extract. I translate it from the French version published in the mid-eighteenth century. The original (I presume) was written like most of his devotions in English, but at the French Revolution the greater part of that manuscript perished.

'I am fixed that the longer I live in this world, the more do I hazard my eternal salvation, and that I cannot be in safety till I am freed of this contemptible body and united with you, O my God! Lord, when will that happy day arrive when I shall taste the vision of Beatitude and be

[1] In his letter to George Legge: 12/22 July 1679.

one with the Saints who praise and will praise you for ever? It will be
at your good time, my God; but Lord, delay not long.'

The memorial he left for his son should he reign, the
guide for a prince of England, is a proof of his sincerity
as of his steadfastness in the Principles for which he had
lived and which he carried with him to this end unchanged.
'Keep your kingly right. But disturb not your subjects
in their goods or in their religion. Neither can a king
be happy if his people be ill at ease, nor a people if their
king be constrained, for he cannot then protect and defend.
. . . Do all to establish freedom of conscience by some
(fundamental) law. Whatever persuasions men use, never
abandon that task till you have achieved it. It is the Grace
of God that gives the Faith, and men are to be gained by
goodness, and example and teaching, not by fear . . .
wage no aggressive war. . . .'
Conspicuous in this advice is the right to guide him,
should he become King of England: '*Preserve the mastery
of the sea*'.

In the very days when that class in England which
had destroyed the monarchy were voting in their parliament the rejection of every Catholic heir, James suffered
his first stroke. It was 1701. He was already in his sixty-
eighth year. He spat blood. They sent him to the waters
in the Bourbonnais (where all those years ago he had
sent Berwick's mother, Arabella—how he must have remembered!). They somewhat relieved him—but not for
long. On Friday, September the 2nd, after a troubled
night, he fell faint at Mass in his chapel of the Palace
at St. Germans, and lost consciousness as the Queen, with
a tenderness which had come on her in these years of his
dereliction, helped him to his room. He was put to bed.
On the Sunday they knew that he was dying. He knew it
too. He made his general confession, and was so weakened

that he again lost much blood and they feared his passing.

But he lingered. They brought his boy, the Prince of Wales, whom he blessed. When they would have taken the child away he clung to his father and James bade them let him be; and turning to him again said, 'Keep the Faith against all things and all men!' *He* had done so indeed.

Also he blessed the last little daughter, 9 years old—'The Consolation'.

As the King lay dying, Louis called, in the Palace of Marly, within a half-hour's ride of St. Germans, a council of some moment. It was to decide whether upon James's death the boy his son should be publicly recognized as King of England, and officially so proclaimed by the French King. The best judgments have debated the matter, and are debating it still. In that same council the Princes of the Blood and Louis himself decided for the course of honour; all the Ministers were for the course of policy. The main argument against publicly recognizing James III was that William would not long last out. He had not the physique of the man whom by intrigue he had supplanted. The small body was breaking up. His legs were swollen. He could only crawl with difficulty in and out of his carriage. He was bent and twisted, and it was manifest that death was upon him. 'The little fellow in black velvet' (as loyal men called, in their toasts, the mole which caused his horse to stumble and threw its rider out of the saddle) did but hasten an event in any case due—I mean the sending of William to his account.

Hence the main political argument against Louis' recognizing the Heir to England. It is always well to buy in the cheapest market, to avoid all unnecessary friction, never to raise an unnecessary difficulty, to let sleeping dogs lie. William's end was near. There was the boy, safe

under Louis' protection. There might he remain. Louis'
pledge of non-interference had not been given to Anne
or her husband, but only to William as an individual, and
when William was gone to explain himself in another
place, it would be time to emphasize the claims of James
III. Meanwhile public recognition would effect nothing.
It was an empty form. It would look like a foreign power's
interfering with the affairs of England (already a strong
argument on the side of the Usurper) and it would rally
to a man who was now supported by but a fraction of the
English nation a much larger number of the doubtful
who were ready to decide of themselves and freely in
favour of the rightful line, but not to accept that line
from the foreigner.

It was one thing to be ardent, as a large proportion
of Englishmen had been, for James II; it was one thing
to be at least in favour, as the majority of Englishmen
certainly were, for the rightful blood so long as James
II (who had been their king, who had fought for them
with such valour, worked so hard in their administration,
and had shown the national character of tenacity so
strongly) was alive to continue his claim—even though
that claim were being advanced from a foreign place of
exile. It was another thing to rally to his son, whom they
had never known. And if such adhesion were to take place,
better work for it by spontaneous, or apparently spontaneous, means than proclaim support of the claimant in a
moment when that support could not possibly come into
effect.

These arguments have convinced the general sense (if
one may so call it) of history. Just as the general sense of
history condemns the revocation of the Edict of Nantes,
so it condemns this other act of Louis XIV: his immediate
recognition of James III after his father's death. I do
not say that that verdict is to be reversed, probably upon

the whole it is sound. Everything being considered— though no man could tell the future, and though we must always remember that a decision taken in the past is taken in ignorance of what we later know has to happen—it would have been wiser upon the part of Louis to have postponed the recognition of the true heir until William's death.

But we must not imagine that nothing but a sense of honour, or of pride, or a desire for consistency, moved that great man when he decided openly to support the claim of the family over which he had thrown his powerful shield. There is also something to be said for the *policy*. Had James III not been recognized openly, then upon William's death a new agitation would be required. Could it be organized in time? The possession of the governing machine is half the political battle. Would not those who possessed the governing machine in England have been able to organize full resistance against a boy of whom it might be said that even his strongest supporter had not admitted his claim? Was it not better that the voice of Europe, as it were, or at least the chief voice in Europe, had told the plain truth and had said that this child was rightful king? Would not such a recognition lead to continued debate, at least, upon his rights, and therefore, later, to actual kingship? I mean, not a debate in Parliament, but in the conversations of men? Would not an apparent abandonment of the lad just where support was most expected, have been interpreted as the complete collapse of the Stuart cause?

It may be so: at any rate, I am convinced that all these arguments weighed upon the mind of such a man as Louis more than those—important as they are to all men —of honour or even of consistency.

As for the talk that he was swayed in the matter by his wife, or at any rate unduly swayed, and mainly determined

by her, I think that those who make it (and many contemporaries did) understand neither him nor her.

Perhaps the best, as it is one of the latest, studies upon
this dominant figure in the story of Europe is that of
Louis Bertrand. His conclusion is that to which I think
sober reflection will lead most men. Louis depended upon
Madame de Maintenon for the happiness of his old age;
he respected her judgment, and he was right to respect it.
He was grateful to her, and there he was doubly right.
But it was not in the character of the man who had taken
so many great decisions, whose lucidity of thought and
whose firmness of judgment were not only unimpaired
but increased as the years proceeded, to have been decided
in so capital a point of policy by the whim or chance
pleading even of the woman to whom he very properly
allowed so much. She had paid her respects to the lad's
mother, as was only decent at such a moment, and of
course Mary of Modena had then desired her son to be
recognized. It is likely enough, or certain, that Madame
de Maintenon agreed. Why should she not? She was of
a strong and generous temper, and the public abandonment of the true heir, even for great political purposes,
would have run counter to a character of that high kind.

But whatever she said or did not say, thought or did
not think, Louis did not decide mainly through her influence. He never did. He recognized James III because,
all things considered—the prestige of his throne, his duty
(and Louis XIV never neglected that), his honour (and
to this he was perhaps even more attached), most of all,
upon balance, his policy—decided in favour.

Therefore it was that the great King came into his
dying cousin's room and announced his decision: therefore it was that James's last recognizable words (so far
as we know) on earth were whispered murmurings of
gratitude, and that the loyal English and Scotch exiles,

falling upon their knees, acclaimed the firmness and grandeur of the Bourbon; therefore it was that when the last thing had happened and the wearied sacrificial man had gone from expiation to his reward, the blare of trumpets was heard in the court of St. Germans, before there was any mourning, and James III of England was proclaimed.

Well, after all, to-day, seeing what happened, we cannot regret it. Indeed, a man—even a man at the head of a state—rarely has to regret doing right. The Stuarts were not to be restored. The English popular monarchy had long been doomed. But when men or things have to die it is as well to die nobly, and it has been greatly said, 'Death for death; better the death of Athens than the death of Corinth.'

But before there was need for this the Viaticum had come. The Priest, entering the death-chamber, held up the Blessed Sacrament asking, 'Do you believe Jesus Christ to be really and substantially present in this Host?' To which the King was heard to answer, fervently, with ardour, gazing on That for which he had given the three crowns and all his House:

'I do believe it. I believe it with all my heart.'

NOTE I

ON THE NUMERICAL SITUATION OF CATHOLICISM IN ENGLAND DURING THE ATTEMPT AT TOLERATION UNDER JAMES II

THE phrase 'Number of Catholics' (as applied to England in 1685-88) is misleading, because there was no 'Catholic body' in our modern sense: that is, there was no distinct society of men and women more or less regularly practicing their religion and separate from a non-Catholic world around them.

The Catholicism of England in 1685-88 was essentially the large surviving fragment of a general social habit which had been almost universal a century before the Restoration, which half England still retained eighty years before James's own accession, of which there was everywhere a lively memory and with which there was everywhere considerable familiarity through the presence all over the kingdom of numerous Catholic landed gentlemen with their Catholic tenants, villages and households and as numerous Catholic trading and working-class families in the towns.

Moreover, the line of demarcation between the Catholic and non-Catholic was not the strict thing it is to-day. Very often a man would avow Catholicism before (apparently) any formal act of conversion. Conversely men would abandon Catholicism and show their abandonment of it by no more than taking part in the services of the Established Church. There was a very large 'floating belt' of neutrals and sympathizers: people who respected the recent memory of actively Catholic parents or the devotion of near relatives; many others who leant towards Catholicism somewhat but were not so moved as to emphasize their attitude; many others who would have proclaimed themselves Catholic in favourable circumstances —perhaps after some delay—but not prepared to trouble much about the affair and prepared to run no inconvenience; many others whose family traditions had been Catholic within a life-time but who had themselves drifted inertly with the increasing Protestantism of the mid-seventeenth century.

On the other hand, all Government and official organization was violently anti-Catholic. Only very rarely could any one hear Mass—a regular Catholic education was almost impossible for the bulk of families and the regular practice of religion (which we take for granted to-day) was utterly impossible to all but a very few. To admit Catholicism publicly and to be known openly as a Catholic was to submit to heavy loss, occasional grave peril and every sort of daily inconvenience: it was prohibition to many activities and a heavy handicap in the rest. A man advertising himself as a Catholic before 1685 was deliberately incurring grievous hardship and helping to ruin the chances of his children.

Therefore, if we take as our basis the numbers of those who *did* so sacrifice themselves, and who, in the face of such suffering, continued the old tradition—violently and continuously persecuted for a century and a quarter—we are reckoning no more than a nucleus: the numbers of those consenting to run such risks and to submit continually to oppression was perhaps half the total of all sympathizers.

What was the *nucleus?* What proportion of the English people was *avowedly* and *publicly* Catholic under persecution in the generation before the Revolution?

We have no exact statistics. It was not an age of statistics. The only written figures happen to be, unfortunately, in a form which renders them not only worthless but ridiculous. Danby, desiring to convince Charles II that toleration was unnecessary because non-conformity (and papistry) were of small numbers, asked the bishops to back him up and send in figures to that effect. But the result was a farce. Hampshire, Wiltshire, Somerset, Dorset, for instance, were set down as having not three adults in a hundred Nonconformists, while for the Papists of all the Provinces of Canterbury (four-fifths of England at least in population) one worthy bishop sends in to Danby, 'jotted on the back of two playing-cards,' the figure 11,000. Barely a third of active London Catholics alone.

This, then, may be neglected. But though we have no direct evidence we have what is most valuable in all such cases, a number of *converging* pieces of indirect evidence. That is, we have a number of quite independent facts which, when they are compared, all point to the same result. These I will tabulate, beginning with the most vague and proceeding to the more particular.

(1) We have the estimate of the beginning of the century that then some half of the people were more or less on the Catholic side.

(2) Some forty years later and more, of five hundred officers killed on Charles's side in the civil wars *over* one-third were avowedly Catholic (the Cromwellian phrase 'a papist army'). That points to a fifth or more of their class as a whole, to which most of the officers of the other side also belonged.

There is a rate of decline showing itself, and

(3) Louis XIV writes, a lifetime later still, of James foolishly, supporting the cause of those who were but 'a tenth' of his country. There, as we shall see, he is giving

but a vague impression and specially emphasizing the smallness of the number. He was wrong, as we shall see; but I quote him to show that even a foreigner arguing *against* Catholic numbers at the *end* of the seventeenth century put them as high as 1 in 10.

(4) In 1676-78 two men give us two interesting judgments which, though quite vague, confirm each other remarkably.

Coleman, an intense Catholic (hanged, drawn and quartered in the Popish Plot), regards the Catholics as a body strong enough to serve as a basis for converting the country and estimates those who would *actively* oppose them at no more than a third of the people.

Meres, of the exactly contrary faction, an anti-Catholic enthusiast, speaking a little later in the House of Commons, says that in the event of a Catholic movement only a third would actively oppose. He also speaks of the very large number of Catholics, and the state of public opinion during the Popish Plot agitation—i.e. in 1678-80—clearly shows how large this Catholic body was. True, that opinion was frenzied and unbalanced, but the panic is at least evidence of a very considerable body of Catholics.

(5) Out of 140 lay peers at least 30 are reputed Catholic when the exclusion of papist peers was resolved. Twenty-three are named. Of these, 20 actually prefer an open avowal of Catholicism to their political places in the House of Lords. Say, one-fifth reputed, one-sixth named, one-seventh sacrificing.

(6) When an inquiry is made in the middle of James II's reign to find out how many country gentlemen will support toleration, about one-third are found in that category. Now, whenever (as sometimes happens in the surviving fragments of the inquiry) religion is mentioned, we find that half those in favour of toleration, that is one-sixth of the whole, are openly and admittedly Catholics

(e.g. Staffordshire: 9 out of 47; Hampshire, 11 out of 68; but Essex only 8 out of 57. Bucks: Catholics not given, but 40 per cent for toleration—and so on).

Here then we have two classes of evidence.

(*a*) (Very vague.) The evidence of general impressions in 1676-88, which has a minimum of one-tenth (from a foreign source), a maximum of the vague phrase 'very large' (from opposed close observers at home), and a further estimate that only about a third of the people are so anti-Catholic as to rise actively in favour of persecution.

(*b*) (More particular.) A rate of from about one-half in 1600 to about one-fifth (or rather more) of the gentry in the middle of the century, and one-sixth to one-seventh of the gentry thirty years later.

The particular evidence relates only to the gentry. But it must be remembered that though the well-to-do had greater opportunities for private education, yet on *them* fell the main burden of the persecution. The enormous fines pressed them to apostatize in a fashion which the poorer Catholics did not feel—or, at least, not continuously. Moreover, the lay lords had trebled in number since the Reformation and the new creations had all been made by persecuting governments. Further, unlike modern times, the proportions in the gentry are a good index in the seventeenth century to total population, for their territorial influence was supreme and a man's tenants and great household and local towns were all influenced by him. Even to-day the very few survivals of continuous Catholic villages with their squires in the north remain as evidence to what a large Catholic body of squires and peers meant when all were territorial and when the great mass of England was agricultural.

But if these considerations, with only statistics of the gentry to support them, be insufficient for more than a rough conclusion, we have one further piece of evidence which approximates to precision. It is most valuable, and is as follows:

(7) In 1696 London, rebuilt, with a very largely expanded trade and a flood of new population, counted half a million souls.

In 1678, with the Plague only thirteen years over and the Great Fire twelve, London, as yet but partly rebuilt, *may* have had 300,000: probably less. By the contemporary map showing the proportion of burnt area to unburnt it should have far less. For the burnt area was the most densely inhabited, it left 75,000 people homeless, and the area not burnt is certainly much less than three times the burnt part.

However, call it at a maximum 300,000. Well, in that year, 1678, just on 30,000 people left London under an order expelling those who confessed Catholicism. That is, at least one-tenth of the population exiled themselves under conditions of extreme danger rather than keep silent on their faith or make an outward show of conformity. No one will believe that this number covers all those who were Catholics, and to call the full proportion one-eighth, at least, instead of one-tenth, is reasonable.

One may sum up and say: In the years of the experiments in toleration, pursued tentatively by Charles II, actively by James II, from one-sixth to one-seventh of the gentry were still openly and avowedly Catholic, and presumably with them their social adherents throughout the nation: of London one-eighth or more; and presumably of the general population some such proportion of between 12½ and 15 per cent. How widely may have extended, over and above these, the belt of those more or less in sympathy with Catholicism, there can, in the nature of things, be no numerical evidence. Our general knowledge of the proportion between those who resist and those who yield to persecution and terror, coupled with the numerous conversions appearing when these were relaxed, and the fear this relaxation caused in their opponents, are our only guides.

NOTE II

CONSULTATION OF THE COUNTIES AND BOROUGHS, LATE 1687

IN LATE 1687, as we have seen, James wished to test the probable results of summoning a new Parliament. Parliament meant, principally, of course, the great territorials, the great landed lords, their following of lesser squires and their ultimate tail of freeholders under the lesser squires. It also meant the burgesses from a great number of towns: a number by this time fixed so that the Crown could not (as it still could do while there was some vestige of real power about it) increase. James was compelled to summon the so-called members from the completely fantastic 'towns' (like Old Sarum, where there may have been a dozen voters in his time, but which was a desert at the time of the Reform Bill); or from Gatton near Reigate, where the electors were once a doctor, a squire, and one other man.

The towns were not quite so much under the domination of the great territorial lords as the countrysides. They were heavily under such domination, but not entirely so. The county representation was simply a matter of these big landowners.

The King ordered a minute and private examination of the territorial interests, to find out how they stood: to find out how these owners of the peasantry and domineerers of the towns would act if he were to summon a new Parliament. And he went at it statistically by a questionnaire.

The questions he asked to have thus privately put were three.

(1) How would these big landed people vote upon the question of toleration if summoned to Parliament?

(2) What support would they give to a candidate who should support toleration?

(3) (A really futile question—seeing the conditions were virtually those of war between popular monarchy and a rich oligarchy.) 'Would they live friendly and peaceably with their dissenting or non-conforming neighbours?'

This set of questions was to be applied to the counties: the boroughs he asked his commissioners to report upon individually. How each borough corporation stood towards toleration. What kind of members they were likely to return, and why.

In our histories the general remark is made that the returns frightened him into not accepting a Parliament. But those returns have never yet, to my knowledge, been analysed. I do not pretend to give here in this brief note a full analysis but only to give the general results in the records of nineteen counties which have been preserved.

We will begin with the boroughs and we will also begin by remembering that in spite of the vast complexity of borough representation, that representation was roughly of three kinds.

(1) It was representation of a considerable body (often from one or two to as many as three or four hundred— occasionally even more), something that might fairly be argued as testing general opinion of householders. This was in quite a small minority of boroughs. (2) It was a mere corporation vote, meaning a handful of the richer men of the place. (3) It was the nomination of a local rich man (e.g. Lord Bedford puts in his son for Tavistock.

Salisbury puts in his for Old Sarum—and so on for dozens of instances).

Now we find on looking down the boroughs of Berkshire, Buckinghamshire, Essex, Staffordshire, Yorkshire, Wiltshire, Kent, Sussex, Somerset, Devonshire, Hampshire, the following state of affairs.

It is reported to James that fifty-six boroughs are safe. It is particularly to be noted that when there is a doubt whether their members will accept the policy of toleration or not, the opinion depends a great deal (*a*) upon the number of dissenters, who are normally favourable to toleration; (*b*) upon whether the representation is under the thumb of a local rich man; (*c*) as to whether it is in the hands of a corporation, i.e. of the clique of local rich men of the commercial rather than the territorial sort (but the commercial men were dependent upon the territorial in these little towns).

Here we have our number 56 for the favourable. Now let us turn to the doubtful. We have 14 only, and of these 14, 3 are marked 'doubtful but hopeful', 2 are marked 'will require management', 1 is marked as dependent upon the influence of two men strong in the locality and opposed to the King, and one other (this is very significant) is safe for toleration because a big rich man, 'a friend of the King', can do what he likes there.

Now let us examine in this list, which I admit to be only a set of samples, but which I think is fairly characteristic, being spread over wide areas and including a large number of counties, the adverse boroughs. We have here twelve only, and of these twelve six are frankly put down as solely depending upon the very rich men in their neighbourhood who are opposed to the Crown. To this list must be added half a dozen on which the reports are given, 'Wholly mercenary: will vote as they are paid', or, as in the case of Cambridge, 'Wholly dependent upon the University, which is adverse'.

I know not what the results would be for the complete analysis of the whole kingdom, and perhaps the materials for it are no longer available. But at any rate here are surviving fragments fairly representative, and the conclusion to be drawn from them is unmistakable.

(1) What James had to fear even in the case of the borough representation, was the organized wealthy class, especially in the form of (*a*) the big landowners, and also (*b*) the corrupt little oligarchies of commercial men in the local towns.

(2) Wherever there was a large body of dissenters he was safe. The dissenting body as a whole was in favour of toleration. I know it is the fashion to-day even for dissenters to praise their remote ancestry for refusing toleration rather than admit the freedom of Catholics to civic life. But that is a calumny on the English dissenters. For instance, where there were many voters and where John Bunyan had most power, the principle of toleration was safe; and no wonder, after what they had suffered. That the same was true of Penn we all know. This particular instance, however, was not so valuable as the general conclusion of the inquiries, that, wherever there was a sufficient dissenting population (all over England in the towns there were great bodies of these, often a large majority) this new principle of toleration was safe.

(3) Where the policy of toleration was strongly opposed there is naturally always a close corporation of local rich men with the power of sending members to Parliament, and in order to secure representatives in favour of toleration James is asked to change the old charters and substitute others.

With such a clearly preponderant tide in his favour

so far as boroughs are concerned (and on that there can be no doubt in the mind of a man who carefully reads the figures), why was it still impolitic (if impolitic it were) to call a Parliament? The Parliament did not mean and could not mean the vote of a popular majority. It was at the best, even when James should have broken up the corrupt oligarchies of the local corporations, an appeal to a small minority of the nation, and to a minority under the control of a few.

Still it would seem upon reading this list of the representative boroughs that according to our modern ideas he could safely have gone ahead, summoned his Parliament, and made toleration what we should call to-day the chief 'plank' in his 'platform'.

To answer that let us turn to the counties, and there indeed we get our answer, for the counties mean the squires who dominated the life of England.

Our remaining statistics cover nineteen counties. The answers were generally given entirely in favour, or entirely against, or doubtful. We get in favour of abolition among these country gentlemen so sounded 336 replies. But we get of point-blank refusals very nearly the same number. It must be remembered that here the inquiry was not undertaken in the form of judgment by the inquirers on how the squires would act, but by plain 'yes' or 'no' addressed to the squires themselves; therefore the real number of potential refusals was much larger. There are certainly in the case of these selected counties, on which alone I have direct evidence, a majority of squires openly against toleration. A very large number, without committing themselves, are clearly opposed to the idea of allowing the Catholics to live as fellow citizens. The total number of these doubtfuls who hedged or who absented themselves, or who put in clauses which clearly show that they are opposed to toleration, is over 400.

The squires then rather than the boroughs were opposed to toleration, and that is what turned the scale. More than two-thirds of them would have refused to help the new policy, and it is remarkable that nearly one-third of them had the boldness to reject it altogether. In the denial of civic rights to Catholics they were prepared under their own hands to stand out against the Crown, and of course the main body of their colleagues were with them. It was this which determined James not to summon them again to share his power in the immediate future. It is particularly worth remarking that a number of them, notably in the county of Devon, stuck to a formula upon which they had obviously previously agreed, and the exact wording is also worthy of remembrance: 'They follow Sir Edward Seymour in declaring themselves doubtful to the first and second questions till it be debated in Parliament how religion by law established may be otherwise secure; but they will help elect only such men as they either know or believe loyal subjects who will both faithfully serve His Majesty in all things *with security to our said religion.*' In other words, they would have no truck with abolition of the Test Act.

NOTE III

ON THE BATTLE OF THE BOYNE

IT IS described in the text how the Battle of the Boyne was no decision and, as a military operation, a failure on the part of the offensive. But why was it fought at all against such a crushing superiority of men and guns? Why was not the retreat continued southwards and westwards until the cost of William's lengthening line of communications should have restored something nearer to equality between the two forces?

The cause of that strategical error was one frequently appearing in the history of war and notorious as lately as in 1914: political motive interfering with military. The Boyne was fought because James hesitated to uncover the capital. He had to uncover it sooner or later, so the decision was unwise; but this fear of the moral effect of letting the enemy occupy territory unopposed, even when it is politically justified, is a source of military weakness. It is also possible that James's staff had insufficient information of the enemy's superiority. It looks like that, when one reads the French complaints (and his own) against what was in reality a respectable effort by half-trained infantry against overwhelming odds and under crushing artillery fire to which there could be no reply.

INDEX

INDEX

CPSIA information can be obtained at www.ICGtesting.com
Printed in the USA
BVOW09s1953120814

362618BV00021B/771/P